This study complements the burgeoning literature on South Korean economic development by considering it from the perspective of young female factory workers in the Masan Free Export Zone, the group whose cheap labor underwrote the initial phases of Korea's economic growth and that continues to be the most poorly paid segment of the Korean labor force. In approaching development from this position, Professor Kim explores the opportunity and exploitation that industrial development has presented to female workers and humanizes the notion of the "Korean economic miracle" by examining its impact on their lives.

The author also endeavors to provide an understanding of the ways in which these women both accommodate and resist the dominating forces of global capitalism and patriarchy. This ethnography looks at the conflicts and ambivalences of young women as they participate in the industrial workforce and simultaneously grapple with defining their roles with respect to marriage and motherhood within conventional family structures. The book explores the women's individual and collective struggles to improve their positions and examines their links with other political forces within the labor movement. The author analyzes how female workers envision their place in society, how they cope with economic and social marginalization in their daily lives, and how they develop strategies for a better future. In exploring these questions, the book considers the heterogeneity of female workers and the complexities of their experience as women and as workers.

Class Struggle or Family Struggle?

Class Struggle or Family Struggle?

The Lives of Women Factory Workers in South Korea

SEUNG-KYUNG KIM

University of Maryland, College Park

CAMBRIDGE
UNIVERSITY PRESS

CAMBRIDGE UNIVERSITY PRESS
Cambridge, New York, Melbourne, Madrid, Cape Town, Singapore, São Paulo, Delhi

Cambridge University Press
The Edinburgh Building, Cambridge CB2 8RU, UK

Published in the United States of America by Cambridge University Press, New York

www.cambridge.org
Information on this title: www.cambridge.org/9780521114653

First published 1997
Reprinted 2000
This digitally printed version 2009

A catalogue record for this publication is available from the British Library

Library of Congress Cataloguing in Publication data
Kim, Seung-kyung, 1954–
Class struggle or family struggle? : the lives of women factory
workers in South Korea / Seung-kyung Kim.
p. cm.
Includes bibliographical references and index.
ISBN 0-521-57062-X (hardback)
1. Women – Employment – Korea (South)   2. Work and family – Korea
(South)   I. Title.
HD6068.2.K6K55   1997
331.4'87'095195 – dc20   96-35843
                                                              CIP

ISBN 978-0-521-57062-6 hardback
ISBN 978-0-521-11465-3 paperback

For Anna, Ellen, and John

Contents

Tables and Figures

Preface:
Field, Subject, Author[1]

A S I have undertaken the long, slow process of converting the personal experience of my anthropological fieldwork into a book, I have been forced to reexamine the ambiguities of my position as a "native anthropologist" and to reflect on the many-faceted relationship between author and subject. The betwixt-and-between position of the native anthropologist has been discussed by various anthropologists (Jones 1970; Choong Soon Kim 1990; Kondo 1990; Narayan 1993; Ohnuki-Tierney 1984). As scholars have become concerned about the nuances in relationships between researchers and their informants/subjects, they have needed to pay more attention to the specific location or positionality of both the researcher and the anthropological subject, and they have stressed the need to incorporate this specificity into writing (Abu-Lughod 1986, 1991; Behar 1993; Clifford 1988; Crapanzano 1980; Narayan 1993; Rosaldo 1989; D. Wolf 1996). The variability in the positionality of researchers has increased as greater numbers of Third World anthropologists have written about people in their home countries. Complex issues of identity also surface when Western-educated feminist anthropologists try to represent lower-class female subjects from their home culture. Setting aside the issue of class differences, no matter how much anthropologists identify with and try to share the position of their subjects, they always remain "other" by virtue of being the ones doing the "studying" (cf. Narayan 1993).

Feminist scholars in other disciplines have also criticized the unequal relationship between researcher and subject in ethnographic research (Acker, Barry, and Esseveld 1991; Gluck and Patai 1991; Mies 1983; Personal Narratives Group 1989; Stacey 1991).[2] Neither in research nor in writing can there be absolute equality between the researcher and the subject. The relationship, I would argue, however, is much more complex and complicated than the binary

1 An earlier version of this preface was published in *Anthropology Today* (1995, 11(3):6–9).
2 Sanjek (1993) offers a compelling discussion on this unequal relationship between anthropologists and their assistants in fieldwork and writing ethnography.

ix

power relationship condemned by many feminist scholars and anthropologists.[3] Ethnographic fieldwork entails constant negotiation with subjects that the researcher intends to represent. Here I explore the dynamics of the ethnographic encounter engendered by a particular political–economic situation of South Korea in the late 1980s and the problem of translating lived experience into text. I examine the relationship between myself as a researcher and a woman who was variously my friend, my key informant and an alter ego to an extent that is unusual in anthropological research.

In order to understand how this relationship developed, it is first necessary to go into my own background[4] and look at the reasons why I was conducting this specific research when and where I was. I came to the United States to study anthropology after completing my bachelor's degree in sociology in Korea. What had attracted me to anthropology was its apparent ability to get closer to human experience through the method of participant observation. Although in the course of studying anthropology I became interested in other cultures, I did not insist on undertaking research in a culture different from my own. In fact, after spending seven years in the United States, I was especially concerned to reconnect with some of the important political issues facing my own society, that of Korea, and therefore became a native anthropologist. Thus, although I made the appropriate efforts to set up my research project in terms of current academic priorities and received funding from several sources, I was motivated by reasons that were political and personal as well as scholarly.

It was my intention to study the lives of women factory workers in the Masan Free Export Zone (MAFEZ) in Masan, a city not far from where my mother still lives. MAFEZ was established in 1970 as part of the government's export-oriented development plan. It rapidly became a significant center for light manufacturing industries owned by foreign companies and employing a predominantly female labor force in low-wage jobs. I knew before I began my

3 Margery Wolf (1992) argues against the accusations made by postmodern scholars that anthropologists inherently violate their informants' stories by reconfiguring and editing. She states that the information given by informants is not ultimately a commodity and that the duty of anthropologists is to interpret faithfully what they are told and relay the information to the wider world.

4 As in the cases of Abu-Lughod, Behar and Narayan, the ambiguities of my own cultural position are important parameters of my fieldwork (Abu-Lughod 1991; Behar 1993; Narayan 1993). Although, unlike these anthropologists, my early life took place within a relatively homogeneous Korean cultural setting, as an adult I studied in the United States, married an American, became the mother of two American daughters and now teach at an American university. Thus, I have acquired a degree of cultural ambiguity.

project that the women who worked in Masan were exploited by nearly any definition of the term. They worked long hours under harsh conditions for extremely low wages. I saw my project both as a way of learning what these women had to say about their lives and as somehow contributing to helping them improve their lives by raising their consciousness (Seung-kyung Kim 1990).

It is necessary to consider my own class background before proceeding further. The social classes of present-day South Korea have little continuity with those of traditional Korea. Colonialism, war and industrialization have combined to create new classes and render previous social divisions obsolete. Nevertheless, there are extreme differences between rich and poor in South Korea. Although my grandparents (who died before I was born) were peasants, my father was a successful small businessman, and my own life has always been comfortably middle class. Along with many others of my class and generation, I was uncomfortable with the feeling of privilege in the presence of so much poverty.

I planned to rely on participant observation to conduct my fieldwork and intended to work in a factory in order to better understand conditions there. This plan presented several problems. First, I no longer had a Korean identification card, so I could not legally get a job. Second, to prevent college students from helping workers organize, the government had established laws forbidding anyone with a college degree from working in a factory. And third, the electronics factories in the Zone did not hire women older than twenty-two. I was able to get around these problems with the help of a cousin, who was a middle manager in a Japanese-owned electronics factory in MAFEZ.

My cousin used his influence to help me get a job there, but he required a firm promise that I would not divulge my identity or try to stir up workers while I was employed. "Strictly observation," he said. I worked in the factory for three months and frequently found maintaining the deception to be burdensome and difficult, especially as I had to pretend to be ten years younger than I really was. Participant observation also proved frustrating because the hours were so long and the work was so exhausting that I had difficulty even maintaining a diary. Quitting my job was the most painful experience in my fieldwork because I had led my friends to believe that I had taken the factory job in desperation, and they were terribly worried about my future without the job. When I met some of them later and explained my project, some were sympathetic but a few were quite angry at my deception.

After I finished working at the factory, I managed to conduct a survey of some of the workers in the Zone using questionnaires. However, as before, the cooperation I needed from authorities to conduct the research had compromised my objectives, and my questionnaires had been purged of any politically sensitive questions. By May 1987, I felt quite frustrated that my project was not making much progress.

At about that time, I began to learn about the Catholic Women's Center from several women workers and from the matron of the dormitory for workers in the Zone. I heard that the Center attracted women workers by advertising classes for women (*yŏsŏng kyosil*) when, in fact, what they taught was Communist ideology and labor law. Workers told me that going to the Center was an exciting experience, but they had been warned not to go there anymore. The matron of the dormitory advised me not to get involved with the Center because the police were watching it closely.

In spite of this advice, I arranged to meet with Ms. Lee, a coordinator at the Catholic Women's Center whom I knew slightly through an acquaintance at the local university. After I explained my project, she agreed to let me participate in the Center's discussion groups. The Young Catholic Workers' Organization (JOC, from the French "Jeunesse Ouvriere Chretienne") set up these groups, consisting of four to five workers each and usually named after flowers: lily, daffodil and others. Each group's first meeting started with the question "Who am I?" Each worker took turns introducing herself, beginning with her birthday and including a brief life history.[5] After that, the group discussed a prepared topic, and went on to talk about working conditions in their factories and how to improve them.

The first discussion that I attended involved reading a book of Korean history written for the common people (*minjung yŏksa*). These histories take a bottom-up approach, in contrast to the elite perspective characteristic of most conventional histories. The book under consideration was an "easy reading" Korean history aimed at a broad audience. After discussing the book, the

---

5 Life histories have been a major interest of anthropologists concerned with positionality, but as the JOC meeting illustrates, people make fairly formal presentations of their life histories in contexts quite unrelated to research. Recording life histories like the ones presented at these meetings became a major part of my research. Coming to terms with the subjective aspect of people's life stories presents problems similar to those involved in understanding the positionality of the researcher. As Laurel Kendall observes, "the truth of an informant's life, like autobiographic truth, is shaped by the circumstances of the telling, and . . . memory and self-presentation are selective and sometimes self-contradictory processes . . . [and] . . . contradictory stories, and even outright fabrications, yield their own windows on the human soul" (1988:12–13).

women took turns talking about their work situations. One woman was at the same factory where I had worked, and three were workers at garment factories. I met Sun-hui at this meeting.

Sun-hui had been working in the Zone at a garment factory that had just gone bankrupt. She was working part time for the Catholic Church while looking for another factory job. She told me she was twenty-six years old and had come from Seoul four years ago. She was more receptive to my project than most workers had been and seemed to understand what I was trying to accomplish in Masan. I was also trying to make arrangements to share living accommodations with workers, and Sun-hui agreed to let me share with her and her roommates. I moved in with them in July and remained with them for the next nine months.

Our room was about three by four meters, so small that when we lay down, there was no room to move. The room was directly opposite an old-fashioned toilet, and whenever it was raining, the smell from the toilet was overwhelming and we were almost unable to eat. We paid 40,000 won ($50) a month for that room plus 8,000 won ($10) for electricity and water. Our landlord and landlady were both factory workers who lived in two rooms of the house with their three children and rented out three rooms (see Chapter 3). Even though the house was old, small and old-fashioned, they were very proud to own a house of their own.

The house was heated by an old-fashioned *ondol* system using coal briquettes. The only furniture in the room consisted of three vinyl wardrobes belonging to my roommates and a desk that belonged to one of them. We folded up and stored our bedding in the wardrobes when we were not sleeping. Our kitchen hardly deserved the name, it was so small. We used a kerosene stove for cooking, and I contributed an electric rice cooker. We took turns cooking, washing and cleaning the room. Whoever was in charge of cooking had to get up at 6:00 A.M. to cook breakfast, which was usually just rice, soup and *kimchi*. Sometimes we ate eggs and other vegetables for dinner, but meat (pork) was a luxury we had only immediately after payday. My roommates often skipped dinner, which they explained was because they were worried about getting fat, but was at least in part to save the expense (see Han'guk Kidokkyo Kyohoe Hyŏbuihoe 1984a). For most workers in MAFEZ, the main meal of the day was the lunch provided by the factory.

Living with them enabled me to participate in their everyday activities and resulted in many hours of conversation. I conducted my first interview with Sun-hui soon after I moved in. We talked for almost three hours about a broad range of topics – how and why Sun-hui moved to Masan from Seoul, how she met her current roommates, how she spent her monthly wage and what kinds of activities she had been involved in at various factories.

We began talking about wages and how much money she allocated for her expenses each month. Sun-hui said, almost laughingly, that she did not send any money to her family because she tried to save about 40% of her wage; she had to pay for her contribution to the household, which came to about 20% of her wage; and surprisingly, she spent almost 40% of her income for what she termed *sagyobi* (money for meeting friends). It seemed a bit strange that she spent so much money for this purpose, but I did not press her to specify the reasons.

She said little about her family, but mentioned that her parents owned a small candy store and that her sister and brother were married and living apart from her parents. Because I did not expect otherwise, I assumed that she was a high school graduate and asked, "So, what did you do after you graduated from high school?" Sun-hui did not object to my leading question and went on discussing her work history:

> After I graduated from high school, I worked for a hat factory at
> Kurodong in Seoul. I am left-handed, so it was hard for me to learn to
> sew. While I was an apprentice there, I cut my hand pretty badly with
> shears. Nobody paid any attention to my injury; a woman just put
> some iodine on it and told me to continue to work. You see this scar
> on my hand? That is from that cut. I really wanted to learn to sew, so
> I moved to another factory, where I became an apprentice to learn
> sewing skills. But I was assigned to do ironing most of the time I was
> there, so I moved again to Chŏngkyechŏn, where I had a friend who
> was a top sewing machine operator. I learned to use the sewing ma-
> chine in two months of working there. After I knew something about
> using a sewing machine, I moved to Puchŏn and pretended to be a
> skilled operator with two years of experience. I spent six months there
> making sports bags. . . .

Sun-hui then explained how she was able to get this factory to improve their policy about Sunday pay so that it conformed with the law:

> Around this time, I had a series of physical and emotional problems. I
> left the factory and spent about nine months working as a domestic
> maid before I decided to come down to Masan. Life as a domestic

maid was easy compared to working in sewing factories. I had a lot of free time to rest, I could sleep enough and the food was a lot better. But I thought that this kind of life was not for me and decided to move again after my health got better. I had a friend whose fiancé was working at a factory in Ch'angwŏn, and we came down together. At first, it seemed that Masan factories didn't have any problems: there was not much overtime work, and labor conditions seemed to be much better than where I had been before. In August 1984 when I came down to Masan, it was easy to get a job at an electronics company in the Zone. I worked for one of them for six months, but then my mother had a serious accident and I had to go back to Seoul to take care of her. When I came back to Masan in 1985, it was almost impossible to get a job at the electronics companies. This time was called "the depression" in the Zone. I went to work for a subcontracting firm while I searched for a better job. I couldn't get a job at an electronics factory, but I heard about this shoe factory, Hyŏpchin. I was not sure about my skills, but I took the job and stayed there until they went bankrupt in May. I worked for this factory for twenty months. That was the longest time I worked at one place.

I asked her how she knew so much about the labor law, but she avoided answering my question directly and mentioned that she learned things while attending the Protestant Church. She also mentioned that she started to go to the Catholic Church and became a member of Young Catholic Workers' Organization after she moved to Masan. She brushed away my question concerning her obvious knowledge of labor law, just saying that she became interested in this issue (workers' rights) after she graduated from high school and started to go to church.

Her life history sounded a lot like the one I used to tell other workers in the factory while I was working, although my story was not as complicated as hers. But I did not, even for one moment, think she was fabricating her story. Now, listening to the tape of the interview, I realize that if I had considered the possibility, I could have seen gaps in her story. Furthermore, I was busy trying to impress Sun-hui during this first interview. I practically lectured her and her roommates about the sins of the multinational corporations, the Korean government and the world economy, as well as trying to convince them that I was a progressive woman even though I was a lot older than they were. During this initial interview, I talked as much as, if not more than, Sun-hui.

For the first two months of living with Sun-hui and the others, I was the primary cook. I got up first, and made rice and some side dishes for our breakfast. The two younger women went to work, and Sun-hui and I went around to visit older married women who had previously worked in the Zone. We became closer and got to know each other more, and after two months we had a sort of heart-to-heart talk.

I used to smoke heavily but did not smoke at all during my fieldwork because it is not acceptable for women to smoke in public. One afternoon I was discussing my plans for interviews with Sun-hui and had an urge to smoke, so I blurted out, "Sun-hui, will it be all right if I smoke?" It risked damaging my reputation with her, but by then I felt secure enough about our relationship to divulge one of my secrets. Her response, however, surprised me. She said, "Don't worry. I smoke too. Since there is no one around today, why don't we buy a pack and smoke?" Smoking among young middle-class women, especially college students, was considered a sign of liberation because it violated conventional ideas about how young women should behave. I did not expect to find a factory woman smoking.[6] This common admission of sinfulness opened up our relationship, and she started to talk about herself more and differently. She told me that she had attended a college (although she did not reveal which one). She also admitted that Sun-hui was a false name, but refused to tell me the real one on the basis that the less I knew about her the better, in case anything happened. Her revelations did not really shock me because by this time, I realized there was more to Sun-hui's life than she had been telling me. I surmised that she was a radical student, but I respected her wishes and did not push any further. After that day, I understood why she was out every night, visiting so many workers and spending her own money. Her way of life made a lot more sense after I heard a little bit of the truth.

At the end of September, my husband came to visit me and we went for a short sightseeing trip to Chŏlla Province. When I told Sun-hui that I planned to visit Kwangju, she gave me a letter to hand deliver to a Catholic nun in that city. When we met the nun, I learned more about Sun-hui's past. She told us she was greatly worried about Sun-hui, especially about her health, because she had been on the verge of collapse when she last saw her in Seoul. Obviously, this was the time Sun-hui left the factory and went to work as a maid. She was

6 Smoking became briefly fashionable among women factory workers after 1988 because of the influence of college students, but the fashion passed quickly, and most factory women still consider it improper for young women to smoke.

also worried about her safety and whether the police were actively pursuing her. From the nun I learned that Sun-hui had moved to Masan to escape the police. She had been deeply involved in a night class for young workers organized by radical students and church organizations. Most of her comrades had been arrested during a police raid, and after that she had to move around to avoid the police. The nun told us that Sun-hui's family was middle class and owned a rice mill factory, and that Sun-hui was a very bright student who had entered the department of education at Ehwa Women's University, with the top examination score.

After I returned I became closer to Sun-hui, confiding in her about many problems I faced personally and professionally regarding the research I was trying to do. Sun-hui helped guide my project and arranged interviews with labor activists for me. I continued to talk and meet with some of the young women I met while I was working at the factory, but my research focus shifted more to women who were involved in unionization and the labor movement. Of course, other people and events also shaped the direction of my research. The nationwide labor uprising in July and August 1987 swept many women workers into demonstrations and strikes and provided my project with a dramatic focus. However, it was through Sun-hui that I met the women who led the movement in Masan (see Seung-kyung Kim 1992). Sun-hui and I participated together in the street rallies and demonstrations and cried together when the police shot tear gas. The experience reminded me of the demonstrations I had been involved with in college.

My last interview with Sun-hui before I left Korea in March 1988 was filled with philosophical questions about social justice, the relative merits of socialist society and democratic society, and considerations of issues of workers' exploitation and the role of intellectuals. She told me:

> I often think about the concept of "social justice" and my place in the quest for this justice, which I define as the distribution of benefits among more people. I do not think any one person can or should have the power to produce this justice, but everyone should try to bring it about. I consider the role of students and religious organizations in recovering democracy for this society to be critical. Along with political democracy, we also need to move toward a society with more equal distribution of wealth. If we can eventually establish a society full of justice and love, I will be very happy. People can contribute to this pursuit on two different levels: a larger and more macro level, and a

smaller and more micro level in changing people's attitudes and values. I consider myself in the latter category.

Most workers do not know about my identity. I do not tell them because the relationship we built on the basis of equal status changes once I tell them, "I am a college graduate, and I came down here to help you to organize." Rather than preaching to them about what to do from the outside, I would bury myself among them and make change from within. It is so rewarding to watch a woman worker change her position from whether to join a union or not to making a statement, "It is all right for me to be arrested for the involvement with a union." Their level of consciousness expands from factory to national issues.

Intellectuals have a role in this process, but first, we need to get over the thought of being superior and leading workers. We need, instead, to be partners, in the true sense, in the same movement. If we do that, then we can open our hearts to each other and we can learn from each other.

During this interview I hardly spoke, and Sun-hui talked mostly about her own place within the labor movement and the student movement. At about this time, I also got to know a lot about her personal life: how much she was in love with a man who was also a union leader in one of the factories. She often told me about her anticipated future being married to this man, and said that together they could work for the workers' community in Masan.

After I left the field, we kept in contact by letters and phone calls. During 1988 and 1989, she worked very hard to help workers of the Tandy Corporation factory in Masan in their unsuccessful struggle against the plant closing (see Chapter 4). However, her letters showed more and more frustration about not being able to do much. Her personal life was not going well either. Her boyfriend had decided to break off their relationship, explaining, "You are not a true proletarian. You come from a middle-class background and you never worked out of necessity, so you don't know how we really feel." And then he decided to marry a woman, also an activist, but from an authentically proletarian background. Sun-hui felt humiliated and defeated. She began to question her role as an organizer. She worried about how hard it was to change workers' consciousness and how unrewarding her efforts were.

Sun-hui left Masan in 1990 to return to Seoul, where she deliberated about what to do with her life. She considered the possibility of attending the

Women's Studies Program in Ehwa Women's University as a graduate student; the possibility of running a day-care facility for the children of workers in an industrial zone; and the possibility of getting married.

In 1991, she married a man who had been involved in the student movement and who managed a small press publishing radical books. She also enrolled in the Women's Studies Program. When I visited Korea that year, she joined me for a week-long visit to Masan, and we went around talking to women workers we knew. It was just like old times. She told me that she felt bad about leaving Masan and admitting defeat. She also felt guilty about returning to academia, which she had previously rejected, as well as about having married an essentially middle-class man.

When I visited her in January 1994, she was still worried about the future of the labor movement, especially of women workers' labor unions and their organizations, but she had come to terms with her role in the labor movement and felt good about the years she had spent in Masan. Sun-hui's role as an organizer was still appreciated by many people in Masan. Workers praised her as a real workers' friend, in contrast to the students who came down to Masan after 1987 to indoctrinate workers (see Chapter 5).

Sun-hui now works as a government employee (*kongmuwŏn*) in a neighborhood office and lives in a small two-bedroom apartment just outside of Seoul with her husband, her two-year-old son, and her mother-in-law. Her modest income provides the bulk of her family's support because her husband's publishing business is not doing well.

As I wrote this, I kept thinking about the parallels between Sun-hui and myself and about how much greater they might have been if I had stayed in Korea. Although Sun-hui was so crucial to my research, I edited her out of my dissertation, and upon reflection, I believe that this was only partly for the obvious political reasons. She was not an authentic proletarian for me either.[7] By writing this preface, however, I am beginning to come to terms with both her and my relationship to each other and to the women who are forced by necessity to work in Korea's factories.

Each fieldwork experience has its own unique characteristics. Sun-hui's initial, fabricated version of her life story reveals the power of an informant within the "negotiated reality" of the fieldwork encounter. However, her story

---

7 Although Sun-hui was not an authentic proletarian, in that she worked in factories for reasons other than financial necessity, it is important to note that she spent a longer period of time working in factories (eight years) than did most women workers in Masan, and that during this time she depended exclusively on her factory income.

also illustrates how anthropology overlaps other aspects of life because her interview with me merely elaborated a story she had already developed for others. Nor was I unique in learning "the truth" about Sun-hui; she had also confided in many of her friends. Although as an anthropologist I had an additional motive to be interested in her story, I also had learned about her as her friend.

My involvement with Sun-hui grew out of the specific political and economic context of Korea in the late 1980s. Both Sun-hui and I had been influenced by the political climate of the universities, both of us had had a desire to promote the welfare of people who seemed excluded and exploited, and both of us went to Masan with ideas about helping women factory workers. The fact that we started from such similar positions helps to explain our instant rapport, her willingness to help me with my research and her influence on my project. The nature of our relationship reveals a blurring of the distinction between researcher and subject and highlights the ambiguities of the native anthropologist's position within her own culture.

Acknowledgments

I have benefited from the help of many people over the past 10 years, from the time of my first fieldwork to the publication of this book, and I would like to thank them. First and foremost, I would like to thank the women workers of the Masan Free Export Zone, where I conducted my initial fieldwork between 1986 and 1988. I had the privilege of witnessing their bravery as they engaged in the struggle to secure their rights and protect their livelihoods. The women who were my research subjects also became my friends, and extended family. Without their willingness to share their joys, sorrows and tears, I could not have completed my fieldwork or written this book. I would like to thank my roommates (Chŏng-hui, I-suk, and Sun-hui) for putting up with me for the 9 months during my fieldwork and providing friendship afterward. They will know who they are, although I have used pseudonyms to preserve their privacy. I would also like to thank Yi Kyŏng-suk and Kang In-sun for their generous support during my fieldwork in Masan and afterward.

Many scholars have provided intellectual and emotional support during my years at the Graduate Center. I owe my greatest debt to Joan Mencher, my dissertation advisor. Before, during, and after my fieldwork, Joan was always there for me. When I lacked discipline, her encouragement compelled me to continue. June Nash introduced me to the subject of the "new international division of labor" and to the importance of doing this research. I am very much indebted to her for guiding me through theoretical issues and providing the constructive advice I needed. Burton Pasternak was the other helpful member of my committee. This book has benefited greatly from his perceptive suggestions and kind words. My special thanks go to Sue Rosenberg Zalk, director of the Center for the Study of Women and Society, and Judith Lorber, coordinator of the Women's Studies Program, for introducing me to the field of women's studies and for their valuable comments on my work.

During my graduate school and my early professional years, I have enjoyed wonderful conversations with the community of scholars of South Korea.

Acknowledgments

Nancy Abelmann has always been there for me whenever I needed to discuss scholarly and personal issues. Laurel Kendall served as the outside reviewer for my dissertation and has continued to guide me throughout my professional years with generous advice. Roger Janelli has always provided encouragement and advice whenever I needed it. I have also benefited greatly from the guidance and encouragement of Choong Soon Kim. I would also like to thank Haejoang Cho, Chungmoo Choi, Eun Mee Kim, Eun-Shil Kim and Dawnhee Yim for their support and comments.

I also owe much to the many people I grew to know during my years at the Graduate Center. Bernice Kurchin has been the most wonderful friend during all these years since we met in 1983, and her family has become my family in the United States. I would also like to thank Rose Caporrimo, Paola Ciardi, Aisha Khan, Audrey Korelstein, Allyson Purpora, Lisa Schnall, Richard Shryock, Ian Skoggard, Alisse Waterston, and many others for useful discussions and for their friendship.

The Department of Women's Studies at the University of Maryland has provided me with a generous, encouraging, and supportive intellectual home. I would like to thank the department for granting a semester leave that was crucial for me to complete this book and for supporting me for tenure. My colleagues Evelyn Torton Beck, Bonnie Thornton Dill, Katie King, Deborah Rosenfelt, and Melissa Matthes have been most supportive during the years I have been at the University of Maryland. My special thanks go to Claire Moses, chair of my department, and Lynn Bolles, chair of my tenure committee, for their unending encouragement and generosity. Cynthia Gaye and Laura Nichols were invaluable in guiding me through the rigors of campus bureaucracy. I would also like to thank Virginia Beauchamp and Nancy O'Neill for copyediting and commenting on my manuscript.

My late father, Kim Sam-bong, and my mother, Pak Kun-Rye, and my parents-in-law, Helen and David Finch, have been most encouraging and supportive while I completed my work. It has required great patience to watch me go through the long years of becoming an anthropologist. My two daughters, Anna and Ellen, who were born after I began this project, have discovered a productive use for the rough drafts, which provided stacks of scratch paper for their drawings. I would like to thank them for growing up healthy in the midst of chaos.

At Cambridge University Press, I am grateful to Elizabeth Neal for guiding me through the whole process. I would also like to thank Louise Calabro for her patience and management of the manuscript and Helen Greenberg for her thorough copyediting.

My research in Korea was supported by a 1986–7 National Science Foundation Doctoral Dissertation Fellowship (BNS440358); a 1986–7 Andrew Silk Dissertation Fellowship, CUNY/GSUC; a 1994 Korea Grant, Association for Asian Studies; and a 1993 International Travel Grant, UMCP. I received support for writing from a 1989–90 fellowship from the Center for Labor–Management Policy Studies CUNY/GSUC; a 1991–2 Lilly Teaching Fellowship at UMCP; and a 1992 General Research Board Summer Research Award at UMCP.

Finally, I could not have finished this book without John Finch, my husband and a fellow anthropologist, who became a "Koreanist" as a result of endless reading, commenting on, arguing about, and editing of this book. My enduring gratitude is more than I can express in writing.

The Preface appeared as "Field, Subject, Author: Fieldwork with a 'Disguised' Worker in a South Korean Export Processing Zone" in *Anthropology Today* (1995). Other portions of this book have appeared as "Export Processing Zones and Worker Resistance in South Korea" in *Anthropology and the Global Factory: Studies of the New Industrialization in the Late 20th Century,* Frances Rothstein and Michael Blim (eds.), New York: Bergin and Garvey (1992); and "'Industrial Soldiers," *Cultural Survival Quarterly,* Winter, Special Issue on Women's Work, Women's Worth (1992); and "'Big Companies Don't Hire Us, Married Women': Exploitation and Empowerment among Women Workers in Korea," *Feminist Studies* (1996). I am grateful to the publishers of these works for allowing me to reprint this material here.

Language Note

I have generally followed the McCune–Reischauer system of romanization for Korean. However, I have used the standard alternative romanizations for place names that commonly appear in English language writing on Korea (e.g., "Seoul"). In cases where I know that a Korean author uses an alternative romanization, I have followed his or her preference. Names of Korean authors are written in the text and in citations according to Korean style, with surname first, except for persons who I know prefer otherwise. In the references I have tried consistently to list Korean authors in Korean style and Korean-American authors in American style.

1

Women Caught between Global Capitalism and South Korean Patriarchy

THIS book examines the lives of young women factory workers in the Masan Free Export Zone (MAFEZ) in South Korea, and endeavors to provide an understanding of the ways in which these women both accommodate and resist the dominating forces of global capitalism and South Korean versions of patriarchy.[1] My ethnography looks at the conflicts and ambivalence of these young women as they participate in the workforce of industrial factories and simultaneously grapple with defining their roles with respect to marriage and motherhood within conventional family structures. It explores their individual and collective struggles to improve their position and examines their links with other political forces within the labor movement. I analyze how women workers envision their place in society, how they cope with economic and social marginalization in their daily lives, and how they develop and actualize strategies for a better future. In exploring these questions, I consider the heterogeneity of women workers and the complexities of their experiences as women and as workers.

My research covers a defining moment in South Korean labor history. In December 1986, when I arrived in Masan to begin my fieldwork, workers appeared politically quiescent, but in the ensuing months, as the country worked through a political crisis, workers in Masan became part of a nationwide labor uprising that challenged the legitimacy of the government. Not only did I witness and participate in the widespread demonstrations for democracy and workers' rights, I developed a firsthand appreciation of the lives of factory workers by taking a job in a MAFEZ electronics factory. Through this personal

---

1 This book is based on anthropological fieldwork carried out in Masan, South Korea, from December 1986 to March 1988, with follow-up visits during the summer of 1991 and the winter of 1994. During my first period of fieldwork, I worked for three months at a Japanese-owned electronics factory. My personal experience of working in a factory and living with workers who came from the same region of Korea as I do helped me to develop an understanding of the subjective experience of workers.

1

experience of working in a factory and living with workers, who came from the same region of Korea as I do, I developed an understanding of the subjective experience of workers.

This study complements the burgeoning literature on South Korean economic development (Amsden 1989; Cho Soon 1994; Cole and Park 1983; Jones and Sakong 1980; Eun Mee Kim 1987; Kuznets 1977, 1985; Lim H.C. 1982; Luedde-Neurath 1980; Song Byung-Nak 1990; Steinberg 1989; Woo 1991) by considering development from the perspective of women workers whose cheap labor underwrote its initial phases and who continue to be the most poorly paid segment of the labor force. In approaching development from this position, the study explores the mix of opportunity and exploitation that development has presented to women workers and humanizes the notion of the "Korean economic miracle" by examining its impact on their lives. My work also complements recent anthropological studies of South Korean conglomerates and their white-collar employees (Janelli 1993; Choong Soon Kim 1992) and addresses the general neglect of women's participation in labor and trade union activities. As a case study of women workers, it contributes to a growing body of literature concerning women's involvement in the labor movement worldwide (Bolles 1996b; Bookman 1988; Cook, Lorwin, and Daniels 1992; Costello 1988; Karl and Choi 1983; Lamphere and Grenier 1988; Milkman 1985, 1987; Sacks and Remy 1984; Susser 1988). This study also explores the connections between traditional roles in family, labor market opportunities, and political mobilization and looks at the dynamics of women's political participation. In so doing, it contributes both to feminist understandings of women, work and family (Beneria and Roldan 1987; Bolles 1996a; Lamphere 1987; D. Wolf 1992) and to the anthropological literature on resistance (Kondo 1990; Ong 1987; James Scott 1985; Willis 1977).

INDUSTRIAL SOLDIERS AND DUTIFUL DAUGHTERS

The transformation of South Korea's economy during the past three decades has been termed an "economic miracle." In a single generation, the country has changed from a poor rural nation, dependent on foreign assistance, to one of the most dynamic manufacturing economies in the world. Essential to this transformation has been South Korea's low-paid but highly productive and well-disciplined labor force.

As South Korea industrialized, vast numbers of men and women migrated to urban centers to take jobs in factories (Sorenson 1988). In 1960, before the drive for export-led industrialization began, women had been only a small part of the manufacturing labor force, comprising 6.4% of workers in the secondary sector. By 1990, the percentage had grown to 28% (Moon 1994:267). Looked at another way, the number of women workers in the manufacturing sector increased from a mere 160,000 in 1960 to over 2 million in 1990 (Economic Planning Board cited in Myung-hye Kim 1992:158).[2]

Female workers' presence has been most significant in the labor-intensive light manufacturing industries, which underwrote South Korea's economic development in the 1960s and the early 1970s during the regime of President Park Chung Hee. Park was a great admirer of Japan's modernization during the Meiji period and held it up as a model for Korea (Park Chung Hee 1970). The incorporation of young women into a national struggle for modernization as low-paid factory labor is only one of many parallels between Park's regime and that of Meiji Japan.[3] Through the end of the 1970s, light industries produced most of South Korea's exports, and female workers comprised more than half of the work force in these industries: electronics 55.2%, textiles 72.4% and rubber footwear 52.4% (Choi Jang Jip 1983:83–84). Female factory workers were predominantly young single women working from the time they completed their schooling until they got married.[4] These women could be hired for extremely low wages, and companies benefitted enormously from low labor costs that made their products competitive on the world market (Hong 1985). Wages paid to women averaged less than half those paid to men for industrial work (Kim Kŭm-su 1986:73; Han'guk Yŏsŏng Nodongjahoe 1987:32).

During this period, "factories were the symbol of Korean modernization and industrialization, and encapsulated the dream of future prosperity" (Eun-Shil Kim 1993:182). President Park asked the people to sacrifice and be patient in order to build a nation without hungry people. Nationalist slogans such as

2 Women have been employed in Korean factories since the early colonial period, but until the 1960s, the country was overwhelmingly rural and the total number of women factory workers was small. For a discussion of women workers in Korean factories during the colonial period, see Eckert (1991:192ff.).

3 See Tsurumi (1990) for a discussion of women factory workers in Meiji Japan.

4 "Young and unmarried woman workers have represented the majority of labor force in the industries for the past three decades. In 1970, 77.5% of 541,200 employed women studied by the Research Center for Human Resource Development were unmarried. . . . The average age of the total female workers was 23.5 years, and it was even lower (22.5 years) in manufacturing industries which hired the majority of women workers. . . . In 1983, 72% of women working in manufacturing sectors belonged to the age bracket of 18 [to] 24. In . . . such feminized industries as textiles, garments, and electronics, 74% to 77% of women workers were between 18 and 24 years old" (Moon 1994:271).

3

Suchul ipkuk ("Exports are the way to build the state") and *Hamyŏntoenda* ("We can do it") were prominently displayed in factories throughout the country to foster a spirit of development and modernization in the new export-oriented economy (ibid.:184).

Factory workers were asked to sacrifice, but they were also promised that their efforts would be rewarded within the next decade. In a January 1970 speech to South Korean workers, President Park said:

> The most basic factor in our pursuit of a self-reliant defense and the foundation for reunification is the power of a completely self-reliant economy, and the most important factor for achieving a self-reliant economy is the expansion of exports. . . .
>
> In order to increase our export volume, we have to produce good quality goods at lower prices than goods produced by other countries and this is impossible if wages are high. What will happen to us if export volume decreases because of high wages and high prices for goods?
>
> I want you to understand that both improvements in workers' lives and the growth of corporations depend on our national development, so I ask for your cooperation to take pride and responsibility for the establishment of the nation. I can assure you that the rapid growth of the economy due to the continuing expansion of exports will provide a prosperous future for our three million workers. (Park Chung Hee 1970:2–3)

Although the gender of workers is not specifically mentioned in this or many other similar speeches, it must be recalled that during this period, exports were dominated by light industrial goods produced by women workers and that the burden of low wages was also borne disproportionately by women workers.

The director of the Office of Labor Affairs repeated the same themes in his 1972 address to workers:

> I promise all of you workers will be amply rewarded for the price you have paid in "blood and sweat" in the mid-1970s for our economic foundation. I assure you that the late 1970s will be a period of "benefits and compensation" rewarding our workers for their sweat and work during the 1960s. Since we have such bright prospects and so much hope, I ask you to be patient today and to work even more

diligently, and devote our spirit and sweat to the economic establishment. (Sanŏp kwa Nodong 1971:4)

On the whole, workers responded positively to the call for sacrifice for the good of the nation. A woman who worked in a garment factory in the 1970s captures the mood of the period:

> We worked very hard. . . . During our factory morning meetings, managers held out the hope that workers would live well in the 1980s. . . . We were told to sacrifice ourselves, to work even if our fingers were bleeding. . . . I had great expectations that in the 1980s I would pay back all my parents debts, continue with my education, and not have to work such long hours. (Quoted in Jeoung 1993:44)

The image developed by the government to promote this spirit of sacrifice was that of workers as "industrial soldiers" (*sanŏp chŏnsa*).[5] The government's stress on loyalty and obedience as the chief virtues of workers frequently utilized a traditional image of young women as dutiful daughters willingly sacrificing themselves for the good of the nation. The ideal image of the woman factory worker is illustrated in a 1970 Office of Labor Affairs poster (Figure 1.1). It features a slender, delicate-looking young woman smiling and wearing a uniform and a hard hat. The caption, translated, says, "Come to our factory and you will learn the real value of labor." A factory with smokestacks forms the background. Clean and happy, as well as industrious, the poster image is a sharp contrast to the harsh conditions of real factories. The woman's hard hat looks rather like a soldier's helmet, but it is not what women factory workers wore for their jobs in light industry. Thus, the poster casts a gendered female worker in a masculine role in a way that exaggerates how these contrasts were played out in real life.

Although government images of women workers sometimes seemed to disregard their gender, gendered identity pervaded women's experience in the workplace. Factories where women worked used a gender hierarchy to maintain work discipline. The work environment was structured so that women performed unskilled and repetitive tasks that men never did, whereas virtually

---

5 The symbolic meaning of "industrial soldiers" should be understood in the specific cultural and historical context of South Korea. As Eun-Shil Kim states, "the project of industrializing the nation was metaphorized as a war against the old Korea, which had been stained by poverty" (1993:182).

Figure 1.1 A woman factory worker in a 1970 government poster

all managerial and supervisory positions were held by men (the only exceptions being women who occasionally filled the lowest-level supervisory positions). This subordination of women within the workplace seemed natural or common sense (cf. Ong 1987) because it derived from the traditional hierarchical relationship between the genders that permeated society outside the workplace.

Women's employers also capitalized on the culturally defined life-cycle expectations of young women by offering them short-term employment. Both

6

workers and their employers accorded little importance to women's factory careers, seeing factory work as a transition phase before women took up their primary adult roles as wives and mothers. The constant turnover in the labor force kept wages down and increased the marginalization of women workers within the factory setting.

Viewed from the perspective of traditional Korean expectations, factory jobs for young women represented both change and continuity. When young women took factory jobs, they acquired an unprecedented public role outside the household, but the low status and meager wages attached to these jobs were wholly in accordance with the low status with which young women were conventionally regarded.

Many aspects of women's position in contemporary South Korean society are rooted in Neo-Confucianism,[6] which was Korea's state ideology under the Yi dynasty (1392–1910). Although Confucianism no longer occupies a formal position in the ideology of the state, it continues to be an important element of Korean cultural tradition (Hye-joang Cho 1986, 1988; Kihl 1994; Robinson 1991; Eunhee Kim Yi 1993) and promotes such core social values as cooperation, filial piety, social harmony, deference to social superiors, and the importance of education.[7]

Traditional Korean Neo-Confucianism stressed hierarchical relationships between men and women, and between elders and juniors. Male and female spheres of activity were kept separate, and women were barred from participation in public life. A woman's only proper roles were within her family and household, and she was instructed to defer to her father until she married, to her husband during her marriage, and to her son when she became widowed.[8]

---

6 "Students of Korean society have long stressed its Confucian character. American observers . . . are fond of saying that Koreans 'out-Chinese' the Chinese in their devotion to Confucianism" (Janelli and Janelli 1982, p. 177).

7 Confucian values still pervade Korean culture, especially in regard to family and gender roles. Social harmony and hierarchical relationships within which persons in subordinate positions are expected to show deference are key aspects of those values. The five basic relationships are loyalty between lord and subject; filial piety between father and son; order between old and young; separate roles between husband and wife; and trust between friend and friend. Except for the last, all of these relationships are hierarchical, and East Asian societies influenced by Confucianism are notable for their emphasis on hierarchy in social relationships (cf. Nakane 1970; Tu 1984). For an examination of the historical circumstances and social implications of the Confucianization of Korean society under the Yi dynasty, see Deuchler (1977, 1992) and De Bary and Haboush (1985).

8 In practice, several factors ameliorated the low status generally accorded to women within Confucian traditions. First, as women grew older, they became entitled to the respect due to

The Confucian concept of filial piety was utilized by the government in its push for sacrifice from workers. Women workers were encouraged to behave as dutiful daughters toward their families, their employers, and the state. The ideal of the dutiful daughter is a powerful one, rooted in Korea's traditional family system.[9] To be dutiful, a daughter should cheerfully accept her low social status and devote herself to the family that is about to expel her.[10] And because daughters are considered only temporary members of their natal families, the dutiful daughter is one of the culture's strongest images of altruistic, selfless behavior.

Recent changes in society, notably urbanization, women's increasing participation in the labor market, and the increasing age of marriage, have provided women with more opportunities to contribute to their natal families and thus to express their filial piety. In spite of its denial of a woman's own interests, the ideal of the dutiful daughter remains central to the self-image of most young women. In fact, many young women take jobs in factories in order to help provide the financial needs of their parents and siblings.[11]

Filial piety and devotion to duty were featured in the government workers' magazine, *Nodong* (Labor). It published a prize-winning essay entitled "I am a Textile Worker," in which Won Yong-Suk describes her thirteen years as a factory worker. Won fulfills the role of dutiful daughter and describes herself as her family's main breadwinner, supporting her parents and four younger siblings. She acknowledges that life as a factory worker was hard but explains:

> I tried to convince myself to be responsible for my family and four
> younger siblings and told myself to carry out my duty as the

elders. Second, women were able to exercise authority within their own households, where the senior woman was considered the inside master (*anchuin*). Third, although Confucian ideology was dominant among the upper classes, it was only one component of traditional Korean culture. Among the peasantry, Confucianism had less influence and never completely extinguished antihierarchical ideas. Peasant women monopolized such important but formally low-status roles as shaman (*mansin*). For discussions of Korean shamanism, see Harvey (1979) and Kendall (1988).

9 Under Korea's traditional patrilineal family system, daughters lost their family membership when they married, so they were not considered permanent members of their natal families.

10 An idealized image of a daughter's filial piety occurs in the popular folk tale of *Sim Chŏng*, in which an adolescent girl agrees to die in order to restore her father's eyesight. The story's continuing popularity illustrates the legacy of Confucian values.

11 Nearly a fifth of the women workers I surveyed in Masan in 1987 responded that the main reason they started to work was to provide full or partial support for their families or to help pay for their siblings' education.

oldest. . . . I felt so proud of myself for helping my seven-member family . . . and thus, I began to enjoy working. (Won 1975:86)[12]

Her selfless devotion to duty and disregard of her own interests made her the ideal worker from the government's perspective.

LOW-WAGE INDUSTRIALIZATION AND THIRD WORLD WOMEN

Although South Korean industrialization has been exceptional in many ways, its global context requires examination. The manner in which women have been incorporated into the manufacturing sector, in particular, is part of a global trend in which capitalism takes advantage of the undervalued labor of young women. The existence of a gender wage gap, with wages of women being substantially less than those of similarly qualified men, is virtually universal, but it reaches its greatest extreme in South Korea (ILO statistics cited in Amsden 1989:204). The use of women in labor-intensive industries in South Korea reveals some striking parallels with earlier phases of capitalist industrialization (especially in the United States), but such features as electronics assembly plants and the establishment of Free Trade Zones (FTZs) are distinctive components of the late-twentieth-century global economy.

From the early 1960s, multinational corporations based in developed areas (e.g. the United States, Japan, Western Europe) began to build factories in Third World countries to manufacture export goods for the world market. Export-oriented industrialization became a popular development strategy for Third World countries, and a new international division of labor was created as multinational corporations sought to take advantage of the low wages paid in Third World countries by dividing the production process among various

---

12 When Wŏn Yŏng-suk wrote her essay in 1975, she was thirty years old, still single and working as a textile worker. In publishing Won's essay, the government has chosen to present someone whose circumstances were atypical among women factory workers. Although one can see that her self-effacement and her total devotion to her family and her company reflect qualities that the government sought to promote, it is ironic that the government featured a woman whose future prospects seem so limited and even gloomy. In fact, she seems to have been selected on the basis of criteria more appropriate to a male worker's career, where a long period of dedicated service might be rewarded. As a female textile worker at age thirty, she would have had no hope of promotion to managerial status, was too old to be a desirable bride and was not even well educated because she left middle school before graduating. When these factors are considered, her story seems more likely to arouse pity than admiration.

9

plants of one firm.[13] The technology-intensive processes were retained in the home country's factories, and labor-intensive parts of the production process were relocated wherever labor costs were lowest (Frobel et al. 1980; Grunwald and Flamm 1985). In many cases, these labor-intensive tasks consisted of nothing more than assembling semifinished components.

The new international division of labor is a product of the collaboration of economic forces in both developed and developing countries. By the 1960s, advances in manufacturing technology enabled corporations to practice "de-skilling," splitting off the labor-intensive phases of production and relocating them in areas of the world where labor was less expensive (Braverman 1974). Technological advances in communication and transportation also facilitated the flight of capital. Simultaneously, many Third World countries were abandoning failed attempts to modernize by import substitution. Hence, many countries undertook export-oriented development strategies, hoping specifically to (1) earn foreign exchange, (2) reduce high unemployment, and (3) transfer technology. Export processing, often located in specific FTZs exempt from tariffs and other regulations, was seen as a quick way to boost the level of exports. Governments in developing countries regarded export processing as the answer to their problem of chronic high unemployment. Typical of this attitude was a Malaysian government official quoted as saying, "We wanted electronics companies because they are so fast-moving . . . they come in and quickly soak up people" (*Wall Street Journal,* September 20, 1973).

Export processing finds the cheap labor it seeks in young women, and export processing industries throughout the world depend on the labor of young, single women sixteen to twenty-five years old (80% to 90%, according to Fuentes and Ehrenreich 1983).[14] Women have, of course, been part of

---

13 Lim describes export-oriented industrialization in historical terms as a phase of monopoly capitalism. She identifies three stages in foreign investment by the United States, Japan, and Western Europe: (1) the traditional colonial mode of production, concentrating on the extraction of primary raw material from the colonized countries and the importing of manufactured consumer goods from metropolitan countries; (2) the import substitute period, concentrating on the establishment of manufacturing industries to replace imported manufactured goods in the local market; and (3) the new international division of labor, involving labor-intensive factories in developing countries manufacturing goods for export to the developed countries under the aegis of multinational corporations (1978:1–2).

14 In the 1970s and 1980s, many researchers wrote about the women workers in the export processing industries throughout the world. A few salient works are Chapkis and Enloe (1982), Elson and Pearson (1981), Fernandez-Kelly (1983), Frobel, Heinrichs, and Kreye (1980), Fuentes and Ehrenreich (1983), Grossman (1979), Kung (1983), Lim (1978, 1983a, 1983b), Nash and Fernandez-Kelly (1983), Ong (1987) and Safa (1981).

the manufacturing labor force since the beginning of the Industrial Revolution, especially in low-paid industries where the work has been considered "women's work" (cf. Gutman 1973; Hareven 1982). Historians (e.g. Dublin 1981; Hareven and Langenbach 1978; Hershatter 1986; Honig 1986; Kessler-Harris 1981, 1982; Lown 1990; Norwood 1990; Tilly and Scott 1987; Tsurumi 1990) have described the mix of exploitation and opportunity that factory work provided for women as they came to participate in paid industrial labor. Freed from the strict labor legislation of their home countries, the multinational corporations have re-created industrial conditions similar to, or perhaps worse than, those found in the workshops of Europe and America more than a hundred years ago (Rosen 1987:22). One researcher describes labor conditions of the export processing industries as "wages on a par with what an 11-year-old boy could earn on a paper route, and living conditions resembling what Engels found in Manchester" (Ehrenreich 1982).

Young female workers in the offshore production factories are not only underpaid but also a highly vulnerable and manipulable work force because of "(1) their behavior, expectations and attitudes (linked to a gender-specific socialization process); (2) their relative youth (and consequent lack of experience); [and] (3) their subordinate position within their own households" (Fernandez-Kelly 1983:72; Lutz 1988).[15] Once they have entered the work force, young women are manipulated to keep them inferior, subordinate and marginal vis-à-vis males. Management utilizes traditional patriarchal ideas (Confucian, Islamic, Christian or whatever prevails locally) regarding women's roles, behavior, and status to control workers and encourage identification with the company (Grossman 1979; Lim 1978, 1983a). In this way, management achieves two main goals: It improves work productivity and it inhibits the rise of any kind of unified resistance to company authority from women workers (Grossman 1979:3–4).

Young women workers in FTZs are frequently treated as minors. In MAFEZ, for example, it was usual for managers and male supervisors to address women workers as children by using their given names and to refer collectively to their

---

15 The forms of domination introduced through the export processing industry interact with local forms of patriarchy to alter existing gender relations, resulting in forms of gender domination that are intensified, decomposed and recombined into new forms of gender subordination. A father may strengthen his authority over his daughters in order to control their wages (e.g. Kung 1976). Wages earned in factories may become part of dowry payments needed to acquire husbands. Women are also subject to men as supervisors and bosses in authority roles separate from family structures (Elson and Pearson 1981:157–159).

11

section or line workers as "my children" (*urijip aedŭl*). Workers felt humiliated by these practices but were uncomfortable about speaking out.

The low status and harsh conditions experienced by women workers in the export processing industry give rise to various forms of protest and rebellion even though, in many cultures, powerful constraints act to prevent young women from directly confronting social superiors (as with young women throughout Asia; cf. Ong 1991:301). Public passivity and fatalism may conceal an inner, private rebellion, leading to protest phenomena such as the mass hysteria in Malaysian electronics factories discussed by Ong (1987, 1988). In situations where the ethnicity or nationality of managers differs from that of workers, this difference can provide a focus for what Ong describes as "cultural resistance" on the part of workers, and activities such as prayers can be both an assertion of cultural identity and a tactic to lessen work. Forms of covert, "everyday resistance" reportedly used by workers include work slow-downs, disruptions of factory routines and petty vandalism.

South Korean FTZs have specific characteristics that shape the form this resistance takes. Because even foreign-owned companies are staffed by Korean managers, cultural resistance is relatively muted, although national pride is invoked in labor disputes. The regimented workspace[16] in South Korean factories is supervised by sophisticated surveillance techniques and affords workers few opportunities for covert resistance. At the same time, the cultural conventions restraining young South Korean women from confronting their superiors are as strong as those existing anywhere in the world. Workers' grievances are thus completely suppressed until they accumulate into explosive confrontations, and these tend to be strongly political clashes between labor and capital that transcend the FTZs.

FTZs were only one relatively minor part of South Korea's development strategy. For a variety of reasons, the country was able to coordinate its push to develop heavy industry with strong international demand for its products. At the national level, it has thus avoided many of the societal problems that have accompanied FTZs elsewhere and drawn some of the strongest condemnations – for example, that expected technology transfers failed to eventuate and that unemployment among men remained high because "foreign companies

---

16 Not only has South Korea had a succession of military governments, but the fact that all South Korean men perform compulsory military service has contributed to the militarization of all aspects of society (cf. Janelli 1993:48).

investing in the FTZs sought young single women, thus creating a new female industrial force where none had been envisioned" (Ong 1991:281). South Korea's economic growth has been accompanied by a low and steadily declining rate of unemployment,[17] and sophisticated technology has become established in heavy industry, even if FTZs have played little part in either process.

Nevertheless, the two South Korean FTZs have been typical components of the new international division of labor, and have much in common with FTZs in countries where development has not matched that of South Korea. The country's gender wage gap has kept South Korean women in a low-wage economy despite the "economic miracle." The Japanese electronics plants in Masan were set up, like the American *maquiladoras* of Mexico, as a mechanism for a company based in a wealthy country to avoid paying wages at the level established in its home area. Like those in other FTZs, factories in MAFEZ have low levels of capital investment and no long-term commitment to local employees. Their presence in the FTZ is based on short-term economic calculations, and they not only use threats of relocation to intimidate workers, but many have actually relocated when local costs rose.

The young single women who comprised the main workforce in MAFEZ expected to leave the paid labor force upon marriage in order to become full-time housewives. Their commitment to the institution of the family was reinforced by the continued existence of large gender wage disparities. Because low wages gave women little incentive to remain employed, it was a better economic investment for a woman to provide support services for her husband than to hold her own job. The poverty of women's labor market options made "the exchange of domestic work for financial support" something to be highly valued (Ferree 1985), and women traded off being a good wife and mother for economic support. Men who held well-paid blue-collar jobs in heavy industry were usually able to fulfill their part of this bargain, but men in more marginal situations often could not, forcing their wives to return to work in subcontracting factories under worse conditions than those prevailing in MAFEZ. Women who became widowed or divorced were also forced back into this doubly disadvantaged workforce.

Although the family was a focal consideration for young South Korean women, the family system marginalized them, as it positioned them between

---

17 "Unemployment has been steadily declining, and in recent years has been below 3 percent" (Cho Soon 1994:19).

their natal families and the families that they were about to form. Their location within society was thus temporarily indeterminate, and their final status depended on their ability to garner resources and think strategically about marriage and the future. Women factory workers in MAFEZ expected their marriage to be the most important economic and social event in their lives, and they devoted themselves to preparing for it. Although Western ideas about romantic love were fashionable, marriage was still viewed as a practical relationship and was preceded by prolonged negotiations between the two families involved. In order for a factory worker to be in a sound negotiating position, she needed both a good reputation and a substantial dowry.

South Korean factory women's careful preservation of their reputations contrasts sharply with what has been reported about workers in FTZs in other parts of the world. With their largely young female workforces, FTZs are arenas where local and metropolitan notions of gender hierarchy are reassembled into novel forms of gender subordination. Workers may find that any freedom from traditional restrictions on young women results in their being labeled sexually loose and immoral. For example, "A news article on Nogales notes a popular image of the Border Program as a place of sexual conquest where everyday talk included 'innuendoes about *maquiladora* managers who fornicate their way down assembly lines or companies that provide stud services as incentives'" (Ong 1991:294). Factory workers in Cuidad Juarez are reported to "augment their wages by working as prostitutes" (ibid.:297). Some workers in Kwantung "hoped to achieve geographic and social mobility by marrying Hong Kong tourists or entering Hong Kong prostitution rings" (ibid.:298). South Korean women factory workers do contend with unflattering stereotypes, but they are greatly concerned about their reputations and the idea that they might casually moonlight as prostitutes is unthinkable. There were a few instances, however, of women who worked in the sex industry and kept factory jobs to disguise the source of their income (see Chapter 3).

The way workers in MAFEZ saved money for their dowries and marriage expenses was a dramatic expression of their strategizing for marriage. In spite of their extremely low wages, single women workers in MAFEZ regularly saved money for their dowries, even if this required them to do without basic necessities or to skip breakfast and dinner. Most workers accorded much more importance to dowry saving than to consumerism. Women thus reinvested their income from factory work into traditionally structured families, a fact that again points to multilayered interconnections between patriarchal and capitalist systems of domination.

CLASS STRUGGLE OR FAMILY STRUGGLE?

Patriarchal gender ideology has its most direct effect on women workers by defining women in terms of their roles in families. Because women regard themselves as little more than temporary workers, they are willing to provide the low-paid, unskilled labor needed for light industry, and their focus on family diverts their attention from labor issues and makes them more difficult to organize. The fact that most women workers are young and inexperienced further discourages them from engaging in political activity.

Gender ideology also shapes women's participation in the labor movement by the way it structures women's employment opportunities. Women find jobs in the factories of small- to medium-sized companies engaged in light industry. Women factory workers are thus divided among many small companies where grievances are likely to be localized and collective actions unlikely to produce major impacts. The exception occurred during the most repressive phases of military rule, when the rights of workers were almost totally suppressed. During these times, the decentralized structure of women's employment made it impossible for the government to eliminate the last vestiges of activism among women workers. Labor disputes involving women workers in medium-sized companies became foci of antigovernment political activity and assumed national importance.

Writing of recent trends in women's labor history in the United States, Ruth Milkman observes:

> Certainly, it was necessary to challenge the total invisibility of women in conventional accounts of labor history. . . . But this led, implicitly or explicitly, toward an overly simplistic and highly romanticized conception of women's labor history. The old myths of women's lack of interest or involvement in labor struggle were effectively supplanted by new myths, which were equally one-sided and, indeed, the mirror-image of the old. In the new feminist orthodoxy, each discovery of female militancy was taken as evidence of a virtually limitless potential for women's activism in the labor movement – a potential thwarted primarily by the disinterest or active hostility of male-dominated unions. While yielding some valuable insights and motivating a substantial body of important research, this approach could not do justice to the complexity of its subject. (1985:xii)

Discussions about women's participation in the labor struggle in South Korea similarly veer between the extremes of leaving women invisible or presenting a romanticized view that overstates women's accomplishments. Women are generally ignored in discussions of such events as the 1987 nationwide labor uprising, whereas scattered strikes conducted by women workers during the height of *Yusin* repression are enshrined as great events even though, in most cases, the government was able to completely suppress all publicity about the strikes for many years.

A tendency related to the romanticizing of women's role within the labor movement is the exaggeration of women's victimization. This has two corollaries: First, when women do confront management, their importance is seen in terms of how brutally their efforts are put down rather than in terms of their accomplishments; second, ordinary workers are seen as nothing but victims. The image of a young woman working extraordinarily long hours for inadequate wages is a compelling icon of suffering. Furthermore, Korean cultural values stress the defenselessness of young women, and in MAFEZ, where the factories are owned by foreigners, nationalist sentiment contributes to the production of an image of the worker as victim and martyr. Literature on the new international division of labor also dwells on the image of the factory worker as victim. Although I do not want to understate the difficult conditions under which women factory workers labor, I was struck in Masan by the ways in which women took the fiercely totalizing experience of factory work and managed to use it as a foundation for more highly valued aspects of their lives.

Sociological and political-economic analyses of South Korean industrialization often lump workers into the single category of the "exploited masses," united by shared victimization (*AMPO* 1977, 1990; Choi Jang Jip 1983; Cho Sŭng-hyok 1984; Cho Soon-Kyoung 1987; Cho Wha Soon 1988; Committee for Justice and Peace of South Korea 1976; Deyo 1987; Im Yŏng-il 1984; Koo 1990, 1993; Ogle 1990; Spencer 1988). However, neither the workers nor their conditions at work are homogeneous. Women come to the factories with significant differences in terms of education and family background. For example, education is the principal criterion that determines whether a woman will get a job in a relatively comfortable, high paying electronics factory or work under sweatshop conditions in a garment factory. The factories intensify those existing differences and create additional ones by their hiring and wage policies. Other circumstances, such as personal or family misfortune, also contribute to differences that greatly affect the quality of life of individual women. The ways in which women themselves perceive status differences have not been adequately addressed in previous studies. I argue that the perceived differences among women workers are crucial in understanding how the myth of social mobility is created and reproduced among women workers.

Throughout this book, I contend that women in factories are motivated by a complex nexus of public and private considerations within which they interpret their individual situations. Chapter 2 describes women workers in terms of their factory experience. I present the results of my research survey that measured demographic and sociological characteristics of the MAFEZ workforce in 1987 and describe how workers were treated and regarded by their employers. Productivity and control were the dominant themes that emerged from my research. With sixty-hour workweeks common, workers' daily lives were completely dominated by the factory experience.

For most women, however, factory work was a means to an end. Their belief that they were temporary workers was both a source of emotional strength, because they could envision a better life in the not-too-distant future, and a source of political weakness, because they did not expect to be in the factories long enough to benefit from improvements promoted by unions. In Chapter 3, I consider how workers experienced their lives as factory workers, which for most women was as a preparation for marriage. Marriage gave many women an escape from the drudgery of factory work, but it generally provided only a single chance for success (second marriages were very rare). A marriage that ended in early death or divorce, or one in which the man was unable to support his family, left the woman in the unfortunate and unforeseen position of having to return to factory work. The labor force of married women workers was clearly on the bottom of any status hierarchy, but few single women expected to ever become part of it.

With the nationwide labor uprising in 1987, many workers in Masan joined with workers throughout the country and became more aware of their collective strength. The strikes that followed demonstrated women's bargaining power, especially by increasing their wages. In Chapter 4, I examine the political actions taken by workers and unions, beginning with the period of the labor uprising and continuing throughout the next few years as political repression returned and factories closed. Throughout this period, the struggle was intense, but victories were ambiguous because rising wages were matched by falling employment.

In Chapter 5, I examine the roots of working-class consciousness, especially the relationship between workers and intellectuals within the labor movement. Students and intellectuals gave workers guidance and support during their struggles, and their political theories were particularly important in providing the ideological foundations on which workers built their own sense of class identity. Nevertheless, intellectuals remained, in a sense, outsiders to the working class, and workers' attitudes toward them were ambivalent. The worker–student relationship has gone through major changes recently, as student opposition to the government diminished following the establishment of a civilian government. Most of the students who were involved in labor organizing have left the movement, although a few have stayed with workers' organizations. In analyzing this relationship, I pay particular attention to how workers and students evaluate the contribution made by students to the labor movement, especially how those still active within the movement feel about middle-class students who took real personal risks to join workers for a few years and then retreated back to a secure position in the middle class.

The contribution made by middle-class activists was important, but working-class consciousness was also rooted in the experiences of workers. Those women who actively participated in labor unions began to see themselves as working class and to consider their previous middle-class identification as a misperception. They began to feel proud of being working class, and many made personal sacrifices for the movement. After they endured hardship, including periods of imprisonment, the constraints of class and gender have rematerialized in the lives of the young women who became labor activists in 1987. Most of them have, as expected, married and left the labor force. Activists from 1987 are still committed members of the working class, but with their new responsibilities as wives and mothers, few remain factory workers. As former workers who are married to workers, they are still involved, but their role is no longer as clear as it was when they were single.

The women factory workers of MAFEZ are a diverse group, but they are united by the factory experience and by a desire for a better life. In presenting the lives of ordinary workers, I illustrate their creativity and perseverance as they struggle to make life better for themselves and their families. Among these workers were a number of truly heroic young women who expanded their mission into a struggle for a just society. Their sacrifices have given voice and unity to their fellow factory workers and have produced important changes in MAFEZ.

2

The Process of Production in the Masan Free Export Zone

FROM its inception, the Masan Free Export Zone (MAFEZ) has been a leading center of South Korean light industry and a major employer of young women in South Kyŏngsang Province. The cheap labor of young single women has been essential to the success of the Zone and its enterprises. This chapter looks at the process of production in the factories of MAFEZ, and the ways in which the workforce was controlled and manipulated to reach high levels of productivity. I begin by describing the Zone and the alliance between the South Korean government and foreign capital that led to its formation. Next, based on my survey of more than 700 women workers, I examine the background of the workforce employed in the zone: Who are they, and how do they come to be factory workers? Finally, I draw on my own experience in working at KTE, a large MAFEZ electronics company, and on extensive interviews with workers to consider the manufacturing process in the Zone's factories: How are women workers used and controlled by their employers? By examining the process of production, I lay the foundation for a deeper understanding of how women are caught between global capitalism and South Korean patriarchy.

MASAN CITY

The Free Export Zone

Masan is a port city located on the southeastern coast of Korea, only a short distance by sea from Japan. It was already a minor manufacturing center in 1970, when it was selected as the site for the larger and more important of two Free Export Zones to be established as part of the national program of export-led industrialization.[1] Initially, MAFEZ was extremely attractive to foreign

---

1 The other Free Export Zone, at Iri in South Chŏlla Province, did not open until 1973. It is much smaller than the one in Masan and is dominated by textile and garment factories.

investors, and by 1975, 101 companies were operating factories there.[2] Many of these factories were very small (with less than US $50,000 in investment) because the government was not very selective in choosing these companies (MAFEZ Administrative Office 1987). In 1978, thirty-three of the ninety-five operating companies employed fewer than 100 workers. When a recession hit the world economy, many companies collapsed and fled without paying severance pay or overdue wages (Han'guk Katorik Nodong Chŏngnyŏnhoe 1980). By 1987, there were only seventy-six companies operating in the Zone (MAFEZ Administrative Office, Monthly Statistics). However, these tended to be larger and better established firms, and employment in the Zone reached its peak in that year. The main industries were electronics (twenty-three companies), metal (eighteen companies), precision equipment (seventeen companies) and garment manufacturing (twelve companies) (MAFEZ Administrative Office, Monthly Statistics).

Given its geographical proximity to Japan, it is not surprising that MAFEZ accommodated primarily Japanese firms (see Table 2.1). Japanese electronics companies were the Zone's most important investors. In 1987, twenty-one of the twenty-three electronics factories operating in the Zone were Japanese owned. The other industries were also dominated by Japanese or Japanese-South Korean joint venture companies, and in 1987, fifty-six of the seventy-six companies operating were Japanese or Japanese–South Korean joint ventures. Although MAFEZ was set up solely for foreign firms, a 1981 modification of the law governing the Zone allowed South Korean-owned companies to operate within the Zone; by 1987 there were ten of these.

In 1987 the companies in the Zone employed 36,411 workers (8,389 men and 28,022 women). The electronics industry employed the largest number of female workers (over 18,000, 65% of the total female employees), followed by precision equipment and the garment and shoe industries (with about 3,000, 12% each). By 1990, the number of companies operating in the Zone had decreased to seventy and the number of workers had decreased to 20,142 (see Table 2.2). The decrease in workers has resulted from plant closings, attrition (mostly resignations by women intending to get married), and voluntary resig-

---

2 The industrial complex of MAFEZ consists of two sections. The first section has a land area of 803,235 square meters and the second section has a land area of 264,539 square meters. Each section contains some factory buildings built and owned by foreign companies and others built and owned by the government and made available for rental by foreign companies. In 1987, sixty companies owned their own buildings and sixteen rented space from the Zone's administrative office.

Table 2.1 *Companies operating in MAFEZ by country (1987)*

	Sole owners	Joint ventures	Total
South Korean	10	N/A	10
Japanese	40	16	56
U.S.	2	6	8
Other	0	2	2
Total	42	24	76

Source: MAFEZ Administrative Office, 1987.

Table 2.2 *Employment in MAFEZ*

Year	Total	Female	Male
1972	7,106	6,052	1,051
1973	21,240	17,275	3,965
1974	20,822	15,196	5,626
1975	22,586	17,026	5,560
1976	29,953	22,787	7,166
1977	30,719	22,927	7,792
1978	30,960	23,298	7,662
1979	31,163	23,280	7,873
1980	28,532	22,183	6,349
1981	28,016	21,782	6,231
1982	26,012	20,029	5,983
1983	30,989	24,491	6,498
1984	33,858	26,697	7,161
1985	28,983	22,342	6,641
1986	34,883	27,018	7,865
1987	36,411	28,022	8,389
1988	33,080	24,975	8,105
1989	23,076	16,595	6,481
1990	20,142	14,346	5,796

Source: Masan Free Export Zone Administrative Office Monthly Report.

nations encouraged by severance pay. There has been no public recruitment since 1987.

The volume of exports from MAFEZ increased steadily from US $856,640 in 1971 to nearly US $1.8 billion in 1988 (Kyŏngnam Sahoe Yŏn'guso 1993:15). However, MAFEZ never provided more than a small proportion of South

Table 2.3 *MAFEZ exports compared to total South Korean exports*
(millions of U.S. dollars)

	MAFEZ exports	Total exports	MAFEZ exports/ total exports
1971	0.9	1,132	0.08%
1977	30.3	10,047	0.30%
1981	696.3	20,671	3.37%
1985	809.3	26,442	3.06%
1986	1,033.4	33,913	3.05%
1987	1,399.5	46,244	3.03%
1988	1,769.2	59,648	2.97%
1989	1,666.7	61,409	2.71%
1990	1,405.4	63,124	2.23%
1991	1,463.4	69,582	2.10%

Sources: MAFEZ 1987; Kyŏngnam Sahoe Yŏn'guso 1993:15; Cho Soon 1994:24.

Korea's exports, and the relative importance of its contribution to the national economy has decreased as other sectors of the economy have grown. Until 1977 MAFEZ provided less than 1% of the nation's exports. The figure increased to 3.3% in 1981, but the proportion of total exports produced in MAFEZ has gradually declined since then (see Table 2.3).

Local residents had little idea of the Zone's purpose when it first opened. One woman who worked in the Zone during the early 1970s said, "When I first started to work there, I did not know what the Free Export Zone meant except that the place was for making exports and [was] mostly owned by Japanese." Many workers told me that they did not know what MAFEZ was until they started to work there. Some even thought that it was a women's school because every morning they saw rows of women walking there.

With the establishment of MAFEZ, Masan City grew rapidly. The population more than doubled between 1970 and 1975. Following the oil crisis and subsequent cutbacks in employment, the population increased less rapidly, averaging less than 1% a year between 1975 and 1980. After the economy recovered, population growth again increased to an average of 3.2% a year between 1980 and 1985. Workers formed a large segment of this population, and by 1989 23% of the population of Masan were production workers (110,987 out of a total population of 473,466). The rapid expansion of the population has led to a crisis in housing, with many people being inadequately housed and overcrowding constituting a serious problem.

The young workers of MAFEZ have also changed the age structure of the population of Masan. "The age cohort of 15–19 comprised 31% of the total population of Masan City in 1970 and the percentage increased to 36% in 1984" (Lee, Hwang, and Lee 1987:37). MAFEZ has become a major manufacturing center within South Kyŏngsang Province. By 1985, the 28,983 workers employed in the Zone comprised 10.1% of the total workers in the manufacturing sector within the province (MAFEZ Administrative Office 1987).

Adjoining Masan is the city of Ch'angwŏn, where in 1975 the government established a heavy industrial estate as part of a nationwide program to develop heavy industry. Machinery and metals are the major industries in Ch'angwŏn. In 1989, these heavy industries employed a predominantly male workforce of approximately 70,000 workers (Kang 1990:138).[3] Ch'angwŏn also grew rapidly during the 1970s and 1980s and had an extremely high proportion of production workers among the city's economically active population. Thirty-eight percent of Ch'angwŏn's population were production workers in 1989 (82,453 out of a total of 214,829) (ibid.:136).

In addition to providing the land and infrastructure of the Zone, the South Korean government sought to attract foreign investors by offering tax incentives, simplified administrative procedures, waivers of the free trade union organization law and other inducements. The tax benefits included an exemption from all income taxes for the first five years and taxation at half the usual rate for the following three years; a total exemption from the business tax; an exemption from acquisition taxes for the first five years and taxation at half the usual rate for the following three years; and a total exemption from all individual income taxes.

One of the incentives that the South Korean government offered foreign investors was a hard-working and compliant labor force. Although labor unions were not illegal, "labor peace" was ensured by a policy that imposed so many restrictions on labor organizing that no unions were formed. After 1980, "joint labor–management councils" (*nosa hyŏbuihoe*) were introduced as a substitute for labor unions. Labor representatives for these councils were chosen by management and therefore could do little besides listen deferentially to the presentation of company policy at council meetings.

---

3 In 1989, the workforce in Ch'angwŏn consisted of 60,000 men and 10,000 women.

Out-Zone Processing

Masan's manufacturing industries are not limited to the Free Export Zone. Subcontractors operating outside MAFEZ assemble components using parts provided by the companies in the Zone through what is known as "out-zone processing." Companies in the Zone rely on out-zone processing for three main reasons. First, factories can increase their manufacturing capacity more quickly by subcontracting with companies outside the Zone. Second, a subcontractor can add short-term workers more easily than a company operating in the Zone. Third, overall production costs are lower outside the zone.

Out-zone processing began as soon as MAFEZ started to operate. The conditions imposed on out-zone processing were that subcontractors had to be owned by Koreans, no more than 60% of the value of the finished goods could be manufactured outside the Zone and subcontractors could not produce finished goods. Also, defective parts received by factories in the Zone had to be repaired in the Zone rather than sent back to the subcontractor that made them. In spite of this regulation, I heard rumors that some factories smuggled parts out to be repaired beyond the Zone.

Both the government and the companies in the Zone encouraged the growth of subcontracting firms. The government saw them as promoting economic development and providing additional employment, and foreign companies welcomed the opportunity to escape the regulations of MAFEZ and reduce production costs.

Although not actually located in MAFEZ, these firms were very much a part of its manufacturing process. For example, one electronics company in the zone used twenty different subcontracting firms outside the Zone in order to meet its annual export volume of over US $100,000,000. Because the production volume of MAFEZ fluctuates with world market demand, subcontracting firms serve as a buffer, absorbing the impact of the booms and busts of business cycles. MAFEZ administrators assert that "without out-zone processing, MAFEZ could not have handled the sharp increase in export volume" (MAFEZ 1987).

Workers in subcontracting factories could be easily dismissed and also served as a "reserve labor pool" for the big companies. This workforce consisted mostly of married women who were older than those hired in MAFEZ. It also included substantial numbers of women under eighteen who could not work legally in MAFEZ. Out-zone subcontracting firms employed a substan-

Table 2.4 *Employment at out-zone firms compared to MAFEZ*

	Out-zone firms	Out-zone employees	MAFEZ employees	No. in out-zone/ no. in MAFEZ
1976	94	4,518	29,953	15%
1980	108	4,620	28,532	16%
1983	207	7,787	30,989	25%
1984	252	8,521	33,858	25%
1985	193	7,509	28,983	26%
1987	347	12,364	36,441	34%
1988	525	16,686	33,080	50%
1991	330	9,348	17,741	53%

Source: Kyŏngnam Sahoe Yŏn'guso 1993:9.

tial number of production workers, and the number of employees in these firms has increased steadily relative to the number of employees in the Zone. In 1987 more than 12,000 workers were employed in out-zone processing (see Table 2.4), equal to about 34% of the number employed in the Zone itself.

Subcontracting firms were run with little investment and less concern for the workers. Owners simply rented a space and tried to produce as much as possible as cheaply as possible. Out-zone processing firms have even started to move to rural areas, where rents and labor costs are lower than in Masan. The quality of the components assembled in these factories was very uneven. Workers in the Zone frequently complained about rejects produced in subcontracting factories. One woman told me:

> I could not understand why the company sent those parts to subcontracting factories. Sometimes, over 10% of components assembled outside are rejects, but supervisors just order us to fix them. However, I learned that the company makes more money if it sends work out to subcontracting factories even with 10% rejects.

One supervisor told me that his company saved 30% of its overhead this way because they did not have to pay bonuses, allowances, medical insurance and so on. Big companies cut expenses by giving orders to subcontracting factories, and owners of those subcontracting firms made money squeezing wage differences from their workers.

25

Facilities for Workers

The infrastructure provided for MAFEZ by the government also included facilities for workers. These consisted of a dormitory, a welfare hall and a health clinic. The first two MAFEZ dormitory buildings were opened in 1973 and together accommodated 600 workers. The dormitory was administered by a committee appointed by the companies operating in the Zone. Following the oil crisis of 1974, the dormitory closed and the committee was dissolved. The dormitory reopened in 1977, and a new administrative committee was organized from the thirty-four companies that employed more than 200 workers. The reopened dormitory facilities accommodated 850 workers.

Additional buildings were opened in 1981 and 1982, so by 1987 the dormitory consisted of four residential buildings with a total of 336 rooms accommodating 2,050 workers from thirty-one companies. Each room was shared by six women and was just large enough for them to roll out their bedding at night. Room and board cost 30,000 won per person per month, paid half by the worker and half by her employer. Only the larger factories were willing to make this contribution, so the dormitory only housed workers from the largest companies. Dormitory facilities included an additional building containing a cafeteria and a public bath.

The matron who supervised the dormitory had been there since 1973. Each building had its own supervisor, who reported to the matron. Each floor and each room had its representative. The floor representative was responsible for taking attendance every night at 10 o'clock. Women had to be in their rooms by that time unless they were working on a night shift or attending night classes. In 1987, 264 dormitory residents were attending high school and 14 were attending college.

The dormitory imposed strict rules on the workers, so parents could send their young daughters to the Zone without worrying about their reputations. The dormitory, in effect, extended family control to the factory environment. If a woman missed attendance call three times, she was reprimanded by the matron and punished by being assigned to clean the bathrooms for a month. If a woman stayed out more than three times without getting prior permission, she was asked to leave the dormitory.[4]

There was a long wait, sometimes more than six months, to get into the

---

4 Even with the strict rules of dormitory living, some women got into trouble. There were even a few cases of dormitory residents getting pregnant.

dormitory. The main reason workers wanted to live there was that it was so cheap. The worker's contribution was only 15,000 won a month. Room, board and transportation cost women living outside the dormitory about three times as much as for those living in the dormitory.

Another reason women wanted to stay in the dormitory was that their reputations were protected. They could tell prospective husbands and in-laws that they had lived there. The matron told me that she frequently vouched for the good behavior of dormitory residents to their future husbands and in-laws.

Despite the low cost of the dormitory and the importance of their reputations, however, many women moved out of the dormitory after a while. They complained about not having enough freedom and about not getting along with their roommates. An electronics worker stated:

> We do not choose our own roommates, so we do not always get perfect roommates. It is not easy to have six women sharing a room and we cannot ask for a transfer even if we do not get along with some of them. Some women play their radios loudly when others would rather have a quiet evening to read. When I live with my own friends, I can ask them not to bother me, but here in the dormitory I cannot do that and I just have to put up with it until I get out of here.

Women also complained about the meals provided by the dormitory. They said, "The food here is worse than the lunch at the factory" or "I do not understand why they cannot come up with better menus." Furthermore, because the meal schedule was so rigid, workers frequently missed meals and had to buy their own dinner outside.

Dormitory buildings were equipped with boiler systems and hot water was supposed to be available all the time, but workers frequently found that their rooms were cold in winter and only the first women to get up had enough hot water for washing in the morning. Workers had to choose between having a little extra sleep and having hot water for washing.

In 1983, the government opened a "Welfare Hall" in the Zone to provide recreational facilities for workers. This facility was little used because workers had so little free time. Classes offered at the Welfare Hall included calligraphy, flower design, and Japanese and English languages, but only a few workers attended them.

Workers also found that the health clinic in the Zone was inadequate to their needs. Medical personnel usually just gave women some pills and told them to rest. The clinic had neither the personnel nor the facilities to cope with industrial accidents. Furthermore, although women could not get much help from the clinic, they did not have the time or money to visit outside doctors when they got sick.

Age Restrictions on Hiring

Most workers in MAFEZ are young women between sixteen and twenty-five years old (see Table 2.5). The strictest age limits on hiring are found in the higher-status jobs in the electronics industry. Because electronics assembly work requires good eyesight and manual dexterity, these companies seek a youthful labor force and usually only hire women between seventeen and twenty-two years of age. They actively recruit young women as they graduate from high school. Workers are allowed to continue to work after they reach age twenty-two or even after they get married, but most women leave the labor force by their middle to late twenties.

Those workers who continue beyond age twenty-six find that they no longer fit comfortably into the factory structure. Among the pressures brought to bear on them is teasing about their anomalous position. One worker told me that she was pressured to quit her job at a MAFEZ electronics company where she had worked for seven years by the teasing of her managers and coworkers. When she was twenty-seven, they started saying things like "When are you getting married?" and "My God, you will be here until you get to be a grandmother." She gave up her job in the Zone and found that the best she could do was to take a job at a factory outside where she made less money and worked longer hours. Ironically, her new factory was a subcontractor for her former employer.

Because the restrictive hiring policies of electronics factories are so well known, some women outside the age limits use someone else's identification card (usually a sister's) when they try to apply for jobs. When I was working at an electronics factory, my coworkers accepted that I was using false identification because they could tell that I was older than the factory's hiring limit. They were also worried that I would not be able to get another job at another electronics factory when I quit.

Women who leave jobs in the electronics industry for any reason are not able to return because of the age limit and must look for jobs either in garment factories or in subcontracting factories outside the Zone, which have more flexible hiring policies but also lower wages and worse working conditions.

28

Table 2.5 *Age distribution (from questionnaires)*

	Number of Workers			
Age	Single	Married	Total	%
15	3	0	3	0.4
16	20	0	20	2.8
17	45	0	45	6.3
18	82	0	82	11.4
19	94	0	94	13.1
20	111	0	111	15.5
21	98	2	100	13.9
22	98	2	100	13.9
23	63	3	66	9.2
24	40	4	44	6.1
25	17	4	21	2.9
26	3	2	5	0.7
27	1	1	2	0.3
28	0	3	3	0.4
29	0	0	0	0.0
30+	0	22	22	3.1
Total	675	43	718	100%

The age limit was temporarily lifted in 1987 because there was a labor shortage in MAFEZ. Even electronics companies then hired older (married) women, but only under temporary labor contracts specifying that the company had the right to lay them off whenever it wished. The labor shortage lasted only through the end of the year, and most older workers were laid off in 1988.

Out of 718 women working in MAFEZ factories who responded to my questionnaire in 1987,[5] nearly 90% were between seventeen and twenty-four

5 Administering survey questionnaires in Masan in 1987 was a difficult task. I received cooperation from people in official capacities only after I dropped any questions that might be at all
controversial, and with my limited access to workers, I was unable to administer my questionnaire to a truly random sample. Nevertheless, I was able to get basic demographic information
from a wide variety of workers in various industries. It was easier to locate single women
workers, and I collected 675 questionnaires from them. A total of 250 questionnaires were
distributed among residents of the MAFEZ dormitory with the cooperation of the matron. I also
distributed 200 questionnaires at the two major industrial high schools. The rest of the questionnaires were distributed at various factories through a network of friends and acquaintances
without the consent of the management. Although my sample was not random, the group
surveyed is diverse, and in general, their answers seem to be representative. An obvious bias is
that many respondents are pursuing education, and my sample also slightly overrepresents

29

years old.[6] There were very few workers in their late twenties or early thirties in the Zone because most women over twenty-six had left the workforce to get married. A small number of married women between their mid-thirties and early forties worked in the Zone and a few companies were known to hire these women, but most women in this age group had to look for jobs outside the Zone. Workers' voluntary resignations benefitted the companies in the Zone by enabling them to maintain a youthful workforce without incurring any costs associated with seniority. This workforce was not only cheap, but able to endure the repetitive and exhausting tasks associated with export processing. The youth and inexperience of the workforce also made it easier for management to control them.

How Well Educated Are Workers?

Electronics companies had more stringent education requirements than garment factories (see Table 2.6). Nearly two-thirds of the electronics factory workers who responded to my survey had completed high school, and most of the rest were attending high school night classes. Garment factories were less selective about the workers they hired, and many of their workers had a lower level of education. More than a third of the garment workers who answered my survey had no more than a middle school education (cf. Fernandez-Kelly 1983; Safa 1981). I even learned of one Masan hat factory that employed mostly workers who were illiterate or had only a primary school education.

In 1977, the government established "standard rules and regulations on

workers in both electronics and garment industries compared to employment statistics from the Zone.

Collecting data from married women was even more difficult. I could not conduct surveys at workplaces, and married women were residentially dispersed. Nevertheless, I managed to collect 105 questionnaires from married women who were current or former workers in the Zone. About half of these were administered directly by me and the other half were self-administered. Of these women, twenty-five were current or former electronics workers, sixty were current or former garment workers, and twenty were from other industries. Again, garment workers are slightly overrepresented. Forty-three of the married women were still working in factories, giving me a total of 718 workers for my survey.

6 The female labor force in MAFEZ is much younger than the general female labor force in South Korean manufacturing industries. For the nation as a whole, the proportion of older women workers has grown steadily since the early 1980s. In 1986, only 45% of the female labor force in manufacturing was twenty-four years old or less (Korean Women's Development Institute 1994:132). In the youthfulness of its female labor force, MAFEZ resembles export processing zones outside Korea, as well as earlier stages in South Korean manufacturing industries.

Table 2.6 *Workers by industry and education*

	Electronics	Garment	Other	Total
Primary school	1	3	1	5
Middle school	14	53	3	70
Attending high school	172	36	13	221
High school	325	53	22	400
Jr. college/college	17	1	4	22
Total	529	146	43	718

special classes for adolescent industrial workers' education" (*sanŏpch'e kŭnro ch'ŏngsonyŏn ui kyoyuk'ŭl wihan tŭkpyŏlhakkŭp dŭng ui sŏlchi kijunryŏng mit sihaengsech'ik*) that required companies to provide night classes for their employees. "The industrial school system was promoted in the late 1970s to attract women production workers" (Jeoung 1993:70). To comply with these rules, companies in the Zone had to allow workers to attend high school classes in the evenings. Approximately 1,850 workers were sponsored by their employers to attend various night schools in 1987. Six night schools in Masan offered classes for workers: a middle school, two regular high schools and two commercial high schools for women and a technical high school for men.

Factories used night school as a device to recruit, retain and control workers. A study of these schools found that they restricted women's participation in labor union activities and the labor movement (Kim Hui-jŏng 1990). If a factory sponsored a worker, she had to stay at the same company until she graduated. If she quit or was fired, she was automatically dismissed from school. Many garment factories, however, did not allow their workers to attend classes when they wanted them to work overtime. One woman told me how her conflict with factory managers, who tried to deny her the right to attend classes, led her to become a labor organizer:

> At Sinhŭng, about a third of the workers were students. The work at a
> shoe factory is hard, so the management used promises of education
> to get young women to work in the factory. But whenever they
> needed overtime work, they would not let students go to school. Stu-
> dents had to cry, fight, and run away to go to school. When I saw
> this, I got angrier and angrier. From this experience, I learned that we
> needed a union to protect our rights.

31

Some electronics companies, by contrast, even set up student lines that were exempt from ordinary overtime work. Most electronics companies also provided some kind of dinner for students before they went to school, but garment companies usually did not provide anything for students. Students who worked at garment companies usually had to buy their own dinner.

About a third of my respondents said that they started to work in order to attend school (see Table 2.7), although only 9% reported that this was their main use of their income. Tuition for high school was a heavy burden for many poor families, and when they had to decide who they could afford to send to school, sons were favored over daughters. Thus, for many young women, the factories in Masan represented their only chance to attend high school.

Many women workers I interviewed expressed their desire for education. The desire for higher education has been expressed in many workers' autobiographies (Chang Nam-su 1984:9, 16–21; Sŏk 1984; Song Hyo-sun 1982:18), and studies of women workers also confirm that one important reason women leave rural areas to work in factories is a desire for higher education (Chŏng 1991:418–419; Jeoung 1993; Kim Eun-Shil 1993:186–193).

Some of the more ambitious workers sought a college education because they hoped to get a better job with a college degree. Education generally provides access to better-paying jobs in contemporary South Korea (Chang Chi-yŏn 1990:174), and the difference between the salaries of college graduates and high school graduates is much greater than that between high school graduates and middle school graduates. Official statistics indicate that different educational levels establish large differences in income between middle- and working-class individuals.

> [C]ollege graduates are paid much higher wages than middle and high
> school graduates. . . . [T]here is a tendency for college graduates to
> be paid a larger share than less educated workers regardless of pro-
> ductivity; the college diploma has become a social status symbol. . . .
> However, the wage differentials by education level have been con-
> tinuously narrowed during the past two decades. (Cho Soon 1994:95–
> 96)

Higher education generally does not provide good jobs for women, however, and one recent study concludes that "the labor-force participation rate of women decreases as their number of years of formal education increases"

Table 2.7 *Reasons for starting work*

Reason	Number	%
Main support of family	14	2
Partial support of family	90	13
Siblings' education	26	4
Dowry savings	80	11
Own education	241	34
To be independent	177	25
For experience	77	11
Other reason	5	1
No response	8	1
Total	718	102%

(Myung-hye Kim 1992:160). Thus, even with a college diploma, these women find it difficult to find jobs because the labor market in South Korea is rigidly segmented by gender at all levels, and by the time they finish their college education through part-time study, they are too old to be hired for the office jobs that employ most female college graduates.

One woman who worked on my line at KTE had attended a junior college for two years. She planned to stop working at the factory and find an office job when she graduated. She was still working in the factory after she graduated because she found that at twenty-four she was too old to be hired for an office job. She had to remain in the factory even after she got her diploma because companies are unwilling to hire women whom they expect will soon leave to get married. She did eventually quit her factory job, but I do not know what happened to her later.

In addition to the workers who went to junior colleges at night, there were some workers who tried to achieve a college education through correspondence courses. Six years were required to complete a four-year college program. Women who started these courses often became disillusioned when they realized that the diploma would not lead to a good job and many dropped out. One woman told me:

> I tried four times to start a college correspondence course, but now I have given up since I realized that a college diploma did not mean much. A lot of union officers were taking correspondence courses, but they all decided not to continue either.

33

Class Struggle or Family Struggle?

Some of the families of workers in Masan were much poorer than others. Although many families sent their daughters to high school, others could not even afford to send them to middle school. There were even a few who, because of poverty, had forced their daughters to work as maids when they should have been attending primary school. One of my roommates began working as a maid when she was only eight years old. The only education she received was two years of primary school while working for a relative in Pusan. Her wages were sent to her stepmother, who told her that she was saving it for her dowry. Workers' family backgrounds affect many aspects of their lives and shape their relationships with each other, as well as their strategies to escape from poverty and exploitation (see Chapter 3).

Where Do Workers Come From?

MAFEZ recruited most of its female workers from Masan City and the nearby areas in South Kyŏngsang Province. Without the employment possibilities of the Zone, these women would have had to travel much farther to find work, at least to Pusan and possibly as far as Seoul. Seventy-one percent of the respondents to my questionnaire were from South Kyŏngsang Province (see Table 2.8), with an additional 8% from either Pusan or North Kyŏngsang Province. A significant minority of workers (12%) came from North or South Chŏlla Province, just east of Masan. Chŏlla Province is largely rural and unindustrialized, but because of regional tensions, many Chŏlla people prefer to travel much farther to find jobs in Seoul rather than go to Kyŏngsang Province. Other regions supplied only a small number of workers to Masan.

The regional tensions between Kyŏngsang Province and Chŏlla Province are acute.[7] People from Chŏlla Province are easily identified by their distinctive accent. Kyŏngsang people look down on them and regard them as backward and dishonest. People from Chŏlla Province, on the other hand, feel that they

---

7 Regional tensions in Korea can be traced back to the Three Kingdom era (18 B.C.–668), when the Korean peninsula was divided into three kingdoms (Koguryŏ, Paekche and Silla) that engaged in territorial wars. Discrimination against the people of the Chŏlla area was institutionalized at the beginning of the Koryo dynasty (918) when Wang Kŏn, the founder of the dynasty, excluded people from the region of Later Paekche (roughly present-day Chŏlla Province) from the ranks of government officials. "The policy of open discrimination against people from the Honam (Chŏlla) region continued throughout the [Koryŏ] dynasty and has become deeply entrenched in the psyche of the Korean people" (Yu 1990:26).

Table 2.8 *Workers by province*

Province	Number	%
South Kyŏngsang	510	71
North Kyŏngsang	45	6
South Chŏlla	67	9
North Chŏlla	19	3
Ch'ungch'ŏng	25	3
Kyŏnggi	2	0
Kangwŏn	13	2
Cheju	6	1
Seoul	4	1
Pusan	14	2
No response	13	2
Total	718	100

are victims of hundreds of years of government neglect.[8] Their resentment has increased in recent years because every South Korean president since 1960 has come from Kyŏngsang Province and because industrial development has been heavily concentrated there. Political dissidence has also focused on Chŏlla Province, especially South Chŏlla Province and its capital, Kwangju.[9]

Women workers in Masan often made comments like "One cannot trust Chŏlla people" or "Chŏlla people are disloyal, and they always cheat you." Even the matron of the workers' dormitory admitted that she did not trust women from Chŏlla Province. She acknowledged that she should not be prejudiced against people from there and tried not to show her prejudice, but she still felt she could not trust them. One Masan worker justified her feelings about people from Chŏlla Province with the following story:

> You really cannot trust these Chŏlla people. I had a very close girl
> friend who came from Chŏlla Province. We met at the factory and be-

8 A study of migrants to Seoul based on the 1980 census concludes that people from the Chŏlla region experience more "discrimination in white collar employment compared to migrants from other regions" (Yu 1990:37).

9 The regional rivalry reached its height during the "Kwangju massacre" in May 1980. Chun Doo-hwan's government sent in the army commandos to suppress an antigovernment demonstration in Kwangju. In suppressing the demonstration, the army commandos killed numerous civilians. The government reported that only about 100 people were killed in this incident, but other sources reported more than 1,000 dead. The commandos involved in the massacre were rumored to be from Kyŏngsang Province. Chŏlla Province people refer to the massacre as genocide by Kyŏngsang Province people (Hwang 1985).

came roommates. After we lived together for almost two years, she suddenly disappeared. She stole my clothes and my savings passbook; that was all my savings from working in the Zone. After that incident, I told people not to trust anyone from Chŏlla Province.

If someone from Kyŏngsang Province stole from her roommate it would have been regarded as a personal problem, but because the woman came from Chŏlla Province it became a regional problem. In the face of these prejudices, it is not surprising that workers from Chŏlla Province felt unwelcome. One Chŏlla woman told me:

I don't know how I can prove myself to be an honest and trustworthy person to these people in Kyŏngsang Province. They already have this set idea about us and they won't change their attitude no matter what we do. It's not fair. How can I like them when they treat me like this?

Apart from their prejudice against women from Chŏlla Province, workers accepted the few workers from other provinces without much tension.

Finding a Factory Job

Because factory work is a low-status job, women who decide to find work in MAFEZ are those with few other employment opportunities. Many of these women seek jobs because their families are unable to perform the support functions that more affluent families provide. These functions include providing secondary education, providing support during adolescence, and assembling a dowry (see Table 2.7). Not only are many families unable to fulfill these functions, but a significant number required the income from these young women for various purposes.

The largest number of women who responded to my survey (34%) reported that they started to work because a job in the Zone would provide an opportunity to further their own education. Most of these workers started to work at ages fifteen and sixteen (see Table 2.9). Young women who graduated from middle school and could not afford to go on to high school must have thought that jobs in the Zone were very attractive. They could earn their own living and continue to go to school without burdening their families with tuition costs.

Fifteen percent of the women responded that they started to work in order to provide full or partial support for their families. Another 4% responded that they went to work to help pay for their siblings' education costs. Both genders

36

Table 2.9 *Age at first employment*

Age	Number	%
12	2	0
13	5	1
14	44	6
15	180	25
16	108	15
17	68	9
18	128	18
19	114	16
20	39	5
21	10	1
22	3	0
23	2	0
24	1	0
Over 25	6	1
No response	8	1
Total	718	100%

considered the education of boys to be more important than the education of girls. Women were willing to make sacrifices to help their brothers continue their education and often expressed concern for their brothers' education. They made comments like "If my brother does not go to college, he won't get a good job."

Although providing daughters with a dowry is a family duty, 11% of the respondents reported that their reason for starting to work was to raise money for their dowry. Using this money to attract a desirable husband and start their own family is their greatest hope for improving their status. Women working to save for their dowries represent both a break with tradition, in that young single women are taking on a function that should have been performed by their families, and a recommitment to the family as the proper way for women to invest in the future. After they began working, even more women reported that dowry saving was the most important use of their income (see Chapter 3).

The increasing individualism of young South Korean women is reflected in the 35% of my respondents who reported that they started to work either to be independent (25%) or simply to gain experience (11%). Although the wages paid to women workers are very low, their earning power gives them a degree of independence from their families and freedom to make decisions as consumers. The mass media encourage consumerism, and some workers try to

Table 2.10 *Movement between industries*

First job	Current job	Number
Electronics	Electronics	371
Garment	Electronics	75
Other	Electronics	35
N/R	Electronics	50
Electronics	Garment	9
Garment	Garment	126
Other	Garment	5
N/R	Garment	6
Electronics	Other	3
Garment	Other	2
Other	Other	32
N/R	Other	4
	Total	718
	Number changing industry	129
	Percent changing industry	18.0%

spend their salaries as if they were middle class, buying clothes on monthly installment plans and dresses that cost more than their monthly salaries. The expressed desire for independence may, however, also reflect the failure of some poor families to provide basic support to the young women who are their least important members.

There were two peak ages at which women found their first employment: right after middle school (ages fifteen and sixteen) and right after high school (ages eighteen and nineteen) (see Table 2.9). Forty percent of my respondents took their first job at age fifteen or sixteen, and 34% took their first job at age eighteen or nineteen. Far fewer women took their first job outside these peak ages.

Women's short careers as factory workers in the Zone gave them few opportunities to move among industries. Nevertheless, 18% of the women surveyed were currently working in a different industry than the one that gave them their first job. It was much more common for women to change industries by moving to electronics factories than by leaving them. As Table 2.10 indicates, 85% of those who changed industries (110 women) moved from other industries to electronics, whereas only 9% of those who began in electronics factories left them for other industries.

Table 2.11 *Source of jobs*

Source	Number	%
Connections	419	58
Bulletin board	209	29
Newspaper	23	3
Government placement	3	0
Training school	6	1
Other	54	8
No response	4	1
Total	718	100

Because jobs in electronics factories were more prestigious, were better paying and had better working conditions than those in garment factories, women sometimes changed industries when they met the age and education requirements of electronics factories. Women in garment factories frequently expressed a wish to change their jobs but were hindered by their education or their age.

Including those who remained within the same industry, 40% of respondents reported changing jobs at least once. The most important reasons (50%) that women gave for changing jobs were related to poor working conditions (ill treatment, too strenuous work or poor conditions). About 10% of those who had changed jobs said that they left because they expected better pay at their next job.

Most women (58%) found their jobs through personal connections (see Table 2.11). Connections were most important in recruiting women for garment factories, where more than 80% of the women reported having been recruited this way.[10] Some garment factories even offered monetary incentives to workers who recruited new workers (cf. Jeoung 1993:60). Connections were somewhat less important in electronics factories, although they were still the way a substantial majority (60%) found their jobs. Recruiting women through

10 Workers are hired through personal connections in other industries in South Korea. An example is the large metal company, Poongsan, where a study determined that at one of their main plants, most male industrial workers were hired through connections: "73.1 percent of all Bupyong plant employees had been hired through the recommendation of friends, relatives, and acquaintances" (Choong Soon Kim 1992:92).

connections helped management to impose labor discipline because they held women responsible for the behavior of those whom they recruited.[11]

The next most important source of jobs was a large bulletin board at the entrance to the Zone that advertised current job openings. These advertisements mentioned job requirements, such as age limits and education, and requested applicants to submit photographs and a resumé. I never saw any job description that mentioned wages. Every day women flocked to see whether there were any better job prospects. Factories also advertised jobs in newspapers and at government placement offices, but these were sources of jobs for only a few women.

THE LABOR PROCESS: CONTROLLING THE WORKFORCE

Working Environment and Working Hours

In their dedication to keeping production costs down, factories in MAFEZ often neglected the safety and health of workers. South Korean factories, in general, had "a casualty rate . . . 5 times greater than in comparable Asian countries and 15 times the rate of Western countries" (U.S Department of Labor 1990:102). Women in Masan often complained about working conditions in their factories, and, as mentioned earlier, this was the most important reason cited by workers for changing jobs. Conditions were especially poor in garment factories. Dust was a problem in textile and garment factories, and fumes from glue were bad in shoe factories. A worker in a shoe factory told me:

> I couldn't breathe when I first started to work at this factory. The ventilation system was really bad. Other workers told me that I would get used to the dust in a month or so. Then, I started to get headaches and had to take aspirin. Now I take aspirin almost every day. I know I shouldn't, but until I get out of this miserable work, it is the only way I can cope with my headache.

Breathing dust caused chronic bronchitis in many workers. The strain of operating a sewing machine for eight to twelve hours a day often led to swollen legs and feet. The prolonged sitting in one position caused constipation for many factory workers.

---

11 Choong Soon Kim also describes how managers try to discipline workers by talking to their patrons rather than confronting them directly (1992:92).

In some factories, workers also had to cope with changing shift schedules. Some garment factories and a few electronics factories had schedules of three shifts to which workers were assigned on a weekly basis. Workers found it hard to adjust to the changing schedules and complained that it was difficult to sleep during the day when they worked the night shift. A garment worker in Seoul described the traumatic experience of adjusting to the factory schedule in her autobiography:

> The shop floor felt almost like being in the army. It was very hard for me to adjust to factory life. . . . I had to work three shifts – starting at six o'clock in the morning, two o'clock in the afternoon, and ten o'clock at night – my living schedule changed completely according to which shift I was on. In my village, we went to sleep when night came and got up when dawn came, but we don't even know what the weather is outside the factory, we are slaves of time. We work at midnight or eat at one o'clock in the morning which we could never imagine doing in the village. Sometimes I wonder what I am doing late at night when I should be sleeping and realize that I am in a really strange place. (Sŏk 1984:14)[12]

Overtime and even overnight work were frequently required of women in garment factories. Working hours in South Korea are the longest in the world (Amsden 1989:205), and South Korean women work even longer hours than men. Workweeks are gradually getting shorter, but even in 1989 women's workweeks averaged 54.1 hours and "[s]ixty-hour workweeks [were] common in many firms" (U.S. Department of Labor 1990:102).

One woman described how frequent overtime work was in her shoe factory:

> We have to work overnight at least three times a month. We work until 4 o'clock in the morning, go home, and have to come back to work at 8:30. It is impossible to get enough sleep. When the shipping date is near, the company sets quotas for everyone and only permits workers who have finished their quotas to go home. No one talks at night since everyone wants to finish as fast as possible and go home. Productivity increases whenever the company announces overnight work.

12 Working conditions in specific South Korean factories are discussed in Pak Yŏng-kŭn (1984) and Sun (1984).

At first, her factory imposed overnight work only on Saturday nights because workers could get some rest on Sundays and management claimed to be worried about workers' health. But later, they added overnight work on other days.

Frequent overnight work and long hours of overtime work created a tense working environment. The tensions sometimes led to arguments and even caused physical fights. The worker at the shoe factory went on to tell about an incident at her factory:

> During the summer time, when we had to work overnight twice a week, everyone was very tired and tense from not having enough sleep. The factory did not operate fans, so everyone was sweating like pigs. People in the factory often used abusive language to each other. One Sunday morning at four A.M., a woman threw a pair of scissors because she was angry that the manager still wouldn't send workers home even though the work was finished. A friend of mine was hit by the scissors and had to go to the emergency room at the hospital. She had to have six stitches in her arm. Workers in shoe factories are short tempered. I don't know whether it is because they are uneducated. My friend couldn't be angry at the woman who threw the scissors, only angry about her fate to be working at that kind of place.

Workers in electronics factories were better off than workers in garment factories. Not only were they paid somewhat better wages, but the work required clean, air-conditioned factories. Nevertheless, even in electronics factories, the work was strenuous and hours were long. Although workers in electronics factories rarely had to work overnight, they frequently put in long overtime hours. At some factories, overtime work followed a seasonal pattern; for example, a factory that produced goods for Christmas orders in the United States regularly assigned workers four to six hours of overtime work every day throughout the summer. Workers at this factory were ambivalent about this overtime work because, although it gave them a predictable chance to earn more money, it also meant that they had no time for themselves.

The KTE factory where I worked typified the working conditions of electronics factories in MAFEZ. It was owned by a subsidiary of a well-known Japanese corporation and was one of the largest in the Zone, employing about 2,500 workers. It produced tape recorders, telephones and black-and-white televisions. KTE occupied a five-story building and also had factories in parts of two other buildings in the Zone. On the fourth floor where I worked, there were approximately 250 workers in two different sections. I was in the preparation section, and in the other section, workers assembled parts on a conveyor belt.

Although assembly work in my line did not seem too difficult at first, after a whole day of work I could not move my shoulders without pain. I did not need any training because the work did not require any skill, only agility and good eyesight. Most of my coworkers complained about their eyes, and many had to wear glasses. I found the work even harder on my eyes when I was loaned to another line for a week. I had difficulty attaching tiny nails to the circuit board even with glasses, and I had to ask the line leader to send me back to my regular place.

Our time at the factory was closely regulated. We were allowed forty minutes for lunch and two ten-minute rest breaks, one in the morning and the other in the afternoon. There were only ten toilets for the whole floor with over 250 workers, so we had to wait in a long line during breaks. Workers in my group sneaked away during the work period when the supervisor was not looking. Supervisors constantly lectured us about going to the toilet too often, telling us to wait until the breaks. Three minutes before the end of the breaks, there was a recorded announcement that workers should be seated at their workplaces. Management continually tried to cut into the small amount of rest time allowed to workers.

Physical exhaustion caused industrial accidents in our factory. I saw one worker accidentally crush her finger under a heavy pressure machine. The supervisor was angry at her, calling her a "stupid bitch" (*pabokatŭn nyŏn*). Although she was required to report the accident, he persuaded her not to do so because accident reports could damage his chances for advancement. Instead, he had her tell the doctor that the accident happened at her home, not at the factory, and he gave her some money to go to a pharmacy. She complied without complaining out of fear of losing her job.

When I was absent from work for one day, the under-manager's helper summoned and scolded me, saying that as a new worker, I should not be absent. "If you are absent, your line leader gets a demerit and it will hurt his chances for promotion." Workers were encouraged to identify with their supervisors and ignore their own rights. The line leader pressured us to come to the factory even if we were really sick: "Unless you are in hospital, you should come to work and then get permission to go home early."

Even when workers came to work sick, however, they were not freely excused. One day, a coworker on my line came to work even though she was quite sick. She pleaded with the line leader to permit her to go home. First, he told her to stay on until lunch. Then he told her to stay on until the break time in the afternoon. Finally, he excused her from overtime but told her that she had to stay until 5:30. She responded sarcastically, "I better stay on for overtime since I am apparently not going to die on the shop floor," but she did go home at 5:30.

The way mandatory overtime work was handled in my factory illustrates how women workers voiced discontent toward management before the 1987 labor uprising. During the spring of that year, the company imposed many hours of overtime work. One time we had to work twelve hours a day on Monday through Friday and eight hours on Saturday and Sunday for three weeks in a row. This amount of overtime work was not typical, but it was not unheard of when a shipping date was close. Usually management did not require us to work overtime on Saturdays, but on weekdays we were never informed about plans for overtime work until late in the afternoon. At first, I could not understand why management could not plan and let us know about the overtime schedule in advance. Later, I realized that the timing of the announcement was deliberate. In this way, management controlled our lives within and outside the factory almost entirely. Our schedule depended on how our overtime was planned. Workers felt unhappy about this practice but limited their complaints to gossip among themselves. Many did not mind short periods of overtime work because the inconvenience was not too great and they needed the extra money.

One Saturday afternoon, the supervisor came over to us and said that we had to work an extra two hours. Most young women's social activities take place on Saturday evenings, so the workers were much more upset about having to do overtime work on Saturdays than on other days. They complained and protested at the announcement. Some women appealed to their supervisors for special permission to leave. Surprisingly, however, almost all of them stayed on and worked. Many women complained among themselves about not being able to keep their appointments and rushed to the public telephone. I asked why everyone did not just pack up and leave and teach management a lesson. "Oh, no, we can't do that," was the typical response. But one woman said, "We can't unite; and if we don't do it all together, only a few of us who do will be reprimanded. So, who would like to be the leader for that?" Furthermore, those workers who did not have plans for the evening did not mind working, so there was no walk-out.

About 10 women out of the 250 working on the floor left work on time that evening. They were formally reprimanded the next day by the supervisor, the

44

under-manager and the manager. The women who had left showed an obvious sense of camaraderie and strained to suppress smiles as they were being scolded. Other workers regarded these women with a mixture of hostility and admiration. Most workers either did not have the courage to walk out or did not feel it was the right thing to do.

Women who avoided overtime work were regarded with suspicion by other workers. I received hostile treatment one day when I felt sick and asked to be relieved of overtime work. I got ready to go home when the bell rang at 5:30 P.M., and a worker looked at me angrily and said, "Why aren't you working overtime when everyone else has to? It is not fair that some people can get off so easily." I felt terrible and decided I could not ask the line leader to relieve me of overtime work again.

When we had to work on Sundays, there was a particular conflict with devout Christian workers. We had four Protestants and three Catholics in our line. The line leader pressured these women to come to work on Sunday, but they insisted that they had to go to church. Eventually the Catholic women gave in and agreed to come to work after attending Mass. The Protestant women insisted that they were committed to church activities for the whole day and could not come to work on Sundays. Our line leader said we had too many workers absent from Sunday work and begged them to come to work. He even offered to go to church with them if they came to work on one Sunday. They still refused, and the under-manager was extremely angry at them. He called them aside and reprimanded them, saying sarcastically, "Why are you so stubborn? Are you going to be a reverend?" The women did not respond, and he finally had to give up on the issue.

The soldering section was recognized as especially dangerous, and women working there received a special allowance of 5,000 won a month. Accidents were common; some women got lead poisoning, and the skin of their fingers turned black. Workers were rotated to lessen the chances of poisoning, but lead poisoning could cause permanent damage that did not become apparent until much later. I heard many rumors about long-term health effects, such as infertility due to lead poisoning caused by work in the soldering section.

Most workers in both electronics and garment factories expected any work-related illnesses to disappear as soon as they left factory work. They were shocked by horrible stories about what had happened to other workers but did not expect anything serious to happen to them. Minor work-related illnesses were overlooked because women expected to leave their jobs before any serious condition developed. Furthermore, the fact that their working conditions were better than those in many factories outside the Zone made them feel that they were not so bad off.

Wages

South Korean women who seek employment encounter a labor market that is sharply divided by gender. Not only are their employment options severely limited, but they are paid at rates that set world records in gender discrimination. "[I]n 1980 the male–female wage gap was greater in South Korea than in any other country for which data are available from the International Labor Organization" (Amsden 1989:203). In the manufacturing sector of the economy, female workers are paid wages that average less than half those paid to male workers (Han'guk Yŏsŏng Nodongjahoe 1987:32; Kim Kŭm-su 1986:73).

Workers in MAFEZ are paid once a month. The monthly wages are divided into two parts: a basic wage and a set of supplements (e.g., an annual supplement, a weekly supplement, a monthly supplement, a monthly physiologic supplement, a food expense supplement, a transportation supplement, an overtime work supplement, a night-work supplement). The complexity of the supplement system makes comparisons between firms or industries extremely difficult because the amount the worker actually receives is the sum of a number of components, some of which are calculated as percentages of others. The system also gives management a set of tools for controlling workers, because if a worker is absent due to sickness or emergency, she loses not only that day's basic wage, but also parts of each of the supplements, so that her actual loss is more than the pay for one day. This system of wages plus supplements is not unique to MAFEZ but is standard in South Korean companies (Janelli 1993:150–151).

In addition to basic wages and supplements, workers received bonuses (see the later discussion). Bonuses were calculated as a percentage of the basic wage rather than from the total monthly paycheck. Workers counted on bonuses as part of their regular income. Bonuses were paid two or three times a year at major holidays (e.g., New Year's Day, *Ch'usŏk*). Electronics factories typically paid annual bonuses of 300–400% of the monthly basic wage, whereas garment factories usually paid 100–300%.

In 1987, a high school graduate at a typical electronics firm received about 3,700 won ($4.60) as the starting daily wage. This provided a basic monthly wage of 103,600 won ($129.50). The supplements paid to each worker varied, depending on their attendance record and hours of overtime work, but supplements apart from overtime increased the typical monthly paycheck by about 15–20% and overtime supplements might increase it by that amount again. Annual wage increases and seniority increases in electronics factories were very small, so workers with several years' experience were paid only slightly more than newly hired workers. At the factory where I worked, a coworker who had been at the factory for five years received only about 10,000 won ($12.50) a month more than I did as a beginner.

The starting daily wage in garment factories was less than that in electronics factories. A woman starting as an apprentice without any sewing skill was paid between 2,800 and 3,000 won ($3.50–$3.75) a day in 1987. The basic monthly wage for an apprentice was about 78,000–84,000 won ($97.50–$105). Even though garment workers started at a lower wage they had more chance for advancement, and in some factories skilled sewing machine operators (A-level) earned a daily wage of more than 5,000 won ($6.25), making a monthly basic wage of 140,000 won ($175).

Women apprentices at garment factories tried to learn sewing machine skills quickly and move to another factory. It took about two years for women to advance to the position of skilled worker, but by switching to another factory and lying about their experience, some women were able to advance more quickly. Managers at garment factories were aware that applicants exaggerated their experience, but the practice was so common that they could not control it. Instead they administered sewing tests to the women they hired.

Women workers found it difficult to support themselves on a monthly basic wage of between 78,000 won ($97.50) and 110,000 won ($137.50). Because the wages were so low, women usually welcomed a few hours of overtime per day to supplement their income. In 1987, with miscellaneous supplements and forty hours of overtime work per month, a worker at an electronics factory could make about 150,000 won ($187.50) a month. This amount was still below what the Federation of Korean Trade Unions (FKTU) estimated as the minimum cost of living for a single woman. The FKTU's figure for the minimum cost of living for a single woman was 177,306 won a month in 1985 (Han'guk Yŏsŏng Nodongjahoe 1987:20). In Masan, the local chapter of the Young Catholic Workers' Organization (JOC) established a figure for the minimum cost of living for a single woman of 185,000 won a month in early 1987. Most workers at the time only made 80% of that figure.

In early 1987, many women told me that they would be happy if they could make 200,000–250,000 won ($250–$312.50) a month (with overtime included). After the July–August labor uprising, wages were increased to about this level, and in 1989 a typical electronics worker received a daily wage of 7,000 won ($8.75), nearly double the wages of 1987. With supplements, workers were making close to 250,000 won a month without overtime work.

"We Are a Happy Family": Invoking Company Loyalty

The electronics companies in MAFEZ used their greater prestige to build a sense of company loyalty in their workers. My job at KTE began with an orientation program. The seventy newly recruited workers (including myself) listened as managers made speeches praising the company:

> Welcome everyone to the KTE family. As everyone here must know, our company is one of the largest in the Masan Free Export Zone and its most closely knit family. Everyone in this company is a family member and we are all extremely proud of that. Everyone here, regardless of our rank, wears our company uniform. Our company is the only one in the Zone where the employees feel such pride that we wear our uniforms not just in the company but outside the Zone too. You will soon feel the same pride and loyalty to the company that you will be happy to be seen as a member of the KTE family.[13]

Managers told us about the company's history, emphasizing that we should be proud to be part of KTE.[14] No one called it a "factory" (*kongjang*); it was always a "company" (*hoesa*). By using the term *hoesa,* the speakers implied that working for KTE was better and more prestigious than a factory job. The new workers, who expected to stay with the "company" until they got married, also felt proud about being selected. KTE was considered a good company to work for. Because it had 2,500 employees and was a subsidiary of a major Japanese conglomerate, it was one of the strongest companies in the Zone. Even before I started to work there, I had noticed many men and women wearing the company uniform as they went to work in the morning.

---

13 Korean companies frequently rely on the metaphor of the company as family. For example, "[t]he relationship between a superior or boss and his employees is often compared to the relationship between head of the family and his family members" (*na ege ttallin sikkudŭl*) (Yi Eunhee Kim 1993:252). Also see Janelli (1993).

14 The South Korean company's conscious effort to indoctrinate male white-collar workers to identify with the company and to defer to their superiors during the orientation period was extensively discussed by Choong Soon Kim (1992:118–132) and Roger Janelli (1993:140–144).

Although the young women who worked in these factories had short careers and were paid very low wages, the Japanese also imported their idea of company loyalty based on an understanding of lifetime employment. New workers went through an orientation that stressed their role as part of a "family." Factory workers were issued company uniforms and were encouraged to consider themselves "company employees" rather than mere "factory workers," a distinction of considerable significance in status-conscious South Korea. Management in some electronics companies even catered to small but personal concerns, such as remembering workers' birthdays and preparing small gifts.

The "New Factory Movement" (*Kongjang Saemaŭl Undong*)[15] introduced by the government in 1973 also encouraged workers to identify with their factories. This movement aimed at augmenting worker productivity, promoting harmony and peace on the shop floor and integrating workers into the enterprise structure. It has been described as "an ideological indoctrination campaign through which the state authorities instilled industrial workers and union leaders with the work ethic and the virtue of submission to managerial authorities" (Choi Jang Jip 1983:497). It used slogans based on family and kinship values, such as "Treat employees like family; I will do factory work as if it were my own personal work" (Choong Soon Kim 1992:176) and essentially asked workers to be as loyal to the company as they would be to their parents.

At KTE, the New Factory Movement coerced workers to contribute free labor to the company. Under this program we were required to be at our positions every morning at least fifteen minutes before work started,[16] and when talks were scheduled we had to come to work even earlier. We were allowed to clean up our work space only after the bell rang. Preparation and cleaning up did not count as part of our working hours but was time given to the factory by workers. Under the New Factory Movement, newly promoted line assistants "volunteered" up to two hours of free overtime work a day for their first six months in their positions.

The company that developed loyalty among its workers most successfully

---

15 The New Factory Movement was an extension of the New Village Movement (*Saemaŭl Undong*) that began in 1970 as a government-directed strategy to improve the rural economy. *Saemaŭl Undong* fostered "diligence, cooperation, self-help, and active voluntary participation and to cultivate grass-roots leadership" (Choong Soon Kim 1992:176). For a critical discussion of the New Village Movement, see Burmeister (1988).

16 Other factories scheduled morning meetings, which required workers to regularly be at work at least thirty minutes before their official work time began.

was Sowa, a subsidiary of Sony, which was one of the few companies not to experience a strike during the nationwide labor uprising of 1987. Before workers did anything, Sowa raised their wages to a level comparable to those of factories that had strikes. One worker at Sowa praised her company as the best one in the Zone:

> We had no need to strike. I know there were some workers who wanted to organize a strike, but I don't see any need for it when our management raised our wages even before we asked. I appreciate our managers' effort to pay attention to this issue, and I am happy that I am working for Sowa.

More radical workers considered that Sowa's management just had more sophisticated ways to exploit its workers. They were concerned that other Sowa workers did not recognize the need for a labor union in their company. Eun-ju, another worker at Sowa, complained:

> I feel so angry that my friends just do not see what the managers are trying to do in our factory. They are just grateful that their wage has increased and the managers voluntarily promised to reduce their overtime work. But they don't realize that this is how the managers block us from organizing a labor union, by persuading our friends to be members of the company family. Whenever I try to tell my friends about the need of a labor union, they just look at me as if I am a communist.

Male Supervisors/Female Workers: Invoking Gender Hierarchy

The traditional hierarchical relationships between male and female, and between young and old, serve to make the subordination of women within the workplace seem natural or common sense. As in many other parts of the world, cheap female labor is used for factory jobs with unskilled, repetitive tasks and minimal opportunity for advancement. Gender hierarchy structures the work environment, so that women never perform the same jobs that men do, and they are usually supervised by men. Women never supervise male workers. Within the rigidly hierarchical, gender-segregated workplace, women are never seriously able to challenge men's control. Ong has described the similar use in Malaysian factories of culturally elaborated notions of gender hierarchy to control and subordinate a low-wage female labor force (1983).

All production workers at KTE were women, and all managers and supervisors were men. Factory work was organized into sections, each with a manager (*kwajang*), an under-manager (*kyejang*), and three line leaders (*panjang*), all of whom were men. Most line leaders, who directly supervised women, had completed high school and thus had a level of educational attainment similar to that of the women they supervised. Unlike the women, however, they were given chances to take examinations for promotion to managerial positions. Management did not have openings for women, so female workers were not expected to advance.[17] Both the manager and the under-manager had women workers assigned to them as secretarial helpers. Each of the three line leaders had a line helper to assist him. These secretarial helpers and line helpers were selected from among the production workers, and these positions were highly desired.[18]

In the preparation line of three women where I worked making gears for tape recorders, my job was to apply grease to the hole of the gear; the next woman attached two springs to the gear; and the third woman used a machine to compress the springs and put the gear in a box. These extremely simple, boring tasks clearly illustrate the Taylorist extremes of "deskilling" and "fragmentation of the production process" which characterize electronics assembly work (cf. Ong 1987:161).[19]

Hierarchical control was also enhanced by the layout of the factory. The floor where I worked was divided into two sections. The larger section had about 130 workers assembling components on conveyer belts. Our section, which assembled basic components, had 120 workers divided into three lines. Each section manager had an office in one corner of the floor. The under-manager's desk was in front of the manager's office, facing the shop floor. In front of the under-manager were the line leaders' desks. Workers of each line were arranged in front of the line leader's desk. Both line leaders and the under-manager could easily observe the work process from their desks, but line

---

17 Although men can reach the position of manager with only a high school education, they rarely advance beyond that level without a college degree. The position of general manager usually requires a college education.

18 Line leaders' assistants work within the factory setting (not in a segregated office setting), but they still regard themselves as clerical workers, not production workers. Because these jobs carry increased prestige, women workers were very keen to get them.

19 Janelli also discusses how white-collar workers in a conglomerate were controlled by assigning them narrowly defined tasks rather than providing them with open-ended assignments that would promote creativity (1993:165).

leaders rarely sat; they were constantly on their feet walking around their lines, keeping an eye on workers and reprimanding those who talked too much or who seemed too slow.

This intensive surveillance is typical of the factories in MAFEZ and other South Korean workplaces (Janelli 1993:163; Jeoung 1993:64). Women workers' autobiographies describe similar levels of surveillance at their factories (e.g., Sŏk 1984:14). As a researcher studying the offices of a South Korean conglomerate notes, "Michel Foucault's observations (1978:170–77) regarding physical layouts and control are resonant here" (Janelli 1993:163).

Age and experience in working for the company also gave male supervisors superior status to female production workers. Managers and under-managers had generally worked in company administration for several years before being promoted to their positions and were at least ten years older than most women workers at KTE. Line leaders also tended to be older than women production workers because they began their jobs after three years of compulsory military service as well as high school. The manager of my section at KTE was in his early forties, the under-manager was in his mid-thirties, and my line leader was in his early thirties. The oldest workers in my line were twenty-six years old.

Managers and line leaders referred to their section or line workers as "my children" (*urijip aedŭl*). In labeling women workers as children, managers implied that they were immature girls. Even when there was no great difference in age between male supervisors and female workers, the men invariably addressed women workers by their given names with the casual suffix (e.g., "Mi-sun-a"), as if addressing their daughters or younger sisters. Whether this form of address was used affectionately or angrily, it always emphasized women's subordinate status, and the older women especially felt uncomfortable about being addressed this way. They often complained about this and envied office workers, who, they pointed out, were addressed as "Miss" with their surname (e.g., "Miss Kim").[20] The way workers were addressed by supervisors was one of the complaints most frequently voiced by workers during the labor uprising in July–August 1987.

---

20 Ironically, factory workers still lagged behind women office workers, who, by this time, no longer wanted to be addressed as "Miss" and their surname, but rather to be addressed in the same way as male employees, with their full name followed by "ssi," e.g., *Kim Mi-sun ssi* (Janelli 1993:168).

Production in the Masan Free Export Zone

Carrots and Sticks: Boosting Workers' Productivity

Up to the early 1980s, Japanese-owned companies in MAFEZ used a coercive strategy to control workers. Management administered a system of demerits and fired women who reached a certain point on the demerit scale. Workers were rated by "sincerity, cooperation with the company, efficiency, attendance, and loyalty to the company" (Committee for Justice and Peace of South Korea 1976:60). A woman who had worked for a Japanese garment factory in MAFEZ in the 1970s described how the system worked:

> It all came down to how docile and subservient you were to the managers that determined your demerit score. You couldn't cross a line leader or manager, unless you wanted to risk accumulating demerit points. We unconsciously competed against each other to be more passive and more loyal to the company. The system was very bad for our morale, because it worked negatively rather than positively. The manager did not award us merit points if we were loyal; he assigned us demerit points if we were not more loyal than other workers. You can only lose under this system, but when we started to work in the Zone we did not know any better. We were just grateful to have a job.

In 1987 some electronics and garment companies used a different system of bonuses and monetary incentives to encourage workers to compete against each other and with other lines. A worker in an electronics factory explained how the bonus system (*konggwaje*) worked in her factory: The amount to be awarded in bonuses was fixed, and the proportion given to each worker was determined by her ranking on a scale of bonuses from A to E. She explained:

> I received the bonus before last at the "A" rate and I was quite happy that I had worked hard and been rewarded. I knew that there were different rates and I heard many of my co-workers complaining when we received that bonus. But I felt that some of them had not worked hard enough, and the system seemed fair. But this time when I received the bonus, I was rated as "B." I thought I worked just as hard as the last period, but I could not ask any questions.

She complained that workers never knew how much they would receive until they actually saw their paycheck. "You can never know why you got a B level instead of an A level bonus." Workers had to compete against each other without knowing where they stood in relation to the quota. This bonus system, with its uncertainty and the way it pitted workers against each other, was very unpopular with workers. During the 1987 labor uprising, workers demanded its replacement by a system of uniform bonuses.

The monetary incentives at KTE consisted of a system of monthly prizes. Prizes were awarded to the line that exceeded its quota by the largest amount, to the line with the fewest defects, and to the line with the best attendance. The prizes aimed at making workers work as quickly as possible and motivating them to be careful about the quality of the product. The attendance prize also forced workers to be responsible for the records of others in their line. If a worker was absent, her line lost its chance for the prize and she was condemned by her coworkers. When a line won the prize, the line members either went out for a group dinner or divided the prize money among themselves.

Garment factories often gave individual bonuses to workers who worked fast and hard. Management made the decisions concerning these bonuses secretly, and workers were told not to discuss their bonuses with each other. This system created a lot of tension and suspicion among workers because they did not know who received what or how the decisions were made. Workers complained to me that the system was unfair because the line leader or the supervisor favored some workers over others when making recommendations for the bonus. Workers had to work hard and be careful not to antagonize their line leader or supervisor.

Some garment factories also had a prize system for perfect attendance for lines. One worker told me that she had to sacrifice her night school trip because of the prize:

> My second year school trip was set for October 1st to 3rd. The first
> and the third of October were holidays, so I thought that I could
> easily get the extra day off. But the company decided to make us
> come to work on those two days instead. I wanted to go anyway, but
> my line leader told me that we could not win the prize if I was absent.
> Management was going to give the winning line 30,000 won and buy
> dinner for all the line workers. The line leader told me that I had to
> pay 30,000 won if I wanted to go. I had already paid 20,000 won for
> the trip, but I decided that giving that up was better than paying the
> 30,000 won. I was really angry.

Companies in the Zone used systems of bonuses and other monetary incentives because these methods enabled the companies to boost production and control the amount they actually paid their workers. Bonuses were not part of the labor contract and could be increased or discontinued at the discretion of the company. The system encouraged women to compete against each other in order to produce more, faster, and without defects. However, it also increased tension in the workplace, as it pitted workers against each other.

Suppression of Union Activity

Although South Korean governments have been generally hostile to workers' organizations, the workers in MAFEZ have operated under special restrictions on union activity. In 1971, the government passed the "Special Law on Trade Union and Mediation of Labor Disputes in Foreign-Invested Enterprises" in order to deliver union-free, docile labor to firms owned wholly or in part by foreign corporations.[21] Attempts to engage in disputes with management during MAFEZ's first ten years (1970–1980) resulted in failure, with the workers involved being fired.

Following the assassination of President Park in October 1979, there was a brief period of political uncertainty. This period, which lasted until May 1980, was known as "Seoul Spring" because of the general hope that democracy could be established in South Korea. The political restrictions of the *Yusin* period were dissolved, and throughout the country labor leaders attempted to replace their unions with democratic unions with elected leadership. The newly active unions led a number of labor disputes, and the number reported during this time (407) was the highest of any period before 1987 (Cho Soon 1994:100).

In Masan, women workers in a Japanese-owned food processing company, Puknŭng, organized MAFEZ's first labor union in March 1980 (Kim and Im 1991:135).[22] The company immediately closed and pulled out of Masan the following month. Five more unions were started before May, but they were forced to dissolve under the emergency decree following the Kwangju incident (ibid.:136).

The regime of President Chun Doo Hwan enacted its "purification of labor union law" in December 1980 and abolished all existing democratic unions (those in MAFEZ had already disbanded "voluntarily"). The government pro-

---

21 Ogle discusses how foreign investors pressured the South Korean government to pass the special law to limit workers' protests (1990:23–25).
22 It is interesting to note that the majority of women workers of Puknŭng were married.

hibited workers from organizing[23] and forced "one hundred ninety union leaders into purification camps," where they were tortured (ibid.:137) and subjected to hard labor.[24] Thus, strikes became impossible again during the early 1980s. As a substitute for unions, the government encouraged "Joint Labor–Management Councils" (*Nosa Hyŏbuihoe*), where management controlled the proceedings and frequently selected the workers' representatives for them.

Labor union activity was liberalized somewhat after 1986, when the government revised its labor laws in response to the prevalence of informal labor activities that bypassed its system of control. The revised laws allowed labor unions to organize without receiving prior approval from the government. However, new unions still had to file for approval with the authorities, and this approval was usually withheld. Workers at Sumida's factory in MAFEZ attempted to organize a union under these rules, but while the union was awaiting official acknowledgment, the company dismissed the union officers and the union never got started.

Apart from the isolated cases just noted, Joint Labor–Management Councils provided the only forum for workers in MAFEZ to present their views before 1987. Although workers had limited input in these councils, the exposure to labor issues provided by the councils inspired many young women to seek a more powerful voice for workers when the 1987 labor uprising broke out.

23 The measures to suppress labor organizing were as follows: First, a petition of at least thirty workers or one-fifth of the workforce (before the change in the law, a petition of only more than two people was required to organize a union) was required for union recognition before the Office of Labor Affairs would register it. Second, the union shop system was abolished. Third, the organization of labor unions was changed from industry-based to enterprise-based. Fourth, any third-party interference in collective bargaining was illegal. Furthermore, bargaining could take place only at the enterprise level between a local union and management (Kim and Im 1991:137; Ogle 1990:54).

24 According to Ogle (1990:55), "purification camps" were "[m]ilitary-like compounds set up in remote mountains away from contact with the outside world. Two hundred some labor leaders from around the country were arrested and sent to these camps. Through intense physical exercise, Spartan existence, self criticisms and moral exhortations, the inmates were to be converted, to see the error of opposing the government's 'good will.'"

3

The Myth of Social Mobility: Its Creation and Reproduction among Women Workers

IT was only in the 1960s, when work in factories became widely available, that factory jobs came to be considered respectable for young women. In traditional Korean society, young women were considered to need moral supervision, and few opportunities existed for them to work outside their homes. High-status families closely supervised their daughters in preparation for marriage, and in-laws controlled the daily lives of young wives. On the other hand, poorer families often coped with the burden of supporting adolescent daughters by sending them to work as housemaids for wealthy families. Even more important than the money that housemaids earned was the preservation of their reputations, and households that employed housemaids were also charged with supervising them to ensure their good reputations. Housemaids were usually rural girls who worked for a few years before leaving to get married, and their employers were often distant relatives, acting as patrons as well as employers.

When the South Korean government began its drive for export-led industrialization, factory jobs were seen as less suitable for young women than jobs as housemaids. Young women and their parents worried that factory settings were coarse and unstructured, whereas they believed that jobs as housemaids protected young women and prepared them for their future domestic roles. People felt that inadequately supervised young women in factories were susceptible to bad influences and in danger of becoming morally loose. And women were reluctant to work for factories because they were worried about their reputations and about how their marriage prospects would be affected.

The government, recognizing that the cheap, productive labor of young women in factories was essential to its program of export-led development, sought to improve the image of women factory workers. Positive images of workers were featured in government propaganda, as they were dubbed "industrial soldiers" (*sanŏp chŏnsa*) and asked to sacrifice for the future. As factory work for young women became more widespread, it became more acceptable. Young women were increasingly recruited into factories, and fewer

57

of them became housemaids. By the end of the 1970s the remaining house-maids tended be to older, married women who did not live in the households where they worked. Those housemaids working in Masan in 1987 made 5,000 won for an eight-hour work day, which was comparable to a factory wage.

Young women were also recruited into other, less respectable occupations. These included working in coffee shops, bars or barbershops. These jobs offered more money than respectable occupations, but their lack of respec-tability put them beyond consideration for most young women. As one elec-tronics worker explained:

> If a woman works in a restaurant or a bar, her chances of getting mar-
> ried to a decent man are almost nil. Even though I earn less working
> in a factory, I would rather be here than working as a bar hostess.

Women working as hostesses in coffee shops or bars are perceived as being little more than prostitutes. When I asked women workers what they thought of bar hostesses, a typical answer was:

> Once women start to work in those places, they will surely become
> prostitutes. They no longer care about their reputation. Since they get
> used to earning money easily they will never come back to doing hard
> work in factories.

As Masan grew, numerous bars and restaurants opened, offering relatively high-paying jobs for young women. However, work in a bar was seen as degrading, and factory workers strove to maintain the status distinction be-tween themselves and women in these kinds of jobs. Although most young women rejected the idea of working as a bar hostess, occasionally women did leave jobs in factories in the Zone to work in restaurants or bars. Hye-sun, a twenty-one-year-old bar hostess, claimed that factory work was too hard and paid too little money. She had been working at coffee shops and bars since the age of nineteen. Like many women in these kinds of jobs, she came from a poor and broken family. Her father had committed suicide when she was seven years old, and her mother was an alcoholic. Family problems kept her from finishing primary school. She began working in factories when she was fifteen, first in a textile factory outside the Zone and later in a garment factory in the Zone. While working in the Zone, she became pregnant. She quit her job and had an abortion. Afterward, she did not want to go back to factory work. Her sister explained: "She was already ruined and she didn't really care what happened to her after that." She took a job as a hostess at a coffee shop and later became a bar hostess. She excused her work by claiming that her bar was different from others:

> My job at this bar is clean. I don't have to go out with customers if I don't want to. I do not even have to drink if I don't want to. A lot of bars force hostesses to drink to hike up the bill, but my employer is different.

At the bar, she was making about 400,000 won per month, nearly three times what a factory worker could earn even with overtime. She went to work around eight or nine o'clock in the evening and came home at two or three o'clock in the morning. She had no plans to get married in the near future but was saving her money to open a small store.

Even though Hye-sun claimed not to want to get married, many bar hostesses hoped to get married and felt that they needed to disguise the fact that they had worked in bars. I knew one woman who worked at an electronics factory during the day and at a bar at night. When I asked her why she kept her job at the factory, she said:

> I don't have to work at the factory since I earn enough at night. But I want to go back to my home village and get married when I save enough money for my dowry [*honsu*]. If I just work as a hostess, I don't think I will have any chance to marry. Since I am working at the factory, I can tell everyone that I was a factory worker. A man will accept that his wife has been a factory worker but not a bar hostess.

Other former factory workers ended up in less respectable jobs in the aftermath of failed marriages. One former factory worker whom I knew took a job in a restaurant after her marriage broke up. Although she had been hired as a cook, she soon found that her boss expected her to be a "hostess":

> I worked in a small village restaurant for three months. I could not put up with the demands to pour drinks for customers and their squeezing my butt, so I came back to Masan and went to work in the Zone again.

Although factory work was certainly more respectable than working in restaurants, bars and coffee shops, it was still a low-status job. Most women would have preferred to do clerical work in an office and would have been willing to accept less money for such a job. The status difference between office worker (*hoesawŏn*) and factory worker (*kongwŏn*) was great. One worker confided:

> I wish I could be an office worker. If I could bribe someone to get that position, I would. I know that I get more money here with over-time, since office jobs don't have any overtime pay. But money isn't everything. I hate the way people call us *kongsuni*. They don't say anything like that to office workers. Even though factory work is re-spectable, it is still low status. I try very hard not to look like a fac-tory worker. I try to wear clothes like office workers, but people somehow know that I am a *kongsuni*.

Many women felt bitter about the way factory workers were regarded, but they also internalized the negative attitudes toward factory workers. Sometimes they said, in exasperation, "What do you expect from us? After all, we are only *kongsuni*," using the derogatory term for themselves.

Some workers were pleased to be working in the Zone, especially those who had experienced great hardships before coming to work there. A twenty-three-year-old woman worker contrasted her job at KTE with her previous job at a textile factory outside the Zone and with farm work:

> At Hanil Habsŏm, we only had two Sundays off a month. Compared to that, KTE gives us many more holidays off. Most workers at Hanil Habsŏm also had to work three shifts. . . . The work at KTE is not as hard as at Hanil Habsom even though it is conveyor work. . . . No matter how hard the factory work is, it cannot be matched to farm work. Thinking about farm work makes me shudder. No matter how much farmers claim that they like farm work, I think they are lying.

Another worker at KTE also considered her current job much better than her previous one outside the Zone:

> The work at KTE is not easy, but the wages are a lot higher and the working conditions are a lot better than at the shoe factory where I worked in Pusan. I don't have any complaints.

Other workers believed that work in the Zone was a hardship and looked forward to getting married as a means to escape from factories. A twenty-four-year-old electronics worker who had been working for six years told me that she really wants to quit her job but planned to work for two more years to save for her wedding expenses:

> I really don't want to work at a factory after I get married. Any job would be better than factory work. It would be nice to run a small business with my husband, maybe an accessory shop or even a portable bar [*p'ojangmach'a*]. . . . These days many of my friends have quit and gone back home to get married. There are three women in our line who are now twenty-seven years old and I really feel sorry for them. I swear I won't stay at work until I am that old. I just feel so sorry for these older sisters at work. If I am not married by then, I will just leave the factory and go home and stay there rather than working here and have other people sorry for me.

A twenty-six-year-old garment worker was even more unhappy, but could not quit because her widowed mother needed her income to sustain the household:

> I want to get out right now and marry the man I am dating, but I can't do that because of my mom. She is alone and she needs my help. I don't think that I can quit working until my brother is old enough to support my mom. I can't even think about dowry [*honsu*], since I haven't saved anything. If I want to save for my wedding, I have to start with nothing and join a rotating credit association [*kye*]. I have worked in this factory since I was seventeen and I really hate it. I told my boyfriend that after we get married I will never touch a sewing machine again.

Some industries in MAFEZ were perceived by workers as being more prestigious than others. Garment and shoe factories were considered to be the worst places to work, and electronics factories were felt to be the best. Factories with better reputations had more stringent hiring requirements and recruited women with more formal education and better family backgrounds (see Chapter 2). Garment workers felt envy, jealousy, and hostility toward electronics workers, and electronics workers felt superior to garment workers. Garment workers commented that "Electronics workers think they are much better than us" and "Electronics workers look down on us because most of them have high school education and a lot of us have only middle school or primary school education." Sometimes, they observed enviously, "Electronics workers get birthday presents, they get more holidays off, and they get more bonuses than we do" or "They wear better clothes than us and their faces look brighter than ours. I don't think they earn much more than us, but I do envy them." Occasionally, they were openly resentful: "Electronics workers are no better than us; after all, they work in factories too, don't they?" One garment worker said:

I think garment workers are more honest. Electronics workers always seem to be smiling, but I don't believe they are always that happy. Workers in garment factories curse a lot and sometimes get violent, but isn't it better to show your feelings honestly rather than to hide them?

Electronics workers were confident of their superiority but rarely commented on garment workers. One woman boasted: "At least we are all high school graduates; garment factories will hire anyone." They noted: "Working conditions here are not bad compared to those of a garment factory." Electronics workers also enhanced their status by referring to their employer as their company (*hoesa*) rather than their factory (*kongjang*). The desire of factory workers to identify with middle-class company employees was encouraged by electronics companies and served to make workers more compliant with corporate objectives.

Whereas electronics workers liked to regard themselves as company employees, garment workers had no such illusions. They knew that they worked in a factory where working conditions were bad, wages were low and treatment of workers was poor. Because there were no grounds for taking pride in their factories, garment manufacturers did not worry about how workers felt about their factories.

WORKERS AND THE CULTURE OF CONSUMPTION

Workers in MAFEZ had little extra money or free time. My job at KTE paid only 3,500 won a day ($4.00) for eight hours of work. The regular workday began at 8:30 A.M. and ended at 5:30 P.M.; two ten-minute breaks, one in the morning and one in the afternoon, and forty minutes for lunch did not count as work time. The normal workweek was six days (Saturday is a normal working day), so Sunday was the only day workers expected to be off. The regular workweek was thus forty-eight hours, but overtime work in the evenings and on Sundays could push this up to eighty hours. (My longest workweek at KTE was seventy-six hours.)

Although the wages of women workers were very low, their earning power gave them a degree of freedom. This freedom was expressed through individualism and consumerism. Most workers in Masan tried to follow fashion trends. There were always cheap accessories that workers could buy without difficulty. For example, there was a ribbon fad at the time of my fieldwork. Practically everyone bought a ribbon and wore it, regardless of how long her hair was. Vendors carried different colors and styles of bows. The trend started among middle-class college women and passed down to working-class women. By the time it reached the workers, the price of the ribbons had become very low, so even they could afford them.

Once they started to work, women became interested in fashion and cosmetics. Immediately after high school, women did not wear any makeup. But after about a year of work, they started to do their nails. Polishing nails was not an extravagant expense. Next, they began to buy lipstick. Many workers used only nail polish and lipstick. Then, at about twenty-three years of age, women started to use liquid makeup and eye shadow. During breaks and at lunch time, they talked about different cosmetic brands and shared them with close friends. KTE ran a small shop where workers bought cosmetics and other consumer goods on credit, with installments taken out of their paychecks.

Workers presumed other workers would conform to expectations for their age category. This proved awkward for me because I was trying to look and act younger than I really was while working at KTE. At first, I had a short, straight haircut and did not wear any makeup. After I had been working for about a week, a worker came over to me and advised me to put on some makeup. "After all," she said, "we are not that young, so we need to use some makeup and you probably should have a permanent. Your straight hair is for a twenty-year-old but not for us." She was twenty-five years old and thought that everyone who was older than twenty-three should have a permanent.

A few workers took up high-fashion clothing. Name brand dresses were extremely expensive, costing more than a monthly paycheck. Many dress shops allowed women workers to buy clothing on credit. Women who bought expensive dresses insisted that they could wear them much longer than cheap dresses, even if it took a year to pay for some of the clothes. Workers watched television and movies and tried to emulate the middle-class lifestyles shown there. They thought, "Why shouldn't we be able to afford it?"

When young workers had free time, they sometimes went out to night clubs (*gogojang*), all-night coffee shops, movie theaters and game arcades.[1] Leisure activities were only a small part of the lives of young, single women workers,

---

1 Chŏng Hyŏn-baek also discusses workers' use of leisure time (1991:417).

but they formed a large part of the image that society had of them as coarse and inadequately supervised. Masan had many night clubs that catered to young factory workers. Few workers had the time or money to go to these clubs regularly, but many went occasionally. For most women, it was a treat that they could afford a few times a year. Women usually went to night clubs in small groups of friends. Couples rarely went to clubs on dates. At clubs women danced by themselves, with each other, or with men they met there. However, although willing to dance with them, young women did not usually want to get involved with men they met at night clubs, preferring to date men they had met in more respectable settings. Most young women were more interested in dancing than in drinking, and usually ordered only the minimum number of beers and side dishes for a table.

While working at KTE, I went to a night club with In-suk, my closest friend at work, and two other coworkers, Yong-suk and Ŭn-mi. We talked about it a lot before finally deciding to go on the Saturday night after we got our bonus. We met at a coffee shop at around eight o'clock in the evening and chatted for about an hour. After that, we went to a night club that we knew was popular with workers. We arrived a bit before ten o'clock, just as the club was starting to get busy. When we arrived, a waiter ushered us to a table and, without asking, brought us four bottles of beer, a plate of fruit and a plate of dried snacks (e.g., peanuts, fish). We felt a bit awkward because no one was used to the night club setting. After a while, we went to the dance floor. We formed a circle and danced together while loud music blasted and psychedelic lighting flashed. When the music changed to a slow dance, two young men came over and asked In-suk and Yong-suk to dance with them. Ŭn-mi and I went back to the table while they danced. It was all right for women to dance together to fast music, but it was too awkward for a woman to dance to slow music with another woman. When we started to leave at about eleven o'clock, the two men approached us again and asked the two women to stay with them. My friends refused and we left. Outside, my friends talked about the danger of getting involved with the young men they met at a night club. In-suk commented:

> How can we stay at a night club with men we don't even know? We
> won't date men we meet at a night club. They wanted to dance with
> us tonight, but they wouldn't want to go out with women they met at
> a night club either. It is best just not to get involved with them.

In-suk's changing attitude toward her family illustrates how the individualism and consumerism that are part of workers' culture brings them into conflict

Table 3.1 *Single women's reported use of income (1987)*

	First priority		Second priority	
	No.	%	No.	%
Own living expenses	153	23	356	53
Parents' living expenses	111	16	72	11
Siblings' education	21	3	59	9
Saving for dowry	313	46	76	11
Own education	63	9	50	7
Other	8	1	10	2
No response	6	1	52	8
Total	675	99%	675	101%

with their families. She was a very sincere, faithful worker and a dutiful daughter, helping out her parents and her brother. Because she lived with her family, she did not have to pay for room and board. But in her first job (outside the Zone), she gave all her salary to her mother and got some pocket money. When she began working at KTE, however, she started keeping one-third of her wages for her own expenses and gave only two-thirds to her mother. She also kept her bonuses for herself, although she used most of the money to buy things that she and her family needed. Her older sister complained about how she had changed since she started to work at KTE, but In-suk thought that it was only fair to keep part of her wages. After all, she said, she was twenty-one years old and she needed to buy things for herself sometimes.

In my survey of single women working in MAFEZ, I asked them to rank the uses of their income in order of importance (see Table 3.1). Not surprisingly, providing their own living expenses was extremely important, with 76% of the women ranking it as their first or second priority. The first priority for the greatest number of women (46%), however, was saving for their dowry (*honsu;* see the following discussion). Despite their low wages, young women managed to save during their time as factory workers. They could do this only by cutting back on necessities, skipping breakfast and dinner, and living in crowded conditions either in the dormitory or in small rooms in Masan. Contributing to their families was also important. Twenty-seven percent of women reported using their income to support their parents as first or second priorities, and education for siblings (12%) was a high priority for some women. Getting additional education for themselves was also a high priority for many women

(16%) because this, like dowry saving, improved a woman's marriage prospects (see the following discussion).

BECOMING A HOUSEWIFE: IDENTIFYING WITH THE MIDDLE CLASS

Most women regarded their work in the Zone as a temporary situation and looked forward to the next stage of their lives. They anticipated being housewives, not factory workers, and looked forward to being middle class rather than identifying with the working class in the present.

Marriage as a Strategy for Social Mobility

Young women workers in MAFEZ expect to marry and see their upcoming marriage as the most important event in their lives. The 1990 census indicates that 95% of South Korean women marry by age thirty (Korean Women's Development Institute 1994:43), and workers do not even consider the possibility of remaining single. In one group where I discussed marriage, workers said, "How can you suggest that we stay unmarried for the rest of our lives? It would be so strange and everyone will feel sorry for us."[2] Twenty-six was considered the best age for getting married,[3] and factory workers who reached twenty-seven and were still single were pitied as "old maids" (*noch'ŏnyŏ*).

Marriage is viewed in South Korean society as a transaction between two families rather than just between two individuals. Even with the recent rise in importance of romantic love among young people, marriage negotiations are still considered family matters rather than individual matters. Although workers usually carried out marriage negotiations by themselves (cf. Cho Oakla 1987), young women in Masan frequently said, "A woman is not just getting married to a man; she is married to a whole family. That is why you need to consider what kind of family a man is coming from." Despite these comments, most young women wanted to make a love marriage (*yŏnae kyŏrhon*), which entailed choosing their own husbands;[4] they would not agree to marry a man

---

2 One worker wrote in her autobiography about how strange she felt about a woman minister of the Urban Industrial Mission, who was over fifty years old and single. She could not understand how a woman could reach that age without marrying (Sŏk 1984:23–24).

3 Both women's and men's age at first marriage has been rising steadily in South Korea. In 1960, the mean age was 21.6 for women and 25.4 for men; in 1990, the mean age was 25.5 for women and 28.6 for men (Korean Women's Development Institute 1994:39).

4 More than three-quarters of the unmarried women who responded to my questionnaire expected to choose their husband themselves.

without getting to know him. Young women categorized ways to get married as arranged marriages (*chungmae kyŏrhon*), love marriages (*yŏnae kyŏrhon*), or half-arranged and half-love marriages (*chungmaeban, yŏnaeban*). The distinction between these different ways of forming marriages is, however, disappearing in modern South Korean society. As Eunhee Kim Yi notes, "Arranged marriages are, to some extent, also based on personal liking and love marriages are often based on the calculation of objective interests" (1993:279). Of the married women who answered my questionnaire, 56% described their marriages as love marriages, 39% described them as arranged marriages and 5% said their marriage was a combination of the two forms.

Women had strong expectations for their future marriages, which they expected would free them from the burden of factory work. A typical expression of these expectations was "I want to marry someone who is sincere and who can support me so that I don't have to work out of economic necessity." They also had strong expectations about the characteristics they wanted their future husbands to possess. Men's character and economic security were the most important criteria that women workers used in evaluating potential husbands. Nearly two-thirds (63%) of the 675 unmarried women who responded to my questionnaire answered that the man's character was the most important factor in selecting a prospective husband. Thirteen percent selected the man's family background as the most important factor, indicating women's expectation to be incorporated into a family, not just linked to an individual. Eleven percent answered that the man's wealth was the most important factor, although most women considered a man's ability to support his family very important. Five percent answered that the man's education was the most important criterion for selection, and 5%, all Protestants, answered that the man's religion was most important.

In considering marriage, women followed various strategies to locate desirable potential husbands and to make themselves more desirable as potential wives. They saved money for a dowry, capital for their future marriage; they worked to advance their educational and social attainment, symbolic capital for their roles as wife and mother;[5] they dressed nicely and used cosmetics to make themselves prettier; and they tried to locate a suitable partner through dating.

5 Following Bourdieu's discussion (1977) on economic and symbolic capital, Janelli describes symbolic capital as assets that "are always intangible and often unrecognized but also contribute to the production of material benefits" (1993:34). Kim Eun-Shil (1993:195) discusses how working-class women perceive education as symbolic capital: "Many working-class women had a good understanding of the symbolic meaning of women's education; women's education was important not only to get good office jobs but also to manage married life well. Women's

Women workers in MAFEZ placed a high value on education and devoted much of their limited free time to studying. Women who had less than a high school education felt disadvantaged as potential wives in comparison with better-educated women and desperately tried to finish high school (see Chapter 2). Many workers who had completed high school tried to take college courses in order to appeal to better-educated men or, if they already had a college-educated boyfriend, in order to match his education. In addition to pursuing further formal education, factory workers were interested in "cultural subjects" such as flower arranging, the tea ceremony, or calligraphy. Both her level of formal education and her knowledge of cultural subjects made a woman more attractive as a potential wife.

Workers in MAFEZ seldom achieved much direct economic benefit from additional education because most better-paying jobs are not open to women. However, by becoming better educated or more cultivated, they developed skills that would be useful if they married a man with a good-paying job and became a full-time housewife. Such men were likely to be well educated themselves and more willing to marry well-educated women.

Dating and Sexuality

Dating and marriage were the two most important topics young women workers discussed among themselves. Conversations of women who were under twenty-two were mostly about group meetings and dating. Women who were twenty-three and older talked mostly about individual arranged meetings, steady boyfriends and wedding plans. Women often confided in their co-workers, and except for a few who were very shy and private, most workers in the same line knew about each other's boyfriends.

It had become acceptable for "progressive new women" to date men they liked in order to decide whom to marry, but it was not easy for young women to meet suitable men to date. South Korean society is rigidly sex segregated, and young women have limited opportunities to interact socially with young men. Jobs and workplaces are segregated by sex, as are middle schools and high schools. As mentioned previously, meeting young men at night clubs or other places where factory workers go for entertainment is considered disreputable.

education was often understood as the index of women's social and biological competence for motherhood; educated women were expected to bring up their children in the 'modern and learned' way."

Thus, arranged individual and group meetings were extremely important in meeting potential partners for dating and marriage.

Factories in MAFEZ cooperated with young women's interest in meeting potential marriage partners because they benefitted indirectly from a system that provided a constant turnover of low-cost female labor. Factories encouraged dating, and supervisors and line leaders even helped arrange group meetings. Arranged meetings took place on Sundays or on Saturday evenings when no work was scheduled, and managers accepted an arranged meeting as an excuse for missing unplanned overtime work at these times.

Dating encouraged workers to become more individualistic, Western and "modern," as it exposed them to consumer culture and nontraditional entertainment. Couples usually dated on Saturday evenings. A typical date might involve going to a movie theater and then to a restaurant for dinner. This was the only time most workers ate expensive food. Many beer halls (*hop'ujip*) in Masan catered to dating couples. Couples also took day trips to the countryside to visit parks and temples on Sundays. In most cases men were responsible for paying all the expenses on dates, but a few women said that they paid half the expenses.

Workers in MAFEZ usually dated men with a class standing similar to their own. Many of these men were production workers from Ch'angwŏn, an industrial estate set up near Masan for heavy industry. Although many women hoped to marry men with better backgrounds, more education and wealthier families than they themselves had, most ended up with husbands whose status was similar to theirs. Women relied on distant relatives and whatever other connections they had in order to meet high-status men. Men with white-collar jobs, especially government jobs, were in great demand for formal meetings, but the men that women met in group meetings or informally through friends were mostly production workers.

Many women met their future husbands through introductions by friends. My coworkers at KTE frequently arranged double dates between their friends and their boyfriends' friends. These informal introductions did not obligate the women to see the men again. Women younger than twenty-two or twenty-three did not take these meetings very seriously and were mostly interested in having fun, but women older than twenty-three were obsessed with meeting prospective husbands and paid close attention to how they looked at these meetings.

In 1987, In-suk, who was then twenty-three years old, met her future fiancé through an arranged meeting set up by her brother-in-law. He was a twenty-eight-year-old skilled production worker who worked with her brother-in-law in a factory in Ch'angwŏn. Her brother-in-law presented his friend to In-suk and her parents as a sincere, good worker who would be a good husband. When I talked to her in 1988, she told me how she reacted to her brother-in-law's suggestion:

> My brother-in-law is very nice to our family and I always thought that I would marry someone like him. When he first mentioned my fiancé to me, I thought that he was too old for me, but all my family thought a five-year age difference was ideal since the husband should be more mature than the wife. I also did not like the fact that he knew too much about my family. There were things that I would not want my prospective husband to know about (like the fact that my mother is a second wife and sixteen years younger than my father).
>
> My family was also pleased that my fiancé is a second son, since I will not have as many responsibilities as I would if I married an oldest son. . . . We have been dating for the past three months and we plan to get married around September. Now I think it is good that he knows all about my family; I don't have to pretend or hide anything from him. He seems like a nice person and he earns decent money so that I will not have to work outside the home.

Other women met prospective husbands through group meetings or club activities. One of my roommates, Chong-hui, met her future husband at the JOC (Young Catholic Workers' Organization) meetings in 1987 when she was twenty-one years old. She told me about her courtship when I talked to her in 1991:

> My parents always told me that I should find my own husband, and they would agree to the person I chose as long as he had no major flaws. When I met my husband at JOC, I did not consider him as a prospective husband. Rather, I thought of him as a good friend. He was very supportive when I was fired in 1989 for being involved in union activities. . . . I dated other men too, but I realized that I really liked him and he seemed to be the right kind of person to marry. He graduated from a vocational high school, he had a good, steady job as a skilled worker at Samsong Heavy Industry and he was a third son. When he finally asked me to marry him, I was ready to say "yes" and we got married in 1990.

Family pressures could make matchmaking especially urgent for some workers. In 1985, Ŭn-sil got pregnant while dating a man she met at a group meeting arranged by her line leader. She started to live with her boyfriend, but his family would not allow them to get married because his older brother was still not married. She eventually introduced her brother-in-law to a sister of one of her coworkers. Her brother-in-law was then thirty-two years old and worked as a truck driver. Her friend's sister was a twenty-seven-year-old garment worker. Thus both of them were in undesirable jobs and also too old to be considered the best marriage prospects. Ŭn-sil explained:

> I was in a hurry to get my brother-in-law married so that my husband and I could have a wedding ceremony. I had to balance both sides for a prospective marriage. I told my friend that although my brother-in-law was old, he had a steady job as a long distance truck driver. He also had a high school education, while she only had a middle school education. At the same time, I told my brother-in-law, Tae-hui would make a good wife for him. She was a hard-working, frugal woman who would take care of his household well while he had to be absent from home. [Tae-hui was present at the interview.] Finally, they agreed and got married this year.

Although young women expected to date before they got married, they were naive about their sexuality and many believed that they could not get pregnant the first time they had sexual intercourse. Women workers who became pregnant felt guilt and shame. No statistics were available about workers' pregnancies or abortions in MAFEZ. However, I heard stories about women workers who did not realize that they were pregnant until the fourth or fifth month and had to have late abortions. An early abortion cost 20,000 to 30,000 won in 1987, and late abortions cost more. I heard about only one place where a woman doctor performed abortions at low cost.

Women who got pregnant unexpectedly were confronted with major changes in their lives. Ŭn-sil told me what happened following her pregnancy:

> I got pregnant while we were dating. I was a virgin and it was the first time we had sexual intercourse. I did not know what to do. In our company, management allowed some women who got pregnant ["into trouble"] time off so they could have an abortion. Women who were considered troublemakers were forced to resign. They gave me time off, but we decided to keep the baby, so I quit my job.

Once a year, a sex education class was offered at the KTE factory. A woman from the YWCA came and lectured on sex and pregnancy. In her talk she emphasized that women should not trust men, and she preached that they should wait until they were married to have sexual experiences. She assumed that most women workers were not sexually active and made no mention of birth control or contraception methods. A sex education program was also offered at the Catholic Women's Center, and it also stressed that women should abstain from sex until after marriage.

Two actions are required before a marriage is fully formalized in South Korea. The first is a public wedding ritual, and the second is the legal registration of the marriage. The wedding ritual is considered the more important of these two actions. Registration is considered a legal technicality, which becomes important only in the unlikely event of a divorce. Many couples do not bother to register their marriages until after a child is born, and some even wait until the oldest child starts school, at which time a record of the parents' marriage is required in his or her documents.

Women workers frequently discussed the topic of living together (*tonggŏ*), along with dating and marriage, but most workers rejected the possibility as immoral. Couples were described as *tonggŏ* when they lived together without having had a wedding ritual or registering their marriage. When I asked them about the subject, most women said, "I won't live with my boyfriend before we are married." But most women knew workers who lived with their boyfriends. Women who were younger than twenty-three years old had very negative attitudes toward *tonggŏ* arrangements, but women older than twenty-three were more tolerant. One twenty-three-year-old garment worker said:

> I used to regard it as immoral for a woman to live with a man, but I have changed my opinion a lot. Right now, I cannot get married because I don't have any money for my dowry. A wedding would cost too much money. I would rather save my dowry money and use it for a deposit on a room. Three of my very close girlfriends are living with their boyfriends because they cannot afford to have weddings. *Tonggŏ* is not a bad idea for those of us who are poor and at the age to get married, because we will eventually marry the man. We are not like young women who get involved without knowing what they are doing.

A former worker in a shoe factory told me that when she was working, most of the workers in her line lived with their boyfriends. Although she knew that many workers lived in *tonggŏ* arrangements, she was surprised when she found out the exact number when she conducted a survey for the Catholic Church. She said that it was easy to tell who was properly married and who was living in a *tonggŏ* arrangement: "Workers who lived with their boyfriends without getting married rarely talked about their men. They just do not act like someone who is married." She claimed that garment factory workers were more likely than electronics factory workers to be in *tonggŏ* arrangements because of their financial situation. Most married women said that although it was not a desirable thing to do, they could understand if a woman of marriageable age lived with her boyfriend for financial reasons, but they were opposed to younger women becoming involved in those relations.

Without a wedding ritual, couples perceive their arrangement as *tonggŏ* and illegitimate. Even though Ŭn-sil had been living with her boyfriend for two years, had registered her marriage and borne a child, she still described her relationship as *tonggŏ* because she had not yet had a wedding ritual (see the preceding discussion). Her ritual had been held up until her boyfriend's brother got married. He had married shortly before I interviewed her in 1987, and she was looking forward to her wedding and her return to respectable status.

In their desire to date and eventually marry high-status men, some women dated college students. It was acceptable for a wife to have less education than her husband, and dating college students was seen as prestigious. However, although college students could be expected to eventually get good jobs, while they were students most did not earn any money and did not have anything to spend on dating. Women workers, therefore, had to pay for most of their dating expenses and sometimes even gave pocket money to their boyfriends.

The class difference between male college students and female factory workers left the women open to sexual exploitation because the students did not feel as responsible toward workers as they were toward women of their own social class. Most of these relationships did not turn into marriages.

One of my coworkers at KTE confided that her boyfriend was a college student. She hoped to marry him, but she was worried about whether his family would accept her. He was the only son of a fairly high-status farm family. She had met his family once, and they received her politely but without enthusiasm. She was especially worried about her dowry because she was twenty-three and had not saved anything. All her income from four years of factory work had gone to support her own family, which was extremely poor. Her invalid father had been a day laborer, and her mother was a market vendor. The money that they used as "key money" for the two rooms in which they lived in Ulsan came

73

from her earnings. She resented the fact that she could not keep her money for her dowry, but her family could not give up their home. Her mother told her that she should be able to save enough in two or three years, but she was uncertain about how her boyfriend's family would react to this plan. In the meantime, her boyfriend was staying in Masan with her and her two sisters while he looked for a room of his own. This was almost a *tonggŏ* relationship and a significant gamble on her part that the relationship would turn into a marriage. If it did not, her reputation would be seriously compromised.

Women who had been jilted by college students warned younger women to be careful of them: "Wake up and face reality. The guy you are dating now will never marry you. Why can't you see that they are just using you financially, emotionally and sexually? I know that because I had the same experience." However, such comments rarely convinced young women to give up their boyfriends. Newspapers sometimes carried stories about how male college students exploited women workers in Masan,[6] and factory workers said that male students considered factory workers easy to get and boasted: "They are more than willing to sleep with us if we want them to."

Lonely young women working in Masan factories could also be vulnerable to sexual exploitation by their bosses. Most managers, under-managers and line leaders were already married and thus unavailable as potential husbands for workers, although they would have been desirable. Divorce is still very uncommon in South Korea, but some workers had affairs with their bosses, hoping that they would divorce their wives and marry them. I learned of a case where this had happened, but it was very unusual.

Casual affairs between managers and workers were more common, and although a woman might benefit in the short term from sleeping with her boss, she would almost inevitably end up out of work, discarded and scorned, while her boss's career would continue unaffected.

While I was working at KTE, one of my coworkers was openly having an affair with the married line leader. Other workers gossiped behind her back and complained that she got special privileges, including release from overtime work. When she married a low-ranking government officer, she left her job and moved to the rural area where her husband worked, but she continued to call the line leader and even came to visit him once. Her behavior was considered

---

6 The *Yonsei Ch'unch'u* carried an article about relationships between male students of Kyŏngnam University and women workers in MAFEZ. Students of Kyŏngnam University protested the publication of the article and burned an effigy of the reporter, but students generally admitted that some students did exploit factory workers.

scandalous. Workers said that it was bad enough to have an affair with a married man while you were single, but it was far worse to continue the affair after getting married. It was always the woman who was condemned, never the line leader. I even heard him boast that because he was her first man, she could never forget him for the rest of her life.

Honsu *and Wedding Expenses*

The young women who worked in MAFEZ were concerned with investing in their marriage and the family in which they expected to spend the rest of their lives. They did this by saving money for wedding expenses and their dowry (*honsu*). *Honsu* consists principally of gifts to the bridegroom, gifts to the bride's in-laws and household furnishings for the new couple. Factory workers both expected and were expected to bring a substantial dowry with them when they married. The size of these women's dowries was remarkable considering their low wages, often exceeding two years' income from factory work. Practically every unmarried worker saved some money for her dowry every month, cutting back on necessities, sometimes skipping breakfast and dinner, and eating only the lunch provided by the company. Forty-six percent of the women who responded to my survey answered that saving for a dowry was their first priority, and another 11% answered that it was their second priority. As women approached the expected age for marriage, twenty-six, the stress placed on dowry saving increased, so that by age twenty-five it was the most important use of income for nearly all workers who remained unmarried (see Figure 3.1). Ninety-five percent of the twenty-five-year-old single women who answered my questionnaire reported that dowry saving was the main use of their income.

Families demonstrate status and wealth in the dowries they provide for their daughters, and the dowries of the daughters of elite families are expected to be lavish. Although the tradition of providing a dowry is ancient, its current level of extravagance and its reach into all levels of society are unprecedented and represent significant "new elaborations upon an older structure of Korean marriage rituals" (Kendall 1985:253). The amount of dowry required of brides has increased dramatically in recent years (cf. Kendall 1985, 1996; Eunhee Kim Yi 1993:289),[7] and now even factory workers are expected to bring dowries of several million won with them.

7 The inflation of the dowry is widely considered to have gotten out of hand. It is now said, for
   example, that the bride for a medical doctor or a lawyer should bring "three keys" with her (a

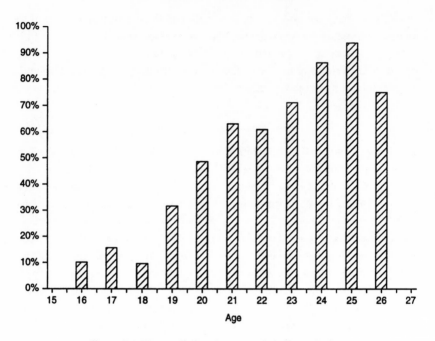

Figure 3.1 Women listing dowry as their first priority.

Before a wedding can take place, the bride's family is expected to prepare gifts for the bridegroom and his family (*yedan*). Gifts to the bridegroom conventionally consist of a watch, a ring, a set of traditional clothing and a Western suit to wear at the wedding ceremony. Gifts to the bridegroom's family include traditional clothing, bedding, cloth, socks and stockings. This tradition has recently expanded to include quite distant relatives (Kendall 1985) and is a significant expense. Also, prior to the wedding, the bridegroom's family sends the bride a chest (*ham*) filled with clothing (*ch'aedan*) and jewelry (*p'aemul*). The largest component of the dowry has to do with setting up the couple's new household. Although the bridegroom's family is expected to provide their living space (for factory workers, this generally means key money for a rented room or two), the bride and her family are responsible for providing all the furnishings for the couple's new home (e.g., wardrobe, bedding, dresser, gas

key for an apartment, a key for a car and a key for an office). This dowry is not only extravagant but suggests that the groom's family is shirking its responsibility to their son.

stove, refrigerator, television, stereo). Both families are expected to share in the actual costs of the wedding, including the wedding hall, the officiator at the ceremony, lunch for the guests and the honeymoon.

The way women factory workers use dowry savings both emulates higher-status families and seeks to improve their own status. By saving for the dowry, these women demonstrate their identification with the middle class and their optimism about achieving a position within it. Marriage is the most important event in determining their status for the rest of their lives, and the amount saved for their dowry is important not only in helping select a husband, but also in how their new in-laws regard them and their position in their new family. As Eunhee Kim Yi observes, "It is well recognized that the status of the bride in the husband's family is primarily determined by how much *honsu* her natal family provides to her" (1993:289).

A generation ago, Korean marriages incorporated very young brides into already existing households run by their in-laws. Nowadays, among factory workers and South Koreans in general, the brides are older and marriages mark the founding of new households based on a neolocal couple (Kendall 1985:261, 1996). Nevertheless, marriage continues to be "seen as a transaction between two families" (Eunhee Kim Yi 1993:287). The daughter is seen as lost to her family, whereas the son's membership in his family is unchanged, and the provision of a dowry is felt to be an onerous financial burden on the bride's family. Kendall quotes an informant who sums up this perception by saying, "When her daughter marries, a mother is lucky if she's left with her own navel" (Kendall 1985:253).

Workers' families were unable to provide dowries for their daughters out of their own resources, so the responsibility of providing a dowry shifted to the women themselves. Nevertheless, assembling a dowry was still seen as a family undertaking and frequently involved pooling family resources. The socially recognized importance of marriage enabled young women to make greater demands on their families than at any other time, and women who had been major sources of economic support for their families demanded and got back some of the money they had earned while working. On the other hand, weddings of older sisters enabled families to make greater than usual demands on the incomes of young factory workers, and many younger workers contributed a large proportion of their income to dowries for older sisters.

Marriage partners were expected to be social equals, and the amount of dowry had to be roughly comparable to that which other women of similar social status were providing. The exact amount of dowry depended on negotiations involving the couple and their families, but it was considered bad form to demand too much because it implied that the woman herself was not worth much.

Although the amounts of money spent for *honsu* by women workers in MAFEZ did not match those spent by middle- or upper-class women, they were still substantial. In 1987, young women workers said, "even a beggar's wedding costs three million won" (about $3,700), and women who had married in the mid-1980s claimed to have spent between 2 million and 5 million won ($2,500–$6,250) for their weddings.

Su-kyong, a former electronics factory worker, told me that she had helped financed her older sister's wedding and then received help from her sister when it was her turn to get married. She spent six years (1979–1985) working in factories both inside and outside the Zone. While working, she lived with her parents in Masan so that she did not have to pay for room and board. She explained how she raised and spent the money for her dowry:

> I spent about five million won when I got married. I had saved about three million won through a rotating credit association [*kye*] and a bank savings plan. One of my older sisters gave me two million won, reciprocating for the money I gave her when she got married. I spent one million won on my husband (to buy a ring, Western suits, a traditional suit, a watch, etc.). I sent his family one million one hundred thousand won instead of getting them presents which they might not want. I used the rest of the money to prepare equipment for the household, and for wedding and honeymoon expenses. My husband's family was satisfied with my dowry and said so. His family contributed seven million seven hundred thousand won for his wedding. We used most of it as key money for the two rooms where we now live.

Retirement funds were important in enabling some women who had spent a long time working at a single factory to finance their own weddings. Su-hyon, a former garment worker who had also lived with her parents, told me how she paid for her wedding:

> I worked for Sinhŭng shoe factory for seven years until 1985 when I got married. I gave my whole salary to my mother to help my family for the first three years while I was working. After that, since my parents told me to take care of my own *honsu,* I started a three-million-

78

won, five-year savings account. When I left my job, my retirement payment came to 2.2 million won. Together, I had over five million won for my *honsu* without the help from my family.

Workers who had to live in a dormitory or share a room with other workers found it very difficult to save, but even women living with their families generally had to contribute to family budgets, which made saving difficult. And, of course, some women had to support families who could not provide them with a place to live in Masan. Tae-hui (see the earlier discussion), who spent eight years working in a MAFEZ shoe factory, sent money to support her family in Taejŏn without saving anything for her dowry. When she left the factory because of poor health in 1983, she received a retirement payment of a little over 1 million won. This was all she had when she decided to get married. Fortunately for her, her health improved, her father had better luck as an unlicensed acupuncturist, and her younger sister was able to contribute to her dowry. Altogether she was able to come up with a *honsu* of 4 million won. Of course, there were other women who were not as lucky as Tae-hui.

Although a sizable proportion of *honsu* was spent on gifts for in-laws, and although marriage expenses included expenditures on conspicuous consumption (e.g., food and elaborate clothing), the furnishings for the new couple's living space consumed the largest proportion of the *honsu.* By saving for their *honsu,* women were thus to a large extent saving for themselves and buying the household equipment that they expected to use for themselves and their antici-pated families. Ideally, a woman brought to her marriage all the equipment she would need to run a household. Her husband's job would be enough to support her and their anticipated children, and she would devote herself to her new role as a full-time wife and mother. Even expenditures that were not recouped immediately would benefit the couple by enhancing their status. In the next section, I examine the gap between this ideal scenario and the situation that many married women actually experienced.

MARRIAGE AND WORK IN THE REAL WORLD

"I Will Never Come Back to a Sewing Machine"

Most women workers in MAFEZ expect to leave their jobs in order to get married and intend to become full-time wives and mothers. Nearly 90% of the single women in my survey said that they planned to leave their jobs on marriage, and even among my sample of married women, many of whom I encountered in factory contexts, 64% indicated that they had left the job market when they got married. Most women cited their position in the family as the reason for not wanting to work after marriage – for example, "I want to be a good wife and a mother" or "It is not good to work after one is married." Some, however, cited the unpleasantness of factory work as the reason for not wanting to continue – for example, "I am sick and tired of working in a factory" or "I worked in a factory too long already."

Single women generally perceived marriage and work to be incompatible and did not believe it was possible for a woman to work outside the home and still be "a wise mother and good wife" (*hyŏnmo yangch'ŏ,* the conventional definition of the proper role for a woman). Single women frequently expressed their desire to fulfill this conventional role and expected that, in the future, they would have husbands who could support them economically. The structure of the labor market reinforced women's moral commitment to the role of mother and wife. Women were happy to exchange "domestic work for financial sup-port" (Ferree 1985), in part because they had such limited options in the labor market. Because women could not earn the same incomes as men, their best economic arrangement was to trade being a good mother and wife for the economic support of a man with a high-paying job. Thus, the segmented labor market pushed women back into the structure of a patriarchal family.

Both single and married women overwhelmingly rejected the idea of a working mother, especially one with young children. Most married women also said that their husbands did not want them to work, and many asserted that any husband who wants his wife to work is not really a man.

In 1987, Su-hyon, a twenty-five-year-old former garment worker, had been married for a year and a half and had a baby daughter. She was considered to have made a good marriage and lived in a nice two-bedroom apartment in Ch'angwŏn. I interviewed her there, and she explained her decision to be a full-time mother and wife:

> I spent more than seven years working in a shoe factory before I got
> married. I never want to see another sewing machine. My husband
> earns 400,000 won a month as a skilled technician. That is not a lot
> but we can live on it. My husband bought this apartment where we
> live. Our mortgage payments are 70,000 won a month. I do not have
> big ambitions. I just want to stay home to take care of my daughter
> and my husband. I worked for a long time. My husband wants me to

stay home too, so why should I go back to a miserable factory job at a sewing machine?

Su-hyon's modest aspirations were typical of many workers in MAFEZ. She found her current role as mother and wife to be congenial and felt she had improved her status significantly with her marriage. Although her family had been too poor to send her to high school and she had spent many years working under harsh conditions, she had married a high school graduate who was a successful blue-collar worker, and she was comfortable.

A few factory workers achieve even more social mobility through their marriages and, by marrying men with middle-class careers, establish themselves firmly in the middle class. I met one former electronics worker who had married very well. Although Na-hyon also came from a family that was too poor to send her to high school, she lived in a comfortable house in a middle-class section of Pusan. Her husband was a college graduate and had a white-collar job in a bank. She looked up to her husband and tried very hard to meet his standards. She was determined to get a college diploma so that she could match her husband's education and had begun a college correspondence course. Although she believed that it was acceptable for a woman to have less education than her husband, she wanted to be equal to her husband's friends' wives. When I interviewed her, she had completed two years of course work and was taking a leave of absence because of her children.

Na-hyon was uncomfortable talking about her experience as a factory worker. Even though she had spent six years at one factory where she was well regarded as a model worker and had been able to earn her high school diploma, she preferred to talk about her comfortable present life, about how much her house was worth, and about her children's piano lessons and private math lessons. Her current economic ambitions focused on opening her own flower shop. She thought of herself as a middle-class woman and tried to leave her experience as a factory worker behind her.

Although she was comfortable and pleased with her middle-class life, it was not without problems. Ever since she had married, she had lived with her in-laws. After her very traditional wedding, she had lived with her in-laws in their village for a month. Then she moved to Pusan, where she shared her two-room apartment with two of her sisters-in-law. After they married and she moved into her house, she had to share it with her husband's younger brother, who was a college student in Pusan. Although she expressed some desire to have the house to herself, she appeared to accept her subordinate position within her husband's family. She was vehemently conservative about family issues, asserting, for example, that sons are better than daughters and that all mothers prefer to have sons. She had one daughter and one son. Her daughter was born first, and she had felt extreme pressure that the next child should be a boy. She said that when she found out that she had given birth to a son, she felt like flying and did not feel any of the pain of delivery at all.

The balance of ambition and self-denial that is needed for a factory worker to move into the middle class is not easily achieved, as the following case illustrates. Chin-yong was a former worker at KTE who had married a manager at her company. Her family's financial problems had prevented her from attending high school, but she took night classes and earned her high school diploma while she was at KTE. She met her future husband at work, where he taught an evening calligraphy class for workers. Even though he was a college graduate and nine years older than she, they dated and eventually married.

She was a very ambitious woman and had difficulty accepting the subordinate role that her husband expected of her. During a period of financial difficulties she took a job as an insurance saleswoman, even though she had two young children to care for. As she became more successful, her husband became more opposed to her working outside the home. In 1987, she was an assistant manager and was earning two-thirds as much as he was. Her husband claimed that she should be able to manage the family's expenses with his salary and refused to acknowledge her contribution to the household. He also accused her of using her work as an excuse to neglect him and their two children.

They had constant violent arguments and eventually took the unusual step of obtaining a divorce. Their marriage had lasted eight years. Chin-yong's husband, of course, retained custody of the children and all their property. In her case, the ambition that enabled her to achieve success undermined her success as a middle-class housewife (cf. Robotham 1973; Zaretsky 1976). Although she had made a good marriage in terms of class, her married life was very unhappy.

Most factory workers did not marry bank officers or factory managers, and many experienced continuing financial hardships after they left factory work. Although most women gave up working in factories before they married, it was fairly common for women to keep some paid employment until their first child was born.

Chong-hui, a worker at a garment factory and one of my roommates in 1987, got married in 1990 to a worker at Samsong Heavy Industry in Ch'angwŏn. Her participation in union activities led to her being fired just before her wedding, but she continued to work until her family was established. At first, she worked as an aide at a day-care center; then she had her first baby. The boy was sickly and died when he was only a few months old. Afterward, she worked as a saleswoman in a department store. When I interviewed her early in 1994, she had just given birth to a healthy son. She was staying home to care for the baby and planned to move to an apartment in Chinhae in a few months. She compared her department store job to factory work.

> It wasn't as easy as it seems. You just see women with makeup smiling and bowing when you go for shopping. But once you are working as one, you find out how hard it is to stand up all day long and repeat the sales pitch for every customer. You do not have time for lunch or even to use the rest room. There are no set breaks like at the factory. After my first week, my legs were so swollen I could not go back to work for three days. You know, while I was working at the factory, I always wanted to be a saleswoman at a department store. But after I started working there, I began to feel that factory work is better in some ways. Many factory women wouldn't believe this, but it's true. At least at the factory, you can sit down. You don't have to work standing up all day. There are lunch breaks and two rest periods, and you can go to the toilet whenever you want even though you have to look around to check where the supervisor is. At the department store, you are the only one at the counter; if you are away there is no one to help the customer. There are no chairs; I brought in cushions so that I could sit down if there weren't any customers. The pay was not much better than factory work either. There is no overtime pay, and you have to work twelve hours a day straight. You are only sure about getting off two days a month; there is no guarantee that you can get the other two days off. (You are supposed to get every Sunday off, but Sundays are the busiest days at department stores.) While I was working for the department store, my husband and I never had a chance to do anything together on Sundays. Also, since I had to work late every night, he volunteered for a lot of overtime work. So we saved some during that time.

Although Chong-hui's departure from the factory was involuntary, her choice of jobs after her marriage was not unusual. Nor was her strategy of continuing to work and save for the family she eventually had. With their combined savings and her husband's blue-collar job they could afford a comfortable apartment, and she planned to stay at home to be a full-time mother and wife.

When financial necessity forces former factory workers back into the workforce, they usually prefer some form of employment other than factory work. One alternative chosen by many former factory workers was to become proprietors of small family businesses. These were very small-scale enterprises, such as restaurants, flower shops, and beauty shops that absorbed all of the couples' savings.

One such enterprise was a tiny restaurant that a former worker at KTE ran with her husband. During the nearly seven years that Suk-ja worked in the factory, she had lived with her parents and turned her paycheck over to her mother. Her parents provided her with a small dowry when she got married and she left her factory job. At that time, her husband worked as a deep sea fisherman. After the wedding, she moved in with his family in a rural village while he continued to work at his fishing job. His job paid well, but it also required him to be at sea for a year or more at a time. Family problems that began when his mother was killed in a car accident forced him to return home and give up his job. After he came back, he and his wife used the savings that they had accumulated, mostly from his wages, to start a small restaurant in Masan. They lost money on the first two restaurants and were now at their third location in as many years. Even though the restaurant was struggling and Suk-ja had to work there all day (twelve to fifteen hours a day), she felt it was better than factory work because she and her husband were working for themselves, and it allowed her to care for her two young sons.

Mothers of young children were especially reluctant to work away from home. Both men and women highly value the role of "wise mother," and women try to manage on what their husbands earn rather than jeopardize that role. In the few cases where women wanted to take outside jobs while their children were young, they were generally unable to find any child-care services.

Hye-in, a thirty-one-year-old former garment worker, wanted to go back to work because she believed that her husband's salary was not sufficient to support her family. But because she could not find any child care for her two boys (ages two and five), she had to stay home and try to make ends meet on her husband's meager salary. Hye-in was a committed labor activist, and her interest in the workers' cause was another factor that made her want to return to factory work.

The Myth of Social Mobility

One option that Hye-in considered, and that was frequently pursued by women with very young children, was doing "home work" in a putting-out system. They were paid a piece rate and usually earned 1,000 to 2,000 won a day. Even though these jobs were low-paid, they were hard to get because so many women were available. Most housewives did not consider home work real work because they did not leave their homes. They believed it was better than going to work in a factory because they could take care of their children. Their husbands were also less likely to object to their working at home.

When I interviewed Hye-in, she was doing home work sewing collars on shirts. She resented the fact that she was still tied to a sewing machine and earning much less than she had earlier when she was at the factory. She was acutely aware of the two major disadvantages of home work. First, it paid poorly. Second, it isolated the workers so that they could not even learn about their shared problems, let alone organize to do anything about them.

> What I am earning now, a little over 2,000 won a day, working at a piece rate [togŭpje], is a lot less than what I could earn at a garment factory working as a skilled sewing machine operator [about 5,000 won a day], but I don't have any choice because there is no child care around here. I know I am exploited working this way, and I feel bad about not being able to do anything to improve the situation. I remember how, even in the seventies, I could organize work stoppages at F-one in the Zone, but I cannot do anything with the married women [ajumma] who do home work. The only ones I know are those who live in this apartment building, and they are grateful just to get orders, so it is impossible to get them to organize.

"Big Companies Don't Hire Us, Married Women"

Most former factory workers did not want to return to factory work, and those who did decide to return experienced severe disadvantages in their search for work. The best jobs were simply unavailable to older women (i.e., those past their mid-twenties). Within MAFEZ, only the lower-paying companies, such as garment and shoe factories, employed significant numbers of married women. Married women could also choose to do home work or work at subcontracting factories, most of which are located outside the Zone. As one woman pointed out:

85

> Big companies don't hire us, married women, so we wind up in sub-contracting factories where there are no fringe benefits at all and no job security either.

The segmentation of the labor market, which kept the wages of women production workers low, discriminated even more severely against married women who continued to work in factories (Society for the Study of Korean Women et al. 1991:73). Married women formed a separate and even lower-paid segment of the labor market. Furthermore, with most of society agreeing that they should not be working, they could not afford to speak out against their situation. Low-paid workers were resented by those in better-paid categories for holding down the wages. Workers in Masan said, "Men's wages do not go up because of women workers, and single women's wages do not go up because of married women's willingness to work at low wages."

Not only were wages for married women low, they generally could not expect promotions or seniority increases. Among the married women factory workers I interviewed, older women were actually paid less than younger women (see Figure 3.2), and a regression analysis correlating age and income produces a downward-sloping line. Jobs for married women were neither as well paid nor as prestigious as those for single women.

Even in factories where single women and married women worked together on the shop floor, they formed separate groups. Single women usually discussed dating and wedding plans, whereas married women were interested in each other's children and family finances. Young women rarely envisioned themselves in the same situation as the married women workers they saw every day, although they knew that almost all of the married women in their factory had once, like themselves, planned to get out of factory work. They pitied married workers, but they did not expect to ever become like them. One worker expressed a typical sentiment:

> I really feel sorry for these aunties [*ajumma*]. They have to work just like us, and then they have to go home and work for families again. I guess that they really need money. But I would never come back to work at a sewing machine again.

Although most workers left the labor force when they got married, many women did eventually return to factory work. Unforeseen financial needs were behind most of the decisions to return to work in a factory, but these included not just coping with family misfortune, such as the death of a husband, but also

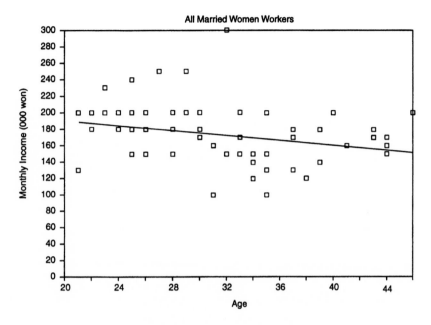

Figure 3.2 Income and age (1987).

plans to make investments in a better life, such as getting money for their children's education or plans to buy their own house or apartment. Although women married to men with the best blue-collar jobs usually believed that their husbands' wages could provide adequately for these needs, many women found that their husbands' wages were unable to provide what was needed to make their families comfortable.

Hye-jong, the landlady of the room I shared in Masan,[8] was a thirty-six-year-old worker at an electronics company in the Zone. Her husband was a guard at T'ongil Heavy Industry in Ch'angwŏn. They were very proud to own their house, even though it was small and old and they had to rent two of the

8 Although Hye-jong considered both herself and her husband to be the owners of the house, most houses (and other property) were legally owned only by the husband. Under the laws in effect in 1987, she would have had no claim to the property in the event of a divorce. Family law underwent a major revision in 1989, and under the current law women are entitled to a share of the property acquired during a marriage, although they still rarely hold formal legal title to their homes.

four rooms to other workers to make ends meet. They had three school-age children (six, eight and ten), but Hye-jong still worked at a factory; otherwise, they would never have been able to afford their own house. She had worked at a textile factory in Taegu before she married. She left work to get married and later moved to Masan with her husband. She explained how she decided to go back to work and how she achieved her present job:

> My husband was totally against my working outside the home, but I started anyway, despite his protests, more than three years ago. . . . We tried to save so we could buy our own house and we bought this one last year. When my husband started to work, he only made 70,000 to 80,000 won; now, after seven years, he earns 260,000 to 270,000 won, which is still not enough for us to live on. We both work three-shift schedules and arrange for one of us to stay with the children at night. The pay is a little better if you work shifts. I could have gotten a job somewhere else with a lighter workload, but I wanted to earn a little more, and this way I can spend more time with my children when they are at home.

Like many former factory workers, Hye-jong had tried a different job before deciding to return to factory work:

> Before I went back to the Zone, I worked as a yogurt delivery woman for just a week. It was too hard since I had to walk all day. I think that factory work is a lot better job than delivery work. First, I don't have to walk; I stay in one place all day. Second, I don't have to pay for my own lunch. Third, I know I will get paid; there was a lot of talk about delivery people being cheated (customers move after a month or two without paying what they owe).

Although she believed that her family needed the extra income, it was a difficult decision for Hye-jong to go back to a factory job. Not only did her husband oppose her plan, but she felt terribly guilty about leaving her children:

> My son was only two years old when I started to work as a yogurt delivery woman. When I was taking the examination at the Korean Yogurt Company, I couldn't read the questions because my tears were streaming down. I didn't think it was right to leave my two-year-old behind. Mothers should be home taking care of their children. My children are not doing well at school because there is nobody to take care of them at home; I feel it is all my fault. They need someone to

go over their homework assignments and to answer their questions. . . . It's true that we were able to buy this house last year because of what the two of us earned together, but I am not sure about leaving my children. I always give in to them when they ask for pocket money since I feel so bad about leaving them. I have to give them money to buy snacks because I am not here to cook snacks for them when they come home. Well, I am working so that they can eat better and can go to college too . . . but I am not sure whether I am doing the right thing. My youngest just started first grade, and I felt sorry for him not having his mother at home.

In-ja was another woman who found that her husband's wages were inadequate to meet their family's needs. She explained how she felt about factory work after spending ten years as a sewing machine operator and why she decided to go back right after her daughter was born:

By 1985, I was really sick and tired of factory work and was willing to do practically anything to get out, and the marriage seemed the best option. I dated my husband for a month and a half before we got married in December 1985. My husband is a welder at Hyosŏng Heavy Industry and earns about 270,000 won (including overtime work). . . . I didn't work when I first got married (the reason I got married was so I wouldn't have to work). But from my husband's wage of 270,000 won, we had to put aside 170,000 won for two savings plans (a 5 million won five-year saving plan and a 3 million won three-year saving plan), which left only 100,000 won. And from this, we had to help my in-laws a little bit every month (about 15,000 won). After all these regular expenses, we didn't have much to live on each month. After our daughter, So-yong, was born in November 1986, there was no way we could live on my husband's wage, so I decided to work again, as much as I hated to do so. I went back to Tŏksŏng Sirŏp even before So-yong was one hundred days old. I thought that if I waited longer, I wouldn't be able to leave her behind to go to work. And I couldn't have done it if my mother didn't live right next door. I cried every day when I had to leave my baby behind before she even opened her eyes.

In-ja also had to cope with her husband's opposition to her working, even though they clearly needed the additional income:

I didn't tell my husband about my job on the first day. I just came home early without staying for overtime work. The next day, when I told him, his immediate response was that we should cancel our savings and I should stay home to take care of So-yong. But I begged him to let me work because I wanted to earn money for our baby's formula and other expenses. These days, my husband usually comes home around nine o'clock. I come home at around eight o'clock, when we work two hours of overtime, or at around ten o'clock when we work four hours of overtime, which we usually do twice a week. From my paycheck of 200,000 won a month, I give my mother 50,000 won for taking care of So-yong and put aside 25,000 won for So-yong's "Education Fund" (she will get 5 million won in ten years), and the rest goes for household expenses. Usually, we use about 125,000 won from my wages plus 80,000 won from my husband's for our household expenses. Whenever I feel tired and sick, I look at my daughter and think that in two years we will have 10 million won to buy our own home, which makes me feel better right away.

In spite of In-ja's contribution to the household, she believed that she had injured her husband by returning to work and felt guilty about it.

After I started working again, I had to be extremely careful what to say to my husband not to hurt his pride. Sometimes when he drinks, he accuses me of "looking down on him because I earn money." Whenever he says that to me, I would like to talk back to him, but at the same time, I also understand how he feels. His pride is wounded by my working outside. I have to watch every word I say to him, and that's hard. I wish that he could understand why I have to go to work, but he doesn't, apparently. If I stay home, we will argue more and more, and I cannot stand that. So it is best for me to go out to work and to save money for all of us as fast as possible.

Although many women who returned to factory work anticipated a better future in exchange for their current hardships, others were forced back into factory work by deteriorating economic circumstances and were struggling merely to maintain themselves. When a husband died, became incapacitated, or abandoned his family, factory work became a permanent condition for women rather than a temporary one.

Ok-ja came from a poor rural family. Although her father had been the principal of a village school, he died when she was six and she received no formal education. Her mother died when she was ten, and after that she was shunted between the households of two paternal aunts. She worked in a small family-owned garment factory until she married at age twenty. She went back to factory work when her youngest child was three years old. After two years at a textile factory, she switched to a hat factory located in MAFEZ. Her husband also worked in the Zone at this time. She told me how difficult it had been for a married woman to get a job in the Zone in 1972:

> There were not many places that hired married women, but I heard there was one company in the Zone. It took me two hours to walk there from where we lived. When I got there, about 150 married women were waiting for interviews for thirty job openings. I was twenty-nine years old, but the manager assumed I was single. When he found out during my interview that I had two children, he asked me how I was going to work when I had to take care of them. I told him that my mother-in-law would take care of them so that I could work without causing the company any trouble. I had to sign a contract specifying, "I will never be absent unless I get really sick," right there during an interview. . . . They were only hiring the married women at that time, and people said that we would be assigned to sections where the work was harder. About fifty of us were hired right there, and we were told to come to work the next day.

Ok-ja worked at the hat factory for five years before she left to run a small store in the market with her husband. They tried several different businesses and worked very hard, and they did well enough to buy a house and think about sending their son to college. Then everything changed; they were cheated when they tried to move the business to a new location, Ok-ja's husband began drinking, and then he became seriously ill. They had to sell their house and, in 1984, her husband died. The family experienced real economic hardship after her husband's death, and Ok-ja returned yet again to factory work. By this time, her daughter was already working for a big textile factory located outside the Zone, and Ok-ja applied for a job at the same factory. In 1987 she was a forty-eight-year-old widow and one of the oldest women factory workers in Masan. She described the conditions in the factory where she worked:

> Wages are low and working conditions are pretty bad, but they have been improving since our labor union became strong. . . . It is hard to

91

work there because of dust, and it is always very hot and humid so the thread won't break. Since they keep the temperature and humidity so high, workers get sick very easily during the winter. I can't sit down while I am working; I have to run from one machine to another constantly. I don't feel aches until I leave the factory at night since I am too busy to feel anything while working. . . . Work at Masan Textile is a lot harder than work in the Zone.

Ok-ja's daughter obtained her high school diploma while working at Masan Textile and was able to get a better job at an electronics company in the Zone. Although Ok-ja had had a hard life, she was not bitter. She lived in one room with her two adult children, and they pooled the money from their jobs to meet household expenses. They believed that their situation was improving again. Her son had completed a few years of college and had a low-ranking government job. She was saving money for her daughter's dowry, and she was also saving money so that she could move to better living quarters. She was looking forward to retirement at age fifty-five and planned to run a small restaurant afterward.

Chŏng-sŏn was another worker who unexpectedly found that she had to return to factory work. She had worked at an electronics factory in the Zone for three years before leaving to get married. She had two children and ran a small dress shop with her husband. When her husband died suddenly, she was unable to manage the shop by herself and had to close it. She and her children went to live with her parents, and she went back to work in the Zone. She felt she was lucky that her mother could take care of her children, and she considered herself very lucky to get another job at an electronics factory, even though the factory was reputed to have extremely harsh working conditions. Taedong was a Korean-owned company that had opened in 1983, and even though it was located in the Zone, it did subcontracting work for other companies located there. It also resembled out-zone companies in employing more married women than single women.

Chŏng-sŏn explained that the company gained some advantages by hiring married women:

(1) Married women do not change jobs easily; once they start to work at one job, they stay for a long time; (2) single women complain too much, and they move to other companies too easily; (3) married women do not complain about overtime work, and because they come to work primarily to earn money, they even welcome overtime work.

Although her working conditions may have been harsh, Chŏng-sŏn said she was satisfied with her job. And, by Masan standards, she was well paid. She earned 300,000 won ($375) a month, including overtime pay. She was the only female worker in the section where she worked and identified totally with her factory. She was sympathetic to her managers and said that if anyone had complaints, they should leave the company instead of making trouble. Her attitudes were apparently shared by her coworkers because workers at Taedong did not go on strike during the July–August labor uprising.

In spite of her satisfaction with her job, however, Chŏng-sŏn still felt torn between her job and her children:

> My only complaint about this job is that I don't have much time to be with my children. In the morning, I leave for work before they get up, and at night, they are usually asleep when I come home. They love it when I do not have to go to work on Sundays. The first thing they ask me when they get up on Sundays is whether I am going to work or not. I am thinking of opening my own business so that they could be with me whenever they want to.

HOW THE MYTH IS REPRODUCED AMONG WOMEN WORKERS

Capitalist use of women as factory workers produced huge changes in the lives of young South Korean women. Their labor was extracted under circumstances that workers in many countries would find intolerable. Working conditions were poor and wages were low, not just by world standards but even when compared to those paid to South Korean men with comparable skills. Nevertheless, by working hard and living Spartan lives – in effect, exploiting themselves still further – women strove to improve their lives through factory work, and many of them succeeded. In spite of wages that several sources have estimated were less than single women needed to support themselves, most women saved a significant proportion of their incomes, which they used to set up new households. Other women managed to support not only themselves but also additional family members on the same low wages.

By looking to the future, factory workers discounted the grim reality that confronted them every day. Hardships were experienced as temporary, and the benefits of economic development seemed to be within reach. Most women factory workers did, in fact, benefit from economic development, although mostly indirectly as the wives of men who had jobs in high-paying industries.

Nevertheless, women generally believed that they benefited from the improving material standards of living in Masan.

The practice of saving for a dowry also provided women with an exaggerated sense of upward economic mobility because it made their lives harder before marriage and easier afterward. Most factory women were willing to put up with conditions of extreme poverty in order to save part of their wages. They lived in overcrowded conditions, ate poorly, and had few recreational activities. When they got married, women were able to use the proportion of their wages that they had saved as workers, as well as sharing their husband's higher wages, and many women experienced a jump in their standard of living. Newly married women generally lived in more comfortable, less crowded conditions than factory workers and also had access to amenities such as refrigerators and cooking stoves that were superior to what they had had as workers.

In spite of their level of exploitation, most women workers in Masan did not see themselves as being on the bottom of the social hierarchy. They were aware that others in South Korea lived in more intense poverty than they experienced. The relatively highly regulated factories in MAFEZ actually were desirable places to work compared to the subcontracting and other factories outside the Zone. Compared to the women who worked in these places, MAFEZ workers felt relatively comfortable and well paid.

Society's hierarchical orientation encouraged people to identify with higher levels of society. Thus, rather than considering themselves part of the working class, many factory workers preferred to see themselves as middle class. Factories exploited this tendency when they could, as when the larger firms in MAFEZ promoted the view that it was prestigious to be associated with them and developed company loyalty among their workers.

The contemporary South Korean obsession with education also fostered a hierarchy among the workers. Women who had completed high school felt proud of their accomplishment. This not only encouraged worker satisfaction with the status quo (especially when the factory had enabled them to attend school), it also divided them from those workers who had not had the same opportunities. Factories benefited from the efficient, disciplined workforce of educated workers and from the tendency of self-satisfied, better-educated workers to identify with the middle class and sympathize with management.

The tendency to identify with those who were better off made women less likely to see themselves as potentially suffering the hardships that they observed among their fellow workers. They tended to blame hardships on family problems or individual misfortune rather than on limited opportunities. Nevertheless, even when former factory workers attained comfortable lives, their situation was precarious. And, when their husbands did not earn as much as expected, or became ill or died, women were forced back into the labor force as low-paid factory workers.

There were other reasons why factory work failed to meet women's expectations in laying the foundation for a comfortable life. Those who were burdened by especially poor or desperate families went into different kinds of factories, were unable to save, married poor men, and remained poor all their lives.

Marriage was the most important event in determining a woman's lifetime status, and unsurprisingly, factory workers were preoccupied with selecting a husband and preparing for marriage. Their best chance for economic security was to marry a man with a well-paid job. Marriages, however, were generally arranged between social equals, so that women usually maintained rather than improved their status when they got married. Women with higher-status backgrounds married higher-status men. Whereas high school–educated workers at large electronics factories married men with good economic prospects, workers in garment factories married men whose economic prospects were less certain.

The married women who reentered the factory workforce exhibited many of the same characteristics as single women workers. Many of them were also saving for the future, no longer to assemble a dowry but perhaps to buy an apartment or to pay for a child's education. Rather than abandon their goal of upward mobility, they extended their sacrifice into their married years. They had fewer grounds for considering themselves middle class, but many did, nonetheless, even though their expectations for a comfortable life may have vanished.

The places where married women worked had worse conditions and paid less than those that employed single women, but married women workers were inhibited from perceiving the degree to which they were exploited by the nearly universal sentiment that the proper role for a married woman was that of a full-time mother and wife, and thus that they should not be working in a factory. Although women who went back to work could justify their decision, they tended to see their situations as individual cases, not as reflecting difficulties imposed broadly on their class. Many women workers could not even feel confident that their own husbands fully supported their decision to return to factory work. Employers of married women benefited from these cultural expectations and got a cheap labor force that would put up with a large amount of overwork without protest.

Although women factory workers expected to achieve social mobility as a result of their years of hard work, in spite of their increased material prosperity they remained near the bottom of South Korean society. Furthermore, for all but a handful, their comfortable lives were insecure. When things went wrong, women found themselves forced back into factories that they had been able to endure previously only because the hardship was temporary. Married women who came back to factory work experienced greater hardships, worse conditions, and less pay, and found themselves trapped at the very bottom of the class system.

4

Labor Militancy and Collective Action

A LTHOUGH most working-class women struggled with adverse circumstances alone, others wanted to do something not just for themselves, but also for their fellow workers who were experiencing similar or even worse hardships. These women gravitated toward the labor movement. The Korean labor movement's struggle toward a more just society has a long history and includes many episodes with close parallels to the situation in MAFEZ. Foreign capitalists have been exploiting poorly paid Korean workers since the introduction of the wage labor system, and nationalism has been an important component of workers' resistance. Interested workers could learn the details of this history in classes taught by labor activists (see the following discussion). This chapter considers this history and how it shaped the way the labor struggle manifested itself in Masan.

NATIONALISM, COMMUNISM AND LABOR IN KOREAN POLITICS

The Korean labor movement began with the introduction of wage labor to the port cities during the closing years of the nineteenth century (Kim Kŭm-su 1986:23). During the Japanese colonial occupation, 1910–1945, the labor movement became closely connected with the struggle for independence (Han'guk Minjungsa Yŏn'guhoe 1986 II:181–188; Kim Yun-hwan 1982:343).[1] Thus, from the earliest times, labor organizations in Korea have combined political and economic goals (Cho Sŭng-hyŏk 1984:121).

As the country underwent rapid industrialization under Japanese colonial rule, the importance of the organized labor movement increased, and a sometimes violent struggle ensued between workers and Japanese and local capitalists backed by the colonial government. Extreme repression by the colonial

---

[1] After 1920, women workers tried to develop their own labor movement by either participating in labor unions organized by men or organizing their own unions (Lee Hyo-chae 1983). A detailed life history of a woman union leader for this period is given by Lee Ae-suk (1989).

government radicalized the labor movement (Kim Yun-hwan 1982:342), forcing it to become "an underground movement with closer ties to the communist movement" (Koo 1993:134).

After liberation from Japanese rule in 1945, the radicalized worker organizations reemerged as a political force and sought to take over factories abandoned by Japanese owners (ibid.). Within three months of the liberation, leftist forces had organized a national trade union, Chosŏn Nodong Chohap Chŏn'guk P'yŏnguihoe (Chŏnp'yŏng), which quickly grew to include more than 500,000 members. Among Chŏnp'yŏng's stated goals were to achieve "a minimum wage," "an eight-hour day," "to abolish child labor," and "to abolish discrimination based on sex and age" (Han'guk Minjungsa Yŏn'guhoe 1986 II:252).[2]

Chŏnp'yŏng also advocated national sovereignty and worker control over industry and refused to accept the U.S. military government (Ogle 1990:9). The U.S. military government sought to suppress Chŏnp'yŏng, and supported the formation of a rival right-wing labor organization, the Federation of Korean Trade Unions (FKTU) in March 1946. The violent struggle between Chŏnp'yŏng and the rightist forces backed by the United States was brought to a close when the Korean Communist Party was outlawed by the military authority in the South in March 1947. By this time, hundreds of leftist labor leaders had been "killed or executed, and thousands were imprisoned" (Koo 1993:135).

The antilabor policies begun under the U.S. military government continued after Syngman Rhee took control of the government of South Korea. The Korean War confirmed the division of Korea into two rival states, cutting off the largely rural South from the more industrialized North. Whereas the North became a Communist nationalist state, ideologically dedicated to workers' power, the South became a conservative, anti-Communist state where workers' political causes were viewed with suspicion. The war left a legacy of extreme anti-Communism in the South, and during the Rhee regime (1948–1960), little labor activity was permitted. Labor organizations outside of the FKTU were politically suspect and seen as potentially treasonable, and the FKTU was used by the ruling Liberal Party as a tool to promote anti-Communism and to stifle any independent political moves by organized labor (Choi Jang Jip 1983:46).[3] In addition to the hostile political climate under the Rhee regime, workers

---

2 For a discussion of Chŏnp'yŏng, see Cumings (1984:351–381).
3 A history of the early period of the labor union movement in Korea is found in Kim Nak-jung (1982) and Kim Yun-hwan (1982); see also Han'guk Nodongjohap Ch'ongyŏnmaeng (1979).

suffered from the economic devastation left by the war and the ensuing period of corruption and inefficiency. There was a huge surplus of unskilled labor, and wages were held down as desperate workers, including women and children, struggled to support their families (Han'guk Minjungsa Yŏn'guhoe 1986 II:274).

Rhee's regime became increasingly dictatorial as he clung to power by rigging elections and amending the constitution in order to hold on to the presidency. Student demonstrations against the rigged elections of March 15, 1960, began in Masan and spread throughout the country, leading to Rhee's forced resignation. The student revolution of April 19, 1960, established the student movement as a significant political force in South Korean politics, and students have remained prominent in the pro-democracy movement since then.[4] The Second Republic failed to generate much support and provided only a brief democratic interlude before it was toppled by a military coup. Its five-year plan for economic growth was never implemented.

EXPORT-LED DEVELOPMENT AND THE DUALISTIC STRUCTURE OF THE LABOR MOVEMENT

The military dictatorship of Park Chung Hee, who seized power in 1961, continued the anti-Communist ideology of the Rhee regime, but it inaugurated a totally different approach to the economy. Although Park's regime was even more openly antidemocratic than the Rhee regime had been, it was strongly committed to the goal of economic development. Park's economic policies focused totally on growth rather than attempting to redress "imbalances in income distribution" or "unevenness in industrial development across geographical regions" (Cho Soon 1994:32). Park argued that a powerful central government was needed to coordinate the economic forces required for development (Amsden 1989:50), although he also promised that the benefits of development would eventually reach workers and asked the people's support to build "a nation without hungry people."

The Park regime had even less tolerance for independent labor activities than the previous regime, and when the labor laws were revised in 1963, unions were reorganized into a centralized system that could be easily controlled. This system replaced the organizational pattern under the Rhee regime, in which

---

4 Sources on the April 1960 student revolution include Kim, Kim and Vicks (1983) and Han'guk Minjungsa Yŏn'guhoe (1986).

labor was fragmented into numerous small enterprise unions (Choi Jang Jip 1983:48–51).[5]

During the first phase of the Park regime, labor was quiescent. "This was probably due to overabundance of labor as well as enthusiasm for the prospects of economic development" (Cho Soon 1994:102). Even as late as the 1960s, the manufacturing industry employed less than 10% of the total workforce, and industrial workers had to be "satisfied with whatever job opportunities became available to them, with little regard to wage rates" (ibid.).

The occasional isolated demonstrations against "wretched working conditions in the many small sweatshops of the garment and textile industries" (Koo 1993:138) and other peripheral industries had little political impact until the dramatic suicide of a worker in 1970. On November 13, Chun Tae-il, a twenty-three-year-old garment worker in Seoul, immolated himself while holding a copy of the Labor Standard Laws in his hand (ibid.).[6] Chun's death succeeded in focusing national attention on the working conditions of South Korea's factories, marking the beginning of a new phase of militant and committed activism within the South Korean labor movement. The incident also brought new allies into the workers' struggle, as college students, urban intellectuals and radical members of church organizations developed a sense of acute moral outrage at the cruel exploitation of industrial workers. This alliance between intellectuals and workers has continued to be important in the labor movement and has helped give cohesion to workers' activities outside the government-run FKTU.

Whereas industrial workers seemed passive and deferential to governmental policy in the 1960s, by 1970 the conflicts latent in the industrialization process began to emerge. The dissatisfaction of the urban poor with their position under Park's regime fueled growing political opposition. Park responded to his poor showing in the polls in the 1971 presidential election by becoming even more openly dictatorial and repressing all political opposition. Under the state of emergency declared in December 1971, universities were closed, union activities were severely curtailed and the labor movement was treated as a threat to national security. Strikes became illegal.

President Park institutionalized his dictatorship in 1972 with the *Yusin* (revitalization) Constitution, which made him president-for-life and sharply cur-

---

5 In order to control labor unions from the top, the government had to approve the establishment of any new unions, and the numerous firm-based local unions were reorganized to form sixteen centralized industry-based unions.
6 Details about Chŏn T'ae-il's life are provided in his collection of writings (1988).

tailed civil rights. The *Yusin* government justified its assumption of dictatorial power by an intensified commitment to export-led economic growth, and especially a push to build up heavy industry. The *Yusin* regime kept tight control over labor activities, allowing unions to grow in size so that they could be used to carry out government policy toward workers.[7]

Under Park's *Yusin* regime, the labor movement developed a dual structure. On the one hand, large unions under the FKTU developed huge memberships (more than 1 million by 1978 [Cho Soon 1994:103]) but remained completely subservient to government policy, while illegal militant actions were carried out by small, independent workers' groups informally linked through student and religious organizations. Strikes and other labor disputes were strongly suppressed by the government but nevertheless occurred throughout the *Yusin* period (1972–1979). There were "133 cases in 1975, 110 cases in 1976, 96 cases in 1977, 102 cases in 1978, 105 cases in 1979, and in 1980, it reached 407 cases" (Kim Kŭm-su 1986:59).

Two religious organizations, the Urban Industrial Mission (UIM) and the Young Catholic Workers (JOC), became the principal advocates of workers' rights in the late 1970s.[8] UIM is a Protestant organization, and JOC is Catholic. As the *Yusin* government became increasingly oppressive, the church associations were left as the sole advocates of free, autonomous labor unions, and they expanded to encompass a range of activities on behalf of workers' rights. They publicized labor issues and provided education and assistance to workers.

These church groups first became involved with workers in the 1960s as a way of expanding church membership (Cho Sŭng-hyŏk 1981), but these activities exposed them to industrial issues, and they began to link the attainment of religious salvation with concern for social justice. At first, church leaders focused their efforts on short-term economic demands and promoted the government's objectives of industrial peace and productivity. But confronted with the misery of South Korea's industrial slums, church organizations came to speak out on issues of distribution of wealth and to criticize the state's growth policy. They also encouraged workers to organize themselves and provided

---

7 Under the Yusin government, the Labor Standard Law was revised to protect the workers, a Vocational Training Law was enacted that required firms of a specific size to provide vocational training, and the government adopted measures to help the workers financially by treating their savings deposits preferentially.

8 For the activities of religious organizations in this period, see Cho Sŭng-hyŏk (1981), Han'guk Kidokkyo Kyohoe Hyŏbuihoe (1984b) and Han'guk Katorik Nodong Ch'ŏngnyŏnhoe (JOC 1986).

them with training and facilities. The resources they provided played a crucial role in developing the consciousness of factory workers.

The assassination of President Park on October 26, 1979, caused a sudden collapse of the restrictions that had been placed on labor activity. Strikes broke out as many unions attempted to reorganize along democratic lines and elect their own representatives. The six months following the assassination were known as the "Seoul Spring" because of the hopeful political atmosphere that prevailed. Opposition forces made plans to install a democratic government and provide for direct election of the president.

The optimism of the democratic forces was destroyed as General Chun Doo-hwan gained control of the army and the nation, eventually establishing himself as president of the Fifth Republic in August 1980. Chun's regime was unpopular from the outset, as his willingness to resort to brutal use of force had been demonstrated in his suppression of the Kwangju uprising.[9] Throughout his presidency, he needed to rely on political repression in order to remain in power and justified his policies by appealing to a need for "national security." Dissident politicians were placed under house arrest, and student demonstrations were outlawed.[10] The new regime also destroyed the new democratic unions and arrested their leaders. Many union leaders were sent to "purification camps," where they were tortured and subjected to hard labor.[11]

The dual structure of the labor movement that had developed under Park continued under the Fifth Republic, but less support was provided for official unions. The declining influence of official unions was accompanied by a drop in union membership attributable to "workers' frustration with formal labor unions" (Cho Soon 1994:104). Labor unions could no longer be organized without receiving prior approval from the government, and authorities usually withheld this approval. Organized labor was left with "no legitimate space in which to operate, and the labor movement was forced into a state of apparent quiescence" (Koo 1993:149). Other changes in the labor law made it more difficult for workers to organize collective actions, such as "mandatory reporting of the occurrence of disputes, the establishment of a cooling-off period, and prohibition of 'third parties' to take part in disputes" (ibid.).

The Chun regime also introduced joint labor–management councils as a substitute for unions in order to limit labor organizations' ability to act inde-

9 For discussions of the Kwangju uprising, see Clark (1988) and Lewis (1988).
10 For studies on the Korean student movement, see Dong (1987, 1988), Lee Namhee (1991) and Lew (1993).
11 The details about these camps began to emerge only after President Chun left office.

pendently. Under the Labor–Management Council Act of 1980, each firm was required to set up a labor-management council in which representatives of labor and management were to "meet regularly to discuss issues of mutual interest" (Cho Soon 1994:104). As intended, these councils became instruments of management policy rather than open forums for workers to air their grievances.

At first, the repressive measures taken by Chun's regime managed to achieve "a surface of political passivity" (Koo 1993:149), but under that surface an increasingly sophisticated opposition was developing. Frustrated workers turned to organizations outside the legal unions as the unions became weak and unwilling to act on their behalf. Church organizations that had been active among workers became more political, and both UIM and JOC embraced organizing workers as an end in itself and began to question the capitalist system. Radical students began to see workers as the key to building a successful political opposition and set out to build a "worker–student alliance" (*no-hak yŏndae*). Thousands of student activists left universities in the first half of the 1980s in order to work in factories as "disguised workers" and to undertake illegal labor organizing. These students provided ideological training for labor activists and helped link grass-roots activists into a politically powerful network. Many students worked with the church organization already involved in the struggle for workers' rights, but others adopted more strongly Marxist positions. The *minjung* ideology (the ideology of the people or masses) that emerged during this period was strongly nationalist and counterhegemonic, and stressed the unity of Korean "workers, peasants, the lower middle class and the urban poor" (Choi Jang Jip 1993:17n). Joint political action by students and workers was instrumental in bringing Chun's regime to a close, even though it failed to achieve the far-reaching reform of society sought by most activists.

WOMEN IN THE LABOR MOVEMENT

Women workers form a distinct segment of the workforce of South Korean industry (see Chapter 3), and consequently their experience in the labor movement has been somewhat separate from that of male workers. Within traditional Korean society, almost all work undertaken by women was within the context of the family, and as we have seen, family continues to be the main focus of the lives of even those women who do work in factories. Thus, even though, from the mid-1960s, women have formed about a third of the manufacturing labor force (32.4% in 1992: Korean Women's Development Institute

1994:129; Lee Hyo-chae 1986), and even though women typically work longer hours than men for lower wages, they have often not been regarded as real workers.[12] Women have had little role in the formal institutions set up by the government to coopt labor such as the FKTU (see Tongil Pangjik Pokjik T'ujaeng Wiwŏnhoe 1985:32) and have frequently been relegated to subordinate roles in antigovernment groups, which also tended (perhaps inadvertently) to perpetuate the notion that political activity is the restricted domain of males.[13]

Nevertheless, those who were involved in organizing workers, whether Christian, Marxist or both, have a long history of advocating sexual equality, or at least the breakdown of existing patterns of gender hierarchy (cf. Jayawardena 1986:213–225). Thus, although women's concerns were often overlooked, they were never formally excluded from labor organizations, and women participated in the labor movement at every point in history from its beginnings under Japanese occupation (ibid.; Lee Hyo-chae 1983, 1989:73–126; Sin 1985:52; Yi Tae-ho 1985:96).[14] Furthermore, the appalling working conditions experienced by women in factories, particularly in the early push for export production, generated much discontent among women workers and aroused the humanitarian concerns of groups like UIM and JOC.

Throughout the entire period of Park Chung Hee's presidency, while male workers were somewhat distracted by a formal structure of the unions designed to coopt them, women workers became increasingly important within the informal labor movement (Tongil Pangjik Pokjik T'ujaeng Wiwŏnhoe 1985:22–25). Women worked mostly in small to medium-sized factories in light indus-

---

12 Extremely bad working conditions are not uncommon in light manufacturing industries where most workers are women, but they do not automatically produce militancy among workers. The export processing industries of Southeast Asia, for example, have been relatively unaffected by labor militancy (Grossman 1979; Kung 1983; Lim 1978, 1983a; Ong 1987). The militancy of Korean women workers does, however, have many historical parallels when poor working conditions are combined with a political context that provides support for militant action. Some of the best examples of radical women's unions come from the United States in the late nineteenth and early twentieth centuries (see Norwood 1990; Turbin 1992).

13 A noted activist with the UIM described her status as the only woman involved in her organization at a high level and recalls "numerous experiences of sexism" (Cho Wha Soon 1988:138).

14 Of those women workers who were active in the labor movement during the Japanese colonial period, Kang Chu-ryŏng, who died in prison fighting for workers' rights, was frequently cited as the most important figure (Lee Hyo-chae 1989:106–107; Yi Tae-ho 1985:96). For a detailed discussion of women's participation in the labor movement during the colonial period, see Suh Hyong-sil (1990).

try, and because their collective actions were generally spontaneous responses to issues that arose in specific factories, women's activism tended to be episodic and discontinuous, with little immediate impact on national politics. Nevertheless, the disconnected actions taken by women in factories across the country were linked together by the church groups and by a growing sense of working-class consciousness. Women's collective actions also provided the labor movement with historical continuity because the combination of repression and cooptation nearly extinguished activism among male workers during the period of the *Yusin* Constitution. Women's unions are generally credited with leading the labor movement during the 1970s (Choi Jang Jip 1993:37; Koo 1993:140, 156; Lee Hyo-chae 1989:264–271; Sin 1985:49–60; Young-mi Pak 1983).

One of the most important labor conflicts of the 1970s involved the workers of Tongil Textile Company. Tongil owned a large factory in Inchon that employed a predominantly female workforce. Their union dated from 1946, but especially between 1960 and 1972, according to Reverend Cho Wha Soon of UIM, "it functioned for the government, not for workers" (1988:55). In 1972, the workers decided to take control of the union, and voted for their own delegates and officers rather than those suggested by the company. The democratic union established at Tongil with the support of UIM was also historic for being the first union in South Korea to be headed by a woman (ibid.:61). Although 1,214 out of 1,383 Tongil textile union members were women (Tongil Pangjik Pokjik T'ujaeng Wiwŏnhoe 1985:32), until the election of 1972 management had always selected men as its candidates. As discussed in Chapter 2, men who work in factories where the production workers are women occupy supervisory or technical positions and are easily persuaded to take pro-management positions. By rejecting management's candidates and substituting their own, the workers had not only placed ordinary workers in charge of the union, but had also begun to undermine the assumption of a natural gender hierarchy that dominated the workplace.[15]

The struggle between the democratic union and the Tongil Textile Company continued until the union was finally destroyed during the tense final years of the Park regime. Management was uncomfortable with the democratic union and its all-female, UIM-influenced leadership and tried repeatedly to crush it. Tongil involved the government and the FKTU in its efforts to help suppress

---

15 Ogle overemphasizes the gender issue in his discussion of Tongil and thus tends to mistake the issue of worker control of the union for concern with "women's liberation" (1990:86).

the union, but it proved to be a stubborn and persistent opponent. Two incidents in the union's struggle are especially important because the tactics used against demonstrating workers aroused indignation at their victimization as workers and especially as women. Female vulnerability was turned into a weapon in the struggle for workers' rights.

The first incident, known as the "nude demonstration," took place in 1976 following the arrest of the union president and another union officer during an attempt to replace union officials with a group selected by management. Supporters of the union occupied the factory for several days before the riot police arrived:

> They surrounded the workers and began forcibly arresting them. Then an astonishing thing happened: the women workers took off their work clothes to protest the arrests. In the hot summer heat of forty degrees centigrade, the workers were mostly wearing only bras under their work clothes; so when they removed these they were half naked. In that state they sang as loudly as they could, thinking that not even the worst policeman would lay his hands on a naked woman's body. But the police brutally arrested them, beating them with clubs, and the helpless women ran and fell, screaming and bleeding. A few women, in a last desperate act to defend the union, even took off their underpants, but the police seized them just the same and threw them into the bus. Some were beaten and dragged to the bus by their hair. Some women lay in front of the bus to try to stop it from taking the workers. It was an agonizing scene. (Cho Wha Soon 1988:65)[16]

According to Reverend Cho, "seventy-two were arrested, fifty passed out from shock, more than seventy were wounded, and fourteen had to be hospitalized" (ibid.).

The union managed to retain its independence, but female union leaders were subjected to another attempt to humiliate them during the election of union officers in 1978. The militant leaders had expected to win this election, but male workers disrupted the proceedings by smashing ballot boxes, spreading human excrement around the union office, and rubbing it on the faces and clothing of the militant women (ibid.:69; Ogle 1990:86; Sok 1984:92–98; Tongil Pangjik Pokjik T'ujaeng Wiwŏnhoe 1985:99–104). The union at-

16 Sŏk Chŏng-nam described the incident vividly in her autobiography (1984:47–50), and other workers provide an account in the union's own history (Tongil Pangjik Pokjik T'ujaeing Wiwŏnhoe 1985:54–61).

tempted to hold the election again the following day, but the company called in the riot police. After the resulting confrontation, the company fired 124 workers, including all the union officers.

The union leaders and other fired workers, blacklisted to prevent them from taking other factory jobs, became full-time political activists and spent the next several years publicizing their confrontation with Tongil and the government and pressing their demands for reinstatement. They used dramatic tactics to draw attention to their struggle, disrupting official labor day ceremonies, unfurling banners in church services and generally drawing attention to the two incidents. Reverend Cho describes a play about the "dung incident" presented at a prayer meeting in Seoul about six months after the firings:

> Actors and audience alike were swept away in a sea of anger and tears. When the drama ended it was naturally followed by an overnight sit-in with the workers shouting, "Secure the three rights of labor! Abolish the *Yusin* Constitution! Step down, Park regime!" (Cho Wha Soon 1988:73)

Although the government succeeded in keeping information about the Tongil struggle out of general circulation, these incidents became well known among opposition groups and came to emblematize the behavior of the regime toward workers. The retelling of the story of the struggle was used to arouse a sense of righteous indignation among labor activists. Specific workplace grievances became overshadowed by the larger issues of the right of workers to organize and the legitimacy of the regime. In the years following the firing of the workers, the political significance of the Tongil struggle grew as the size and strength of the opposition movement increased and the fired workers' account of their struggle (published in 1985) became a key text in *minjung* literature.[17]

The other key labor struggle by women workers during the *Yusin* period produced an immediate political impact, precipitating the chain of events that led to the assassination of Park Chung Hee. The Y. H. Company was a Seoul-based wig manufacturer that had begun operations in 1966 and had by 1970 become the largest wig maker in South Korea, employing 4,000 workers and exporting over US $1,000,000 annually (Former Y. H. Labor Union 1984:19).

---

17 The preface of the *History of Tongil Textile Labor Union* was written by Cardinal Kim Su-hwan.

In 1975, the workers at Y. H. succeeded in forming a union and elected a woman as the union's president. In its initial stages the union received advice and met at facilities provided by JOC and the Catholic Church, but as the struggle intensified, it turned increasingly to advice from intellectuals associated with the *minjung* movement. The company resorted to intimidation tactics in an effort to destroy the union. After four years of conflict between the company and the union, the company closed its factory and, amid accusations of fraud and misappropriation of funds, its owner fled to the United States with its remaining assets. The workers who had been left without jobs demanded that the factory be reopened and took over the factory in protest. After riot police brutally evicted the workers from the factory, workers moved their protest to the headquarters of the opposition New Democratic Party, and about 200 women occupied the building.[18] In spite of the fact that the party was supporting the workers' protest, riot police were again sent to evict the workers. The police arrested everyone who was in the building, and during the arrests, one young woman "leapt or was pushed to her death" (Eckert et al. 1990:371).

Because of the involvement of the opposition party and the death of a striking worker possibly at the hands of the police, the Y. H. incident received much greater publicity than previous labor conflicts and became known beyond the activist core of the labor movement. The incident provided a rallying point for the opposition to Park's regime. New Democratic members of Parliament demanded that the police action and the death of the worker be fully investigated, and the government responded by expelling the party's leader, Kim Young-Sam, from Parliament. Massive antigovernment demonstrations broke out in support of Kim Young Sam in his home region of Pusan and in Masan. The government declared martial law in Pusan and Masan, and as the clique around President Park debated further measures to be taken in response to the open opposition to his dictatorship, Park was assassinated by his own chief of the Korean Central Intelligence Agency, who claimed that he acted "to

---

18 Although Koo states that "party politics became accidentally involved in labor activism" (1993:141), Ko Un, the *minjung* poet who wrote the introduction to the Y. H. Union's book about their struggle, mentions that the strategy of occupying the opposition party's headquarters was discussed by union members with their intellectual sympathizers as a way of politicizing their struggle, and that New Democratic Party officials had been in contact with the strikers before the workers were evicted from the factory (Former Y. H. Labor Union 1984:12,185).

save the nation from the blood bath that Pak [sic] intended to rain down upon Masan and Pusan" (Ogle 1990:92) as punishment for the demonstrations.

In spite of the prominence of militant women's unions in the labor movement of the 1970s, their relative importance decreased in the 1980s as heavy industry became more important to the South Korean economy. Women workers remained concentrated in small and medium-sized companies, where strikes rarely involved as many as 1,000 workers, and individual company closures posed no threat to the national economy. Furthermore, because women nearly always left factory work before age thirty, it was difficult for unions of women workers to maintain continuity. The women's labor movement of the 1970s was a series of independent incidents that were connected and given political importance by church groups. They stand out mostly because all other forms of political opposition to the *Yusin* system were so effectively suppressed. Ironically, brutal treatment applied to women workers enhanced their political importance. The 1970s produced martyrs for the labor cause and a thread of continuity throughout a period of severe repression, but workers gained few, if any, lasting victories at this time. At the end of the *Yusin* regime, working conditions in South Korea's factories remained poor, workers were still poorly paid, and labor organizing was still difficult and dangerous.

In its first years, Chun's regime effectively suppressed labor organizing as well as all other forms of political opposition, but in 1984, when the regime relaxed its grip on society, there was "an upsurge of militant union activity" (Koo 1993:150) involving a broader range of participants than before. The formation of a rival non-FKTU union at Daewoo Motors demonstrated that labor militancy had spread to male workers in a large factory owned by a conglomerate. The 1985 strike at Daewoo Motors was important enough for the head of the Daewoo Conglomerate (*chaebŏl*) to become personally involved in negotiations, and he was present when the union's officials were arrested for organizing an illegal strike (Ogle 1990:111).

Women were not in a position to have so much social impact merely by organizing strikes in their own factories, but although overshadowed by the new militancy of male-led unions, female workers continued to be involved in labor disputes that sometimes had national significance. Another Daewoo-owned factory that experienced labor conflict in 1985 was Daewoo Apparel, a small manufacturer of women's clothing at Kurodong Industrial Estate near Seoul. The factory had only about 100 employees, and as Ogle comments, "ten days of work stoppage and turmoil . . . would probably have gone unrecorded except for the fact that the conflict burst out beyond the walls of the company" (ibid.:112). After the three women who led the independent union at Daewoo Apparel were arrested, their coworkers struck in solidarity, and their strike was joined by workers at other firms in Kurodong Industrial Estate (a light industrial estate employing a predominantly female labor force). The strike also drew "wide support from students and dissident groups, who staged sympathetic demonstrations outside the factory gates almost every day during the ten-day-long solidarity strike" (Koo 1993:151).[19] Although the strike was broken up, with arrests, beatings and thousands of workers fired from their jobs, Koo notes that many of these wronged workers became labor activists[20] and that the Kurodong strike marked the introduction of important new tactics "centered on promoting solidarity struggles among workers across several factories located within the same industrial area" (ibid.). It also demonstrates the continuing importance of women labor activists in the period leading up to the nationwide labor uprising of 1987.

THE 1987 LABOR UPRISING AND THE FORMATION OF UNIONS

The Collapse of Chun Doo Hwan's Regime

Chun's regime never overcame the stigma of its violent origins, especially the Kwangju incident.[21] Any respect for Chun was also undercut by persistent rumors of corruption among those close to him, in contrast to Park Chung Hee's reputation for incorruptibility. South Korea's increasing material prosperity only highlighted the difference between its dynamic, successful economy and its backward, repressive government. Each attempt the regime made to accommodate opposing political forces by relaxing political restrictions was countered by vehement outbursts that the government struggled unsuccessfully to contain. "By 1987, if not long before, it required considerable effort to find

19 In his 1993 article, Koo does not note that the Daewoo Apparel strike involved women workers, and he implies that women ceased to be significant within the labor movement after the 1970s: "Whereas the labor movement in the 1970s was led by female workers in light manufacturing, the new labor movement was dominated by male workers employed in the core industries of the South Korean economy" (156).

20 In 1994, I interviewed two women who had been involved in the 1985 Kurodong strikes and had made labor organizing their life work. One of them was still working in a garment factory. She had been fired after the 1985 strike but had pressed her case and been reinstated in 1989.

21 Brutality remained an issue throughout the Chun regime. The death of a Seoul National University student, Pak Chong-ch'ŏl, during a police interrogation in January 1987 provoked an outcry in the press that forced the government to admit to using torture in police interrogations.

anyone – regardless of socioeconomic background or political affiliation – who genuinely liked and respected Chun and his family" (Eckert et al. 1990:377).

The constitution of the Fifth Republic imposed by Chun following the 1980 coup limited him to one term as president, but his regime intended to maintain political control of the country by the clique that had engineered the coup. Chun's designated successor was Roh Tae Woo, a former general, who had been associated with him in the 1955 class of the Korean Military Academy and had supported him during the coup. Chun's control over the electoral college made the election of Roh a virtual certainty in the elections scheduled to be held in 1987, so opposition demands for political rights centered on amending the constitution to allow for the direct election of the president.

When Chun rejected the calls for a constitutional revision and appeared willing to take any measure necessary to force Roh on the country, the opposition grew in both numbers and intensity.[22] Street demonstrations were no longer restricted to radical students but now included thousands of ordinary middle-class participants. "Throughout June 1987 the streets became a battle zone between the riot police and masses of demonstrators" (Choi Jang Jip 1993:37). The precedent of the Philippines, where the dictatorship had been overthrown by "people power" the year before, loomed over the South Korean political scene as people wondered whether Chun would be forced from office or whether he would again resort to military force to repress political opposition.[23] It was clear, from the size of the demonstrations and the broad sympathy demonstrators were receiving from the public, that only enormous use of force could contain the opposition. "This wide middle class participation changed the attitude of the Chun regime and also influenced the U.S. perception of Chun's viability" (Koo 1991:491).[24]

Uncertain of how much internal or external support it could command, the Chun regime changed its course suddenly and dramatically. On June 29, the ruling party's presidential candidate, Roh Tae Woo, announced his acceptance of direct presidential elections and a series of democratic reforms in his "June

22 Protesting against Chun's decision, "Religious leaders strongly denounced Chun's order with fasting and prayer and led a nationwide campaign of resistance. Intellectuals, writers, lawyers and university professors issued statements demanding constitutional change and direct elections" (Ogle 1990:101).

23 The plan to hold the Olympic Games in Seoul in 1988 also drew international attention to the political crisis in South Korea and increased pressure on Chun to resolve the situation peacefully.

24 Koo (1991) discusses the role of the middle class in the recent democratization struggle in Korea.

29 Declaration."[25] The sudden acceptance of the opposition's principal demands achieved its desired effect, and the middle class stepped back from its confrontation with the government (Choi Jang Jip 1993:38). Furthermore, the newly emancipated opposition proved unable to remain focused on the task of removing Chun's clique from power. The two main opposition figures split the vote in the December presidential election, enabling Roh to win even with a direct and relatively free vote.

Although the Declaration placated a proportion of the opposition, it failed to address the concerns of workers, farmers or the urban poor.[26] Nonetheless, the reforms it promised "provided the opportunity for unionism to explode out of the confines in which it had been shackled" (Ogle 1990:115). "As the regime's ability to exercise its repressive power diminished momentarily, a violent wave of labor conflicts erupted and spread swiftly across the country, halting production at almost all major industrial plants" (Koo 1993:156). Workers seized the opportunity to exercise their rights and demanded "democratic labor unions," "wage increases" and "better working conditions."[27]

The first strikes occurred on July 5, in Ulsan at a subsidiary of Hyundai. The workers there organized a democratic labor union, sparking similar movements at other Hyundai subsidiaries. Workers at Hyundai subsidiaries established an umbrella organization, the Hyundai Group Labor Unions Alliance, to encompass the whole conglomerate by early August. The struggle for democratic unions was quickly joined by workers at heavy industrial plants throughout Kyŏngsang Province, and by mid-August the nationwide labor uprising included workers in all industries in all parts of the country. "Between July and September 1987 about 3,500 labor conflicts occurred, more than the total number of labor disputes during the entire Park and Chun regimes" (ibid.).

Although workers sought higher wages and improved working conditions, "the main issue of labor conflicts during this period was the organization of

---

25 Although Roh Tae Woo made the June 29 Declaration, there has been wide-ranging speculation about who was the main engineer of the Declaration. According to newspaper articles in 1994, Chun Doo Hwan came up with the idea as the last resort to save his regime and to secure Roh's succession.

26 The main points of the Declaration were Roh's agreement to hold direct elections, to release political prisoners, to restore civil rights (including those of the opposition figure Kim Dae Jung), to allow a free press and to end human rights abuses. It also allowed all sectors of society to practice self-regulation and ended strict government control over many aspects of life.

27 According to Koo, "it was the very nature of proletarianization – its rapidity and intensity – and the extremely poor working conditions that provided the impetus for the working-class struggle" in 1987 (1990:669–681).

independent unions and dismantling company unions" (ibid.). "The disputes invariably were charged with emotion, usually magnified by the lack of trust between the two parties" (Cho Soon 1994:98). Actions were taken before demands were presented. Sit-in strikes often preceded negotiations (Han'guk Kidokkyo Sahoe Munje Yŏn'guwŏn 1987:48–49), and "in virtually all cases, both parties demonstrated unusual brinkmanship, coming to agreements at the last minute" (Cho Soon 1994:97–98). Cho attributes this pattern of conflict to the "relatively immature" industrial culture of South Korea and to the fact that "both workers and management are still inexperienced in negotiation" (ibid.:99).

The July–August labor uprising also revealed the new and unprecedented solidarity of the South Korean working class. Enormous numbers of workers in all industries participated in strikes and demonstrations, and although the movement had connections with students and intellectuals, it was led by workers.

The Labor Uprising in Masan

Throughout 1987, Masan had been the scene of antigovernment demonstrations that attracted ever-increasing crowds. By June, downtown Masan was blocked off for hours several times a week by confrontations between thousands of demonstrators and riot police. Demonstrators denounced the regime of Chun Doo Hwan as they blared appeals to the citizens of Masan to join them, and many did. The smell of tear gas was everywhere despite people's effort to wash it away by pouring water on the ground. Demonstrations frequently started at the entrance to MAFEZ, and riot police set up a permanent encampment along one section of the street bordering the Zone. Looking out the window of the room where I lived from January to July, I witnessed these confrontations nearly every day.

Roh's June 29 Declaration had no immediate impact on the demonstrations in Masan, which continued with denunciations of him and President Chun. Furthermore, after workers in Ch'angwŏn joined the nationwide labor uprising on July 21, workers became more involved in demonstrations in Masan, and more slogans relating to workers' issues were added to the placards and chants. At the end of July, I saw workers from Ch'angwŏn gathered in downtown Masan at the entrance to the Zone. They wore their company uniforms and covered their faces with scarves for protection against tear gas. They chanted, "Secure democratic unions," "Improve working conditions," "Down with

Table 4.1 *July–August labor uprising in the Ch'angwŏn–Masan area*

	Total companies	Total workers	Disputes	Workers involved	New labor unions
MAFEZ	74	36,800	44	25,000	20
Ch'angwŏn	167	65,800	74	40,000	40*
Others	50	30,000	20	7,000	3†
Total	291	132,600	134	72,000	43

*Including twenty new democratic unions that replaced twenty company-run unions.
†These include large companies such as Hanil Textile and Masan Textile outside the Free Export Zone.
Source: Kang In-sun 1991:29.

Chun Doo Hwan," and so on. When they went out to the main street, they were joined by students from Kyŏngnam University and Ch'angwŏn University, and the demonstrators were met by riot police and dispersed with tear gas and clubs.

By early August, the movement had been joined by workers in MAFEZ. Before the end of September, more than half of the companies (forty-four out of seventy-four) operating in MAFEZ had experienced sit-in strikes (Table 4.1). The workers' four main demands were wage and bonus increases, better treatment, improved working conditions and seniority allowances.

On many evenings, I joined the demonstrations with other citizens and students. We walked in relatively organized groups, holding hands and singing workers' songs and antigovernment songs. We usually walked about two or three miles to a public square, where we chanted slogans before being dispersed by the police. During the middle of August, women workers held demonstrations in the Zone nearly every day. I sometimes brought my camera with me when I went to observe the activities near the front gate, but I was never able to take pictures before the police attacked the crowd with clubs and tear gas.

The 1987 nationwide labor uprising created a strong sense of solidarity among South Korean workers, and the women working in MAFEZ shared in that solidarity. During the strikes, women workers grasped the opportunity to empower themselves. In spite of the many factors discouraging women workers from adopting radical positions, participation in strikes and demonstrations was nearly universal. The uprising also prompted the emergence of a radical leadership from within the ranks of factory workers. The actions of these deeply committed leaders shaped events following the uprising, and women whose working-class identity was forged during the uprising continue to be important to this day in labor organizing in Masan.

THE DEVELOPMENT OF DEMOCRATIC UNIONS IN MAFEZ

Sudden and intense as the uprising was, by the end of September the street demonstrations had almost stopped. Instead, workers held daily meetings at the Labor Counseling Center at the Catholic Women's Center in order to discuss how to sustain the newly founded labor unions. Twenty unions had been started in August and September at companies operating in the Zone. The Labor Counseling Center held classes on unions and labor laws, which were packed with ordinary workers, some of whom had just become union officers. Instructors included students and labor leaders from around the country. Both workers and instructors were very enthusiastic about discussing labor union issues. The heated discussions frequently extended these evening classes into morning.

Spontaneity and confrontational tactics marked the struggle for workers' rights that followed the labor uprising. Demands for higher wages and decent working conditions generally took precedence over organizing unions, and in many cases strikes broke out before unions were organized. Most workers strongly supported demands for higher wages, and companies quickly conceded the need for pay increases. Wages in the Masan–Ch'angwŏn area increased by "10–20%" (Kim and Im 1991:23) in the aftermath of the uprising.

Although companies were forced to pay higher wages, they strongly resisted any efforts to increase workers' power and often resorted to brutal tactics to crush unions. Companies used various forms of intimidation against leaders and tried to place relatively privileged male workers (who identified with the company) in control of unions. Workers' support for unions also weakened after pay increases were agreed on. By the end of 1987, most of the new unions had been disbanded or replaced by company-run unions, and only six democratic unions survived in MAFEZ.

The end of a democratic union, however, did not mean the end of the struggle. In the following section, I describe how the struggle unfolded in four MAFEZ factories. Although two companies closed their MAFEZ factories, and although neither of the remaining two still had a democratic union in 1994, the struggles were not without achievements, which contributed significantly to working-class identity in Masan. The strength and commitment of the leaders who have emerged from the struggle are remarkable. They have endured beatings and arrests and persevere in the struggle for the rights of workers.

Quick Cooptation by Management: The Company-Run Union at KTE

Most of the unions started during the labor uprising were taken over by management before the end of the year. KTE's union was one of these. In August 1987, Han'guk Tongkyŏng Chŏnja (Korea Tongkyŏng Electronics or KTE) employed about 2,300 women and 200 men. Although I was no longer working there, I knew many of the women who organized KTE's first union on August 17. Among the organizers was Chu Yŏn-ok, who is currently on the staff of the Masan–Ch'angwŏn Women Workers' Association. She became interested in labor organizing through her involvement with the Catholic Women's Center, which started even before she began working at KTE in June 1987. She was already twenty-four years old and referred to herself as an "old maid." She had spent five years working outside the Zone at Hanil Textile Company until she completed her night high school course and moved to KTE. There were seven other former workers from Hanil Textile working at KTE at that time, and Yŏn-ok became their informal leader. Although she was already interested in workers' rights through her involvement with the Center, it was not until the 1987 uprising that women at KTE began to consider forming a union. She recalled how the workers started to organize their union:

> During July and August, many new labor unions were being orga-
> nized in other factories. I kept asking the staff of the Labor Counsel-
> ing Office in the Catholic Women's Center whether any other workers
> from KTE came to ask for help. When in early August I learned that
> some workers had asked, I arranged to meet them on one Sunday af-
> ternoon. . . . Although I did not know about them then, there were
> two *hak-ch'ul* [student activists] working at KTE, and they were the
> ones who had brought workers to the Center. At the meeting, we
> discussed how and when to go on strike, as well as how to organize a
> labor union. In order to organize a union, we needed signatures of a
> minimum of thirty people. We agreed that each of us should bring
> three workers next time. . . . When we met on the evening of the
> 17th, we still didn't have thirty people. . . . I remember that Sun-hui
> *ŏnni* [older sister] did a lot of things for us at that time. She brought
> in a South Korean flag, placard, other things. But most importantly,
> she provided workers needed to organize the union since we did not

have the necessary 30 workers. She went off to the Auxilium dormitory for Catholic workers and recruited any KTE workers who were willing to come. At last we had thirty-six workers and we could organize.

When workers brought the necessary paperwork to register the union at City Hall on the 18th, the application was rejected on the basis that thirty-six signatures were too few given that there were nearly 3,000 workers at KTE. While the women protested the decision made at City Hall, about 170 male workers (mostly technicians and line leaders) organized a rival labor union. Women workers had to elect their union officers quickly, and it turned out to be difficult. Yŏn-ok recalled how they managed it:

> We learned that only workers who had worked over one year could become officers of the union. Most of the eleven people who came to the first meeting were new workers. I started in June, one *hak-ch'ul* started in December, the other in April. The only person who was suitable to be the president was Yi Tu-hui, who had worked for over three years. After electing Tu-hui as the president, we needed to find more workers who were willing to become officers and I raced among the different factory buildings to find them.

Even though it was difficult to recruit workers for the union, nearly everyone supported the strike for higher wages. On the 19th, about 2,000 women workers staged a sit-in strike, and the company simultaneously announced that it was closing temporarily (August 19–21). On the 20th, the women workers again filed their application, this time with the signatures of 274 women workers, and the union was approved to be the representative of the factory. The women who organized the union refused to accept men as union members. Yŏn-ok explained why they distrusted the men:

> The reason why we refused to work with men was that they were the ones who oppressed us on the shop floor. The line leaders were men who directly controlled us: when I was absent one day, I had to stand up isolated all day and had to write a note promising that I would not miss work again. So you see, we were oppressed by men directly; they were masters and we were slaves. There was no way we could work together.

The collective bargaining lasted for a week (August 23–29), and the company accepted seven of the demands made by the union, including a 600-won

(14%) increase in the daily wage. By the 30th, 800 workers had become union members.

In spite of the successful negotiations, the company spent the following month trying to undermine the union. It harassed union officers, tried to discourage women from joining and demanded that the union appoint men as union officers. On September 21, the day before the election of union representatives, ten male managers forced the union officers to resign by holding them prisoner for nearly twenty hours. Yŏn-ok talked about how the men took over the union and turned it into a company-run union (*ŏyong nojo*):

> Throughout the night, they abused us verbally and physically. They even followed us to the toilet and waited outside the stall. After that horrible night, we were exhausted and defeated, and we agreed to sign a statement that said that we resigned under the threats from male workers; we refused to sign a statement that said we resigned voluntarily. After this incident, the management tried to send six of us who were core members to a "special training program" in order to isolate us from other workers, but we refused to go.

On September 24, the managers forced the workers to elect a man as the union president. Workers were not allowed to leave the room unless they had cast their ballot for the company's candidate. The intimidated workers, therefore, approved a male worker as the union president.

Yŏn-ok decided to stay with the union. Although it was not the democratic union that she wanted, she was willing to work for change within the system. She became the union's vice president in May 1988 and was elected president in May 1989. While leading a wage negotiation struggle in March 1990, she was arrested and imprisoned for several months. The company used her allegedly illegal activities as justification for firing her.[28] In 1994 the union at KTE was still company-run, and Yŏn-ok was still an activist.

A Japanese Factory Closing and a Union "Victory": Sumida Electronics Company

One of the most dramatic labor struggles in MAFEZ was waged by the workers of Sumida Electronics Company. The workers at Sumida had a reputation for activism even before the 1987 labor uprising and had already made several

---

28 The Asia Watch report *Retreat from Reform* includes Chu Yŏn-ok and the union's then vice president, Kim Chŏng-ja, on its list of jailed unionists and labor activists (1990:137).

unsuccessful attempts to establish a democratic union. Their factory was established in 1972 by a Japanese electronics company, and by 1987 it was one of the largest factories in MAFEZ, employing about 2,000 workers assembling electronics parts. In June 1986 they had formed a Planning Committee to Organize a Labor Union, and a group of sixty-eight workers took the first steps toward setting up a union in January 1987. The company managed to obstruct their efforts by firing one of the organizers and intimidating the rest, so papers were never actually filed with the social affairs office at City Hall. By this time it was technically legal to organize unions in MAFEZ, but the process was always blocked by the government or factory management, so no unions actually existed.

When the uprising began, Sumida's workers were among the first to start their union. Sixty-six Sumida workers officially organized their union on August 11, 1987, and elected a woman production worker as president. The following day, the union officers filed the notice at City Hall announcing the establishment of the union. The company declared a "vacation" and closed the factory for four days. Two days after the factory reopened, the workers occupied the building and declared a sit-down strike. From August 19 to the 26th, about 2,000 workers occupied the factory, demanding wage and bonus increases. On the 26th the company came to terms and accepted several of the sixteen demands submitted by the union. By September 9, the union membership reached 1,600.

From September 23, the union began publishing its newsletter, *Hamsŏng* (A Great Outcry). Sumida's union was among several which issued newsletters after they became well organized. The newsletter contained information about labor laws, news items, and reports about the union's achievements, as well as cartoons, poems, songs, and letters aimed at raising the consciousness of their members. It appealed to their members to be strong and resist efforts of the company to persuade them to withdraw from the union.

Two *hak-ch'ul* who had worked at Sumida since 1986 were important in helping the workers to organize. Unlike factories in the Seoul area, which were near major universities, MAFEZ factories had very few student activists in 1987.[29] As mentioned previously, it was illegal for college students to use false identities to take jobs in factories. In 1988, the company discovered that Yi

---

29 Although I was aware of only three *hak-chul* during the time I was conducting my fieldwork, I later learned that fifteen had been working in MAFEZ at the time of the nationwide labor uprising.

Son-hui (real name, Pak Hae-kyong), the woman in charge of the education section of the labor union, was a disguised worker. Pak Hae-kyong explained her role in Sumida's union:[30]

> I started working for Sumida in June 1986 and was involved in
> launching the planning committee to organize a labor union. . . . Dur-
> ing July and August 1987, I helped set up the labor union. I was in
> charge of education and producing the newsletter. . . . The manage-
> ment found out about my identity in early 1988 and accused me of
> being a communist. I was so grateful that the union members stood by
> me even when they found out I was a disguised worker. When the
> management threatened to fire me, the union declared that it would
> hire me back on its staff if that happened. After the workers knew
> who I was, it was a lot easier to deal with them.

Although the company argued that the union could not legally hire anyone who was not currently a worker, they were afraid that the union would organize a strike, so they did not fire her.

Sumida's union was one of the strongest in MAFEZ and successfully re-sisted the company's efforts to take it over, but rising wages made Sumida's MAFEZ factory much less profitable. The company began contracting out its operations: moving the production lines, taking heavy machines out of the Zone and reducing its investment in equipment. It also moved its main produc-tion site to China.

Sumida stopped hiring new workers and allowed the workforce to decrease through attrition. First, they laid off married women workers who had been hired under one-year contracts during the 1987 labor shortage. From October 1988, they began encouraging workers to resign voluntarily, offering sever-ance payments of two months' wages as an incentive. Because of decreased orders, the factory stopped operating on Fridays and Saturdays. The company began paying wages in installments or delaying payments, maintaining that they did not have enough money to cover wages. The atmosphere in the factory became tense because of the prospect of the factory's closing, but management continued to cut the workforce.

The number of workers fell to 1,500 in April 1988, 1,300 in October 1988,

---

30 I had a chance to talk to Pak Hae-kyŏng at the office of the Masan–Ch'angwŏn Women
Workers' Association when I visited Masan in early 1994. She was married to an activist and
had just returned to work at the Association after having given birth.

800 in February 1989 and 530 in July 1989. By September 14, 1989, the union began negotiations with management about (1) maintaining 500 workers; (2) providing three months' advance notice in the event of a mass layoff; and (3) paying workers one year's wage in the event of a mass layoff. On October 14, during the negotiations, a fax arrived from Japan. In it, Mr. Kushino, the chairman of the MAFEZ company, declared bankruptcy and instructed the managers to close the factory immediately and dismiss the 450 remaining workers (*AMPO* 1990:59). Workers who had not been paid for September or October were to be paid from funds raised by selling off the remaining assets of the factory.

Not only was this far short of the terms that the union had hoped to receive, it did not even comply with South Korean law, which required that at least back wages and severance payments be made. The union declared that it could not accept the layoff notice, and the final phase of the struggle with Sumida began.

Union members continued to work and organized a negotiation team to go to Japan. The parent company was still solvent; the bankruptcy covered only the Korean factory. The fired workers made contact with labor activists in both South Korea and Japan. They held public demonstrations in both countries and received sympathetic coverage in South Korean and Japanese newspapers. The negative publicity forced Sumida to come to terms with their former union, and on June 8, 1990, after 238 days of struggle, the company agreed to pay overdue wages and additional compensation to workers. The agreement specified the following: (1) the Sumida Electronics Company withdrew its bankruptcy and layoff notice issued on October 14, 1989; (2) the company agreed to pay back wages, annual and monthly allowances, retirement pay and retirement compensation through the end of October 1989 to all workers (about 450); (3) the company agreed to pay a retirement bonus of two months' wages to every worker; (4) the company agreed to pay the ninety-one union members who continued the struggle 396,000,000 won to cover wages from October 1989 to May 1990, as well as compensation for a livelihood and employment fund; and (5) the company agreed to pay within a week of the agreement.

The company paid up, and the union members held a public meeting at the Catholic Women's Center on August 8, 1990, to evaluate their struggle and celebrate the victory. Pak Hae-kyong told me how she felt about the struggle and the workers who were involved:

> It was a hard fight against Sumida, but the union members who re-
> mained did get some compensation. I felt bad about those few

workers who could not stay with us in fighting and had to leave just
before we reached the agreement.

Sumida's struggle was received as a big victory for women workers, who had
humiliated the company into apologizing for their behavior and received a
reasonable compensation for their long struggle. Because Sumida had closed
before the December 1989 crackdown on radical labor unions, its leaders
escaped arrest.

A Prolonged Struggle against an American Multinational: T. C. Electronics

One of the most dramatic and complex labor struggles in Masan was the one
between T. C. Electronics and its union. The struggle began in August 1987
with the formation of the union and continued well after the factory closed in
April 1989. Both sides were disappointed by this outcome because both management and workers maintained throughout the conflict that they wanted to
keep the factory open. In 1987, T. C. Electronics was the largest U.S.-based
company in Masan. It employed 1,800 workers: 1,700 women, who were
mostly production workers, and 100 men, who were mostly managers and
technicians. The factory had been established in 1972 and was owned by the
Tandy Corporation. Its main products were stereo components, computer components and telephones.

The workers at T. C. were relatively late in joining the labor uprising. Their
strike began on the afternoon of August 20, 1987, when about 1,000 workers
stopped work and issued a demand for higher wages. Sixty workers organized
a union that evening and registered it at City Hall the following day. They
elected Kim Chŏng-im, a twenty-three-year-old worker, as the union's president. She supported the strike, although she knew little about how to lead a
union. She accepted the job because no one else wanted it, and over the next
few years transformed herself from a weak, frightened young woman into a
strong-willed union leader.

The company responded to the strike by announcing that the factory would
be closed for two days. The women who had organized the union spoke to a
crowd of 300 workers assembled outside the closed factory, and 250 more
workers joined the union. Male technicians demanded that the women "Stop
the strike and talk to the president. . . . We will try to solve your problems if
you promise to disband the union." That evening, union representatives met
with the company's president and presented him with a list of demands. The
most important of these were for a 30% increase in wages and a 50% increase

in annual bonuses, the abolishment of mandatory overtime and Sunday work, and the payment of a seniority allowance.[31]

Of these demands, management agreed to only one: abolishing mandatory overtime work. Negotiations over wage increases broke off because the company considered the amount demanded to be too high. Male technicians later approached the union officers and demanded that they abandon the union: "Do you know anything about the labor law?" they asked. They harangued the women: "Our parent company in the United States does not have a union, and if you start one, the company will surely move the plant to another country. Then who is going to support 1,800 workers? Forget the union; we can work with the Labor–Management Council System."

The factory reopened on the 24th, with the company making some concessions to the workers. Wages and bonuses were increased by about half the amount the union had demanded; however, the company also insisted that the union be disbanded. All of the workers except the three officers withdrew from the union. The company sent these three women to a "special training program" and transferred them away from the production line.[32]

Although T. C.'s first union was crushed in less than a week, the workers had learned how to organize themselves. They were able to organize quickly and effectively during the next phase of labor disputes in 1988. During these confrontations, male technicians again supported management against the women in the union and beat up several women who were trying to recruit their coworkers.[33] Several of the union women were hospitalized, but the labor union survived the confrontation. By mid-1988, 900 of the 950 women still working at T. C. Electronics had joined the union (T. C. Former Labor Union Members 1991:66–67). The company was disturbed by these developments and began to talk about closing down. The chairman of the Tandy Corporation in the United States threatened to move some production lines out of South Korea because of the "general level of cultural change and political uncertainty" (quoted in *The New York Times,* August 26, 1988). However, he also stated that the company did not plan to pull out of South Korea.

The company warned workers that orders from the parent company were

---

31 Workers throughout the country presented their factories with similar lists of demands during the July–August labor uprising.

32 Usually these special training programs were designed to reward model workers. In this case, however, management used them to remove politically active women from the factory.

33 In factories where all production workers were women, most democratic unions did not admit men because they did not want men to take over control of the union.

decreasing. They instituted a hiring freeze in Masan and tried to move machines to subcontracting factories outside the Zone. Union members threw themselves in front of the movers in an effort to stop them from removing the machines from the factory. The company sued the union for blocking the removal of equipment and for obstructing daily procedures on the shop floor in February 1989. On March 6, they announced that the factory was closing temporarily.

Both sides hardened their positions during these confrontations. Management accused the union members of slowing down productivity and interfering with shipping deadlines. The union accused the company of hiring thugs to disrupt the operations of the factory so that it could use "declining productivity" as an excuse to close. The company also described the confrontations at the factory as being between men and women workers, and thus unrelated to management policies.

On April 4, 1989, Tandy Corporation declared that it was closing its factory in Masan and dismissed its entire staff. They issued payments for the wages for March, the legal retirement pay and the legal severance payment (two months' wages) to workers following the legal requirements for closing the factory.

The core members of T. C.'s union continued their public struggle for more than a year following the plant closing. They refused to accept the payments or the closing, and they occupied the factory building, demanding that the company reopen it. When they were ignored by Tandy, the workers became desperate. About twenty of them formed a suicide corps (*kyŏlsadae*), equipped themselves with paint thinner and agricultural chemicals and went to Seoul to occupy T. C.'s research institute. They found the company president in the institute and took him hostage. They held him for six days before he escaped. Their demand for direct negotiations with the parent company in the United States indicated that they still believed that the problems that had occurred in the Masan factory were due to local mismanagement rather than intrinsic to the structural problems of export processing zones. Perhaps if the head office understood their desperation, they thought, it would be sympathetic and reopen the factory. However, the union's kidnapping of the president of their South Korean subsidiary did not convince Tandy to negotiate, but rather confirmed them in their decision to close their factory.

Because Tandy is an American company, its conflict with Korean workers became linked to nationalist issues that were important in South Korean politics. Radical nationalists objected to the presence of large numbers of American troops in Korea, to the ties between the United States and South Korea's unpopular military government and to the presence of foreign-owned companies in Masan. Anti-Americanism was an important aspect of the ideology of the student radicals who had been helping workers to organize. In this final phase of their confrontation with Tandy, strikers incorporated anti-American sentiments in their protests. On the third day of their occupation of the research institute in Seoul, they hung a banner outside the window:

> We only want to go back to work. It is all right if the American-owned company leaves. In fact, they should leave. Foreign-owned multinational corporations will always leave Korea if they do not make enough profits. They do not care about their social responsibility. We would like to work for a Korean-owned company. (T. C. Former Labor Union Members 1991:96–97)

Strikers walked on American flags and chanted anti-American slogans in Masan: "If you want to leave, Yankees, then go. But repay all the profits you exploited from our blood and sweat for seventeen years." Despite these elements of anti-Americanism, however, the union's primary goal was always to have the factory reopen in Masan.

The more radical union activists were not surprised by Tandy's intransigence. They were interested in organizing workers as part of a larger struggle and considered the closing of factories in MAFEZ inevitable, if not desirable. For radicals, the problem was a much larger one than whether one factory would remain open or not.

The international business community was shocked by South Korean labor activism. *The Economist* reported: "A few militants have pressed absurd demands. One American company, which eventually gave up and decided to close its factory, was told by a union organizer that it should not be allowed to leave Korea until it had repaid all the profits it had ever made there" (*The Economist* May 1990:33).

The police forced the workers out of T. C.'s research institute, and the women occupying the factory began to leave. However, negotiations about compensation were still continuing in December 1989 when the police invaded the factory and forced the remaining fifty union supporters out. Kim Chŏngim, the union president, and twenty-one workers were arrested and sent to jail.[34] A few union members made one last attempt to reoccupy the abandoned factory in January 1990, but the police immediately expelled them. The union

34 The Asia Watch report *Retreat from Reform* includes Kim Chŏng-im and the union's vice president, Lee Yŏn-sil, on its list of jailed unionists and labor activists (1990:139).

125

formally abandoned the struggle with a public evaluation forum held on May 25, 1990, and the fight with Tandy was finished.

Kim Chŏng-im served eighteen months in jail. When she was released, she was hailed as a labor hero (*t'usa*) by her family and former coworkers. She then returned to Masan, where she resumed working for workers' rights and married a labor leader from Ch'angwŏn. (See Chapter 5 for an extended discussion of Chŏng-im's career.)

Establishing a Union with a Segmented Workforce: Married Women Workers at Soyo Enterprise

The workers at garment factories were confronted with a particularly difficult task when they tried to organize their unions. Production workers in garment factories consist of both married and single women, who form separate groups that see themselves as having little in common (see Chapter 3). One garment factory where a union was successfully established in 1987 was Soyo Enterprise, a Japanese-owned factory that produced riding clothes for export to the United States. In 1987, the company employed 114 production workers, of whom 100 were women. The workforce at Soyo was evenly divided between married and single women. The starting wage was 3,580 won per day ($4.00).

On August 12 seventy workers at Soyo established a union and elected Yu Ŭn-sun president. The union members chose both a married woman and a single woman as vice presidents so that both groups would be represented, and the remaining positions on the executive committee were filled by single women. The next day, the officers registered their union at the city labor office and reported back to the members. Over the next few days, the executive committee distributed questionnaires to the workers about the problems of wages, working conditions and disrespectful treatment by managers. The union approached management with a list of demands based on the survey. These demands were:

1 An increase of 1,000 won in the daily wage.
2 An increase in the annual bonus from three months' to five months' salary.
3 Pay for recognized national holidays.
4 The establishment of a family subsidy.
5 The provision of pay for round-trip transportation to and from the factory.
6 Better treatment from managers.
7 Freedom to organize a labor union.

The company refused to negotiate with the union, and on August 18 about 100 workers began a sit-in strike. They chanted, "Let's wrap up the company president and export him." The workers continued to come to work and go home at their usual time during the strike. The company still refused to negotiate, insisting that the workers "operate the factory first and negotiate later." They threatened to close the factory unless the workers halted the strike.

On the 21st the company agreed to negotiate with the union. Management offered a daily wage increase of 200 won; an annual bonus increase of one month's salary; payment for round-trip transportation; and the addition of six more paid holidays. But they refused to provide the labor union with facilities at the factory and threatened to close permanently unless the union accepted these terms.

The union announced that these terms were unacceptable and continued the sit-in strike. The company retaliated by closing the factory indefinitely on August 23. The following day, the workers came to continue their sit-in strike and started a long discussion about whether to support the union.

On August 24, 1987, I went with two of my roommates to see what was happening at the Soyo Enterprise factory where workers were on strike. My roommates were workers at Soyo. A poster hung on the factory door announcing that the factory was closed indefinitely. More than 100 workers were gathered on the sidewalk and street outside. They had planned to strike that day, but they had expected to be admitted to the factory, and were upset and angry that the company had closed it. Most of their anger was directed at the company, but workers were also divided among themselves about how to deal with the lockout. The situation was tense. Some workers confronted me: "Who are you?" "What are you doing here?" "Who sent you here?" My roommate intervened and said, "She is my sister. Her factory is closed today, so she came to see me." After that, they accepted my presence.

Union supporters chanted, "Hooray laborers! Hooray labor union!" (*"Nodongja Manse! Nodongjohap Manse!"*) and the unstructured, emotionally charged discussion lasted for about three hours. Many workers had opinions for or against the strike. Yu Ŭn-sun, the union president, wanted to continue the strike and press for the union's original demands. The most militant workers advocated breaking into the factory to occupy it.

Married women workers gathered at one end of the sidewalk. With families relying on their income, they were the ones most threatened by the closing, and many were desperate to have the factory reopen. Those who spoke argued that the company's offer was an acceptable starting point. They implored the executive committee to listen to them and end the confrontation. They pleaded that they needed work and, unlike single women, they could not get other jobs easily if the factory shut down permanently. They shouted angrily, "We told you that they would close the factory. What are you going to do about it? We don't have jobs anymore. Are you going to get us jobs? We are not single women like you; it won't be easy for us to get other factory jobs." Ŭn-sun was visibly worried because she feared that most of the married women were against her.

In the afternoon the workers decided to hold a vote by secret ballot on whether to continue the strike. Ŭn-sun confided to me that she did not want to submit the strike to a vote because she thought many workers were not yet ready to support her position. Nevertheless, she agreed to the vote, which came out overwhelmingly in favor of the union's position; ninety-five workers had agreed to continue the strike. Ŭn-sun later confessed to me that she had been surprised by the result, and especially by the support the union had received from married women. Whereas the married women who had spoken during the public debate had voiced their opposition to the union and argued in favor of accepting the company's offer, in the secret vote married women had come together with their single coworkers to support the union.

The unity among the workers surprised both sides. After learning of the vote in favor of continuing the strike, Soyo's management approached the Labor Office of Masan City and asked them to arbitrate a settlement with the union. On August 28 both sides agreed to a settlement that included a daily wage increase of 500 won ($0.60) and an increase in the annual bonus from three months' to four months' salary.

Soyo's union continued to be active until December 1989, when, during a strike, all the union officers were fired. The union president, Ŭn-sun, was arrested and imprisoned for a year.[35] The union was replaced with a company-run union (*ŏyong nojo*), which has since disbanded. Ŭn-sun continued her involvement in labor organizing after her release. She married a labor activist and worked for the Ma-Chang No-Ryon (Masan–Ch'angwŏn Coalition of Labor Unions) until her children were born. She plans to get involved with the Women Workers Association when her children are a bit older. (See Chapter 5 for an extended discussion of Ŭn-sun's career.)

---

35 The Asia Watch report *Retreat from Reform* includes Yu Ŭn-sun on its list of jailed unionists and labor activists (1990:139).

5

The Making of Working-Class Identity: Students' Theories and Workers' Lives

THE rapidity with which the South Korean working class emerged as a self-aware political force is one of the remarkable aspects of recent Korean history. During the past few decades, as industrial workers have increased in number, they have come to participate in political activity on a nationwide scale and show growing signs of class consciousness. As Koo observes, "In the 1950s or even in the 1960s, one rarely heard people talking about social classes in Korea" (1993:131).[1] By the 1970s this situation had begun to change, and during the 1980s the working class emerged as the country's "most visible class force" (ibid.:132). In this chapter, I examine some of the key ideological and cultural forces that contributed to its developing consciousness and show how workers in Masan fit themselves into this working class.

Class, as Thompson argues, has to be understood as "a social and cultural formation" (1966:11), "a relationship and not a thing" that "happens when some men [sic], as a result of common experiences (inherited or shared), feel and articulate the identity of their interests as between themselves, and as against other men whose interests are different from (and usually opposed to) theirs" (ibid.:9). In South Korea, a politically aware working class developed with extraordinary rapidity, because rapid industrialization created the necessary community of people with shared interests but also because a repressive state drove its intellectual opposition into the workers' movement. The presence of intellectuals allowed workers to develop sophisticated and coordinated political action, which otherwise might not have been possible in a workforce composed mostly of relocated peasant farmers. Ironically, working-class militance resulted directly from repressive government policies.

A class is made up of real people, and it is important to consider the

---

1 The hostile climate that the Korean War left toward even vaguely Marxist ideas was, of course, also a factor suppressing class discourse during the 1950s and 1960s.

experience of specific individuals in order to understand it. The working class includes not only those who work in factories at a given point in time, but also those who are identified with and broadly share the interests and status of factory workers (e.g., workers' dependents, laid-off workers and union officers). Women who go into and out of factories in the course of their lives normally remain in the working class.

As Joan Scott (1988) notes in her criticism of Thompson, the concept of "the working class" is conventionally formulated in a way that pays inadequate attention to women's roles and experiences within it. Not surprisingly, women tend to be overlooked in the consideration of the South Korean working class. Even though women factory workers have been numerous from the beginning of Korean industrialization, women have tended to have shorter factory careers than men. Thus, they have been thought of as less than true workers and, therefore, marginal to working-class political action.[2] Furthermore, women's position in society, specifically their roles as wives and mothers, serves to decenter their experience as workers in the view of both men and women. However, the question should not be "Are women workers real workers?" but rather "What else are they in addition to being workers?" The social obligations that women have as daughters, wives and mothers of men who work in factories also weave them firmly into the fabric of the working class.

Working-class consciousness does not derive in an unmediated form from the experiences of workers in factories, but rather from how these experiences "are handled in cultural terms: embodied in tradition, value-systems, ideas, and institutional forms" (Thompson 1966:10). The rapid evolution of the South Korean working class means that it has been exceptionally open to a variety of outside influences. Workers themselves are mostly rural people who have brought with them (among other cultural baggage) a tradition of resistance to class and foreign domination rooted in the harsh events of recent history (see Abelmann 1990, 1996). Intellectuals, including college students and religious figures, have played an unusually large role in the development of working-class consciousness by providing connections between diverse experiences of

2 During the period of extreme political repression (the 1970s), political actions by women workers predominated (see Chapter 4). However, when relaxation of government restrictions on organizing allowed male workers to establish effective organizations, women's activities were quickly relegated to secondary status, even by activists and sympathetic observers (e.g., Koo 1993:156).

subaltern groups and by giving workers access to political concepts derived from industrial contexts outside South Korea. *Minjung munhak,* or working-class literature, is the most concrete manifestation of this new working-class consciousness (Koo 1993:151). The South Korean working class is thus characterized by a distinctive literature and politics, as well as by its position in the relationships of production. As Bourdieu observes, "a class is defined as much by its being-perceived as by its being" (1984:483). The South Korean working class has become a highly visible social formation, both to itself and to members of other social classes.

How, exactly, do the participants in the working class develop its consciousness? This is a question of great practical and theoretical importance. How well do workers comprehend their situation? To what extent are they misled into false consciousness by mistakenly identifying their interests with those of the groups who dominate them? (The socially dominant may make overt efforts to encourage this identification, as, for example, in the orientation programs at MAFEZ electronics factories [see Chapter 2], or domination may be accomplished in more subtle ways without necessarily entailing active participation by the dominant group – for example, when workers try to copy middle-class fashions and lifestyles [see Chapter 3].)

James Scott denies that subaltern groups are ever totally mystified about their domination and argues that under systems of wage labor, as in virtually all systems of domination, members of the subordinate group "retain considerable autonomy to construct a life and a culture not entirely controlled by the dominant class" (1985:328). Although I believe that Scott does not give sufficient weight to those subalterns who naturalize or otherwise misunderstand the circumstances of their oppression, the core of his work remains compelling. Human beings do understand a great deal about their social context, and one should not lose sight of this basic fact. As an anthropologist, I believe it is especially important to trust one's subjects to grasp the essentials of their circumstances. Because I think that women factory workers are best positioned to understand their lives, I have endeavored throughout this work to provide an accurate presentation of their ideas and experiences.

In the following section, I examine the relationship between women workers and students in the South Korean labor movement and consider the following questions: What were the ideological motivations of students? How did they participate in the labor movement? What impact have their activities had?

Class Struggle or Family Struggle?

THE AWKWARD RELATIONSHIP BETWEEN STUDENTS AND WORKERS

The Ideological Foundations of the Student Movement

Intellectuals, especially college students, have played a critical role in the development of working-class consciousness. Student activists have led the opposition to the succession of military dictatorships that ruled the country in the post–World War II period (Dong 1987, 1988), and their political alliance with workers dates to the 1970 suicide of Chun Tae-il, a textile worker in P'yŏnghwa market in Seoul.[3] Chun's suicide was the first incident in an increasingly militant and committed activism of workers and marked a turning point in the labor movement. The incident also "set the framework for intense self-reflection" among politically active students (Choi Jang Jip 1993:34). The plight of workers generated a sense of acute moral outrage. College students, urban intellectuals and radical members of church organizations all became increasingly concerned about the problems faced by industrial workers (Kwon Sun-taek 1986). Students led a "night class" movement to educate workers and to teach them about social theories and political action.[4]

At about this time, the government of Park Chung Hee entered its most repressive phase, severely restricting all forms of political activity as part of the *Yusin* system. A few students interested in establishing political ties with workers began to enter factories as disguised workers (*wijangchwiŏbja*). Their practice of taking factory jobs for the purpose of organizing workers became widespread following the Kwangju massacre[5] and the resulting growth of militant antigovernment sentiment among students. In addition to promoting workers' rights, student activists now sought to mobilize the working class in order to bring down the government of President Chun and establish a more just and democratic political order. Factory work (*kongjanghwaldong*) became perceived as an essential step for a politically committed student. It was illegal for students to take factory jobs, so factory work established one's willingness to risk prison and torture to achieve a just society.

The student–worker alliance (*no-hak yŏndae*) provided the ideological

---

3 For detailed information on Chŏn T'ae-il, see Chŏn T'ae-il (1988).
4 For a discussion of the "night class movement" by college students, see *Yahak Pip'an* ("Critique of Night Class") by Ilsongjŏng Publishers (1988).
5 Sources disagree about the death toll of the Kwangju massacre. The government admits to about 200 deaths, but others claim that the actual toll was over 2,000. For more information on the

focus of South Korea's dissident movement throughout the 1980s. Intense government suppression of both movements led to increased radicalization, as well as to cooperation between factions that advocated widely divergent goals. Students and workers achieved broad-based popular support as they led the demonstrations and strikes of 1987 that forced the government to undertake major political reforms (Christian Institute for the Study of Justice and Development 1987b).

Student activists were particularly important in organizing women workers because women were concentrated in sectors of industry that relied on them as cheap labor between the age when they left school and when they got married. Women production workers are thus overwhelmingly young and have short careers in the factories, which handicaps their efforts to develop leaders. Students, with their ideological links beyond the individual factories, have helped provide women workers with the continuity and resources to organize.

At the center of the students' political activism is their vision of what constitutes a just society. This interest is made especially urgent and compelling by the specific situation of South Korea within the geopolitical conflicts of the late twentieth century, and the country's experience of social and economic transformation (Ilsongjŏng Publishers 1988). To help achieve a just society, students were willing to make extraordinary sacrifices.

The role of student activists has recently undergone major changes. The establishment of a civilian government in South Korea, as well as the collapse of the Soviet Union and Communist Eastern Europe, have helped undermine the broad-based antigovernment coalition that focused political action in South Korea in the 1980s. At the same time, the increase in wages paid to production workers has diminished radical sentiments among workers even as a sense of working-class identity has become more firmly established among them.

Student activists were united in their desire to achieve a just society, but factions differed among themselves according to their evaluation of the Korean political economy, their convictions about who should be the principal agent for change (intellectuals, students or industrial workers) and what means were to be used to achieve the desired goals. I have used the diverse experiences of former college students and labor activists to examine the achievements and contradictions inherent in the student–worker alliance.

Kwangju massacre, see Hwang Sŏk-yŏng (1985) and Kwangju Taegyogu Chŏngui P'yŏnghwa Wiwŏnhoe (1987).

Class Struggle or Family Struggle?

The Contribution of Student Activists

In the 1980s many students believed that it was necessary to get involved in the student movement (*undongkwŏn*) in order to demonstrate a social conscience. Chi-hyŏn, a thirty-three-year-old woman who was active in labor organizing at Inchŏn, recalled how she became interested in social activism during the turbulent years of 1979 and 1980:

> I entered college in 1979. I believe everyone who entered college around this time felt that it was urgent for students to struggle to correct the path of the Korean government. In 1980, the "Kwangju Massacre" took place and the campus was closed for a long time. I began to wonder about what contribution I could make to this country. I used to dream about becoming a successful scientist, but that seemed too distant and selfish a goal in that political situation. I joined a small discussion group of churchgoers that was not considered too radical.

This woman became deeply involved in the labor movement, and experienced several arrests and periods of imprisonment, but participants in the student movement varied according to their degree of commitment and their willingness to make sacrifices. Yŏng-ŭn, a thirty-one-year-old woman, who now works as an editor, spoke of her fear of getting caught and imprisoned.

> When I was a college student, from 1982 to 1986, everyone was interested in the student movement. We had to be because of the political situation of that time. I always felt I should be part of the student–worker movement, but I also was afraid of the possibility of going to prison and being tortured.[6] Nevertheless, I participated in the "Night Class Movement" during 1985–1986. Until this time, I was always marginal to the movement even though I participated in street demonstrations whenever they happened.

Kyŏng-hui, currently a high school teacher, remembered that at her college, being part of the student movement was almost mandatory:

6 Many student activists experienced physical and mental torture while they were imprisoned. One of the most notorious cases was the sex torture (*sŏng komun*) of a woman student activist, Kwŏn In-suk. Her experience was publicized in 1986 and caused national outrage. She describes the process of her involvement in the labor movement, and her commitment as well as her conflict, the details of the torture, the experience of imprisonment, and her decision to make her case public in her 1989 autobiography.

Although I was not forced to get involved, the ideological pressure
was such that I just had to. I joined a radical circle of my college
when I became a junior, although I was never at the core of the group.
The meetings made it very clear what needed to be done. I was convinced that it was necessary to go to work in a factory.

Within the student movement, women were at first relegated to marginal
roles. Chi-hyŏn remembers:

During the 1970s . . . women were not encouraged to join a circle. . . . The circles during this time were male-oriented, and very
conservative and hierarchical. There were a very few women who
lasted in this environment, and they had to become like men, smoking
and drinking, as well as street fighting during demonstrations. They
had to prove that they were worthy of membership in the circle. After
1979, circles began to accept women members as regular members,
but women were not given important positions. Because of this closed
environment of the movement circles, women students in Seoul National University organized their own circle for the first time in 1981.
Many of us had double membership during this early period, being
members of both existing circles and the new women's circles. I became the first woman president of my circle when I was a junior. Although I was the president, our circle was not considered to be
important, so I was able to graduate without much problem in 1983.

As women established a greater role within the student movement, they
began to be taken more seriously. In later years, many women activists were
expelled from universities for their political activities.

According to one study, by the mid-1980s, more than 3,000 college students
became disguised workers; in 1985–1986 alone, the police arrested "671 such
agitators" (Ogle 1990:99). In Masan, where I conducted my research, there
were only fifteen students trying to organize a workforce of 29,000 women in
1987, but in other parts of the country the student activists ran into each other at
their factory. Chi-hyŏn recalled:

I went to work [as a disguised worker] at a small electronics factory
with 140 employees in Inchŏn. And guess what? Of those 140
workers, there were about 10 disguised workers. Immediately, I could
tell who were activists (*hwaldongga*). That small factory was over-
flowing with *hwaldongga*.

Some students found that even when they took jobs in factories, they did not have the kind of impact they had hoped for. Kyŏng-hui explained.

I worked for six months at an electronics factory until I could not bear it anymore. When I quit, I justified my decision to myself by admitting that I was not an effective organizer. It was too hard for me to work at a factory, and I really did not want to continue.

Yŏng-ŭn, who tried to organize a garment factory, felt more conflict. She was not an outgoing, talkative, or warm person, and although she tried to change, she could not. She spent a year working as a sewing machine operator in three different factories before she quit in 1987:

I only worked. I did not organize any workers within the factory. I did not make any friends. I quit because I felt that I was not making any difference. I just worked. I did not bring any radical ideology to spread in the factory, nor did I organize workers to start a strike. The need to do something pushed me into the movement, but I never considered myself to be a movement person.

Becoming a student activist required sacrifice, but succeeding as a labor organizer exposed women to personal danger. Chin-ok, who was a disguised worker in Masan during the nationwide labor uprising, described her experiences:

I was expelled from college when I was a junior for being involved in a night class [*yahak*] movement. I had to run away from the police. I came down to Masan, and I started working in 1987 and had been at [my factory] for six months before the uprising. When we tried to organize the union in 1988, I got actively involved and took charge of the education section. As the head of that section, I taught union members about the labor law, workers' rights, and Korean history. Not long after I started to be active, the management began to suspect that I was a disguised worker and started to spread rumors that I was a Communist [*ppalgaengi*] and I had been sent to [my factory] to start a Communist revolution. When I distributed flyers criticizing the "Save the Company Corps" (*kusadae*) in front of the Masan Free Export Zone, the men dragged me and five other workers into the factory and hit us over and over again. They especially targeted me, saying, "Since you are a *ppalgaengi*, we would not be doing anything wrong if we killed you." But, they told each other, "Do not leave any

136

marks," and hit my head with steel helmets. They also pulled out clumps of my hair.

Labor organizing often led to arrest and imprisonment, but this also validated the organizer's political status. Women believed that their confrontation with the government was heroic, and they were proud to have been arrested. Furthermore, prison provided women with an opportunity to reflect and study and reinforced their commitment to their cause. A woman who has worked at organizing (male) workers in Ch'angwŏn for the past eight years explained:

> I never regretted the period I was imprisoned since I read a lot and had a chance to reflect upon what I had done. The prison experience reconfirmed my conviction about helping workers, and I came out a stronger and more committed person. I have never regretted my decision to dedicate myself to the cause of workers. Workers should be the leaders of the revolution, and we, students and intellectuals, have to assist them to become progressive workers so that they can carry out the revolution.

Commitment and dedication were required of all organizers and are especially marked qualities in those who have remained active in the labor movement. Su-hui, who worked for the Pusan regional alliance of labor unions, summarized her role:

> My life would not be meaningful if I led it differently. For me, what I am doing is extremely fulfilling and important; that is why I am still here when everyone else has left. In order for a revolution to succeed, there have to be a few core people who are committed to the cause, no matter what happens to them, and I want to be one of them. Historically, it is clear that revolutions are carried out by a small number of people. Many people join a revolution along the way, but only a few actually carry it through.

The sense of providing a vanguard for revolution produced in some organizers a sense of superiority that could seem to be arrogance. On the other hand, student labor organizers often believed that their superior status was a barrier to acceptance. Sun-hui, who was very active in organizing women workers in Masan in the 1980s (see the Preface), described how she concealed her identity from workers as well as from the police:

Most of workers do not know about my identity. I do not tell them because the relationship we built on the basis of equal status changes once I tell them, "I am a college graduate and I came down here to help you to organize." Rather than preaching to them about what to do from the outside, I would bury myself among them and make changes from within.

In Inchŏn, Chi-hyŏn emphasized that students needed to get around class barriers by becoming like laborers, shedding their middle-class lifestyle and identity.

I told many *hwaldongga* that first they should be ready to become a good, model worker before trying to organize workers. If they are not good workers, others would not follow them.

She went on to criticize student activists whose commitment was insufficient to allow them to adjust their lives to the slow and often unrewarding task of organizing workers:

The problems with those so-called *hwaldongga* are many. First, they are impatient. They would like to do something very quickly. They feel that they have to do something, so they start a strike that cannot succeed. And then they just leave. No wonder many politically conscious workers despised students and did not want them. Second, they are not good workers. They cannot be since they go to late night meetings and discussions with drinking and smoking. They do not get enough sleep, and come to work late and cannot work efficiently. . . . Third, they leave quickly if they feel unwanted. They need to be patient and wait to be accepted by workers. I have seen so many women students leave the factory after three or four months. I wonder why they started to work at all. Factory work should not be a hobby for students.

Other successful organizers made similar criticisms of student activists. Nevertheless, many of those who found that they were not successful as organizers still believed that they could make a contribution and felt hurt by the movement's rejection of them. Hae-ran, who had attempted to organize workers and later became an active member of a feminist group, criticized the narrowness and exclusiveness of the student movement:

138

I wished the student movement people were more understanding and embracing of those of us who failed to carry out factory work successfully. There were many of us who wanted to continue to be a part of the movement, but we felt unwelcome; we were treated as weaklings at best and as traitors at worst.

Workers' Perception of Student Activists

Student activists have made an undeniable contribution to raising workers' consciousness, connecting workers in different organizations, and giving workers' struggles greater continuity. They have helped make workers aware of their collective strength and of what their bargaining power can accomplish, especially by increasing their wages. "[W]ithout the active participation of students and church groups in the labor arena, working-class formation in South Korea might have been much slower" (Koo 1993:162). But student activists remain outsiders to the workers' struggle. Sŏk-hui, a thirty-six-year-old woman who is the president of the union in her garment factory in Seoul, described their contribution:

> I believe that students did a lot for us laborers by teaching us about unions and social justice and helping us organize. However, there is a fundamental difference between us and them: their fighting ground is their head [ideology], while our struggle involves fighting with our own bodies. Furthermore, because student organizers come from many different ideological and theoretical schools, different organizers try to indoctrinate us into their groups, and lead us to argue among ourselves.

Pyŭng-nim, the vice president of the same union, complained:

> I hated the way students got involved for a limited period and also hated that the workplace became their experimental ground. For quite a while, I felt betrayed and distrustful. But now I think that everyone has their own location in society. There needs to be a movement that can embrace and consolidate the student movement and the labor movement. I would like to have a social movement that includes everyone who is willing. . . .

139

Similar sentiments were expressed by a union activist in Masan. She said:

> I do not hate student activists. But I do not have much respect for
> them either. There are positive contributions that they made for
> workers in Masan, but they did more damage than good for us. [At
> our factory] we had one student activist . . . but she was not the driv-
> ing force of our struggle. If anything, she stayed at the periphery.
> However, we did receive a lot of help from student activists outside
> the factory. . . .

The changed political situation and the decreased interest of students in the
labor movement has also contributed to the gap between workers and students.
Sŏk-hui, the union president quoted earlier, continued:

> I don't think that there are many student activists left in factories now.
> There may be a few, but almost all have left to go back to school, so
> they are now an endangered species. It's not like in the 1980s. It is
> natural that they go back where they came from, because they have
> done their share. But watching them go back to their middle-class life,
> I feel betrayed. They have their family background and their educa-
> tion, so that they can start at some other place. But we cannot leave
> our factory work that easily. We are stuck here.

Unacknowledged Affinities

Although students, by their own account, are outsiders in the labor movement,
they have much in common with the women they are trying to organize. Both
middle-class students and working-class production workers are members of
new classes created by the rapid industrialization of South Korea, and individual backgrounds have many areas of overlap. Some factory workers have
brothers and sisters in college, and many college students come from families
that are not wealthy. Nevertheless, the differences that are emerging between
the middle class and the working class are real. Middle-class incomes are much
higher than those of factory workers.[7] Even former student activists, whose

7 Official statistics indicate that different education levels establish large differences in income
between middle- and working-class individuals. "[C]ollege graduates are paid much higher
wages than middle and high school graduates. . . . [T]here is a tendency for college graduates to
be paid a larger share than less educated workers regardless of productivity; the college diploma
has become a social status symbol. . . . However, the wage differentials by education level have
been continuously narrowed during the past two decades" (Cho Soon 1994:95–96).

resumés make it difficult to get regular jobs, can still tutor school children and earn about twice as much as a factory worker.

Women production workers and women student activists are also both channeled into their respective roles by the restrictions the society places on women.[8] Working-class women have few options for employment besides factories that exploit them at low wages in labor-intensive industries, but middle-class women also have limited options. Most female college graduates expect a few years of employment as office workers before getting married and becoming housewives, but for those who had become interested in social issues as part of the student movement in college, this was not enough. The role of labor activist, even though it was illegal, gave women a chance to participate in political processes that aimed to establish a more just society and to address problems such as the military dictatorship and the political division of Korea.

Despite their daily experiences with discrimination based on gender, women student activists saw gender issues as of secondary importance compared to class. They complained among themselves about the hierarchical and patriarchal structure of the student movement, but they rarely discussed their grievances with men, and women who did bring up gender problems were generally dismissed by male students as not taking class issues seriously enough. In spite of sharing experiences of sexual subordination with the workers they organized, these commonalities were seldom noted by female labor activists. An exception is the Reverend Cho Wha Soon, an activist with the Urban Industrial Mission, who points out that "Women workers are probably the class that has borne the greatest burden of historical oppression created by human society up to now" (1988:136) and who advocates a parallel movement for women's liberation. It is only very recently that the issue of equal pay for equal work has been taken up by women workers themselves.

Students' interest in organizing workers and their idea of a just society were closely connected to a quest for national identity. Foreign countries, particularly the United States, were seen as dominating Korea politically and economically. The idea of *minjung* ("the masses") was central to efforts to counter the hegemonic power of the government and its foreign supporters (Abelmann 1990). The term *minjung* implied both the broadly shared interests of the Korean people and opposition to the forces that had historically oppressed them. As Choi Jang Jip states, "the *minjung* is not a fixed or limited sociopolitical entity,

---

8 There are recent Ph.D. dissertations dealing with the ways Korean society has restricted women; see Moon (1994) and Yi Eunhee Kim (1993).

but embodies a dynamic, liberating subjectivity that arises from a history of oppression" (1993:17). Even though the working class in South Korea was formed recently, in its oppressed status it was seen as having continuity with resistance movements extending back to the late nineteenth century. Students believed they had a common national interest with workers, and also that workers were the least compromised by cooptation by outside forces. Establishing political ties with workers legitimized students' political activities.

Although students and workers were drawn together by *minjung* ideology, their aims within the movement often differed. Students would not have been in the factories if they had not been dedicated, idealistic and self-sacrificing. The notion of a just society that attracted them to the cause was an abstract, long-term goal. Workers were in the factories because they needed to earn a living. They were unified not by ideology, but by a set of common problems focusing on low pay, long hours, poor working conditions and harsh treatment. To paraphrase George Orwell, what the ordinary woman worker expected from a just society was simply "better wages and shorter hours and nobody bossing you about" (cited in James Scott 1985:349).

Students advocated confrontational strategies and considered workers' acceptance of a meager improvement in their tangible rewards as "false consciousness." Students reasoned that workers occupy the bottom strata within a capitalist society, and that improvements granted to them by the ruling class to pacify them did not change this fact. Student activists aimed at leading workers to a higher level of understanding of their social location and sometimes regarded the improvements in workers' lives as hindering their progress toward achieving class consciousness. Although some workers came to identify with the goals set by students, many did not, and after unions achieved modest success in improving wages and working conditions, militant union leaders frequently found themselves abandoned by rank-and-file workers.[9]

Student activists are currently much less numerous in factories than they were at the end of the 1980s. Some of those who have left the factories and resumed their middle-class lives may feel satisfaction at having advanced their cause. The military government has been replaced by one led by civilians. Workers are much more conscious of their class interests. Working conditions and wages are improving. However, although many workers now believe that

9 An example of mass defection from a union that was seen as too militant by the rank and file is discussed by Kim Chang-ki (1991). At the Pohang Iron and Steel Company, union membership plummeted following a prolonged confrontation between union leaders and company management.

they should organize themselves without help from outsiders, they still resent the ease with which activists resumed their middle-class status.

For the most radical activists, the cause has not been won. Both the South Korean government and the capitalist economic system are still in place. They regard their former comrades with suspicion and worry that the gains in working-class consciousness are eroding. They have remained in the movement because they believe that they are still needed and expect to play a role in anticipated future struggles.

Prior to the 1987 labor uprising, Catholic Church organizations were the only ones that paid much attention to the women workers of Masan. In 1971, shortly after the establishment of MAFEZ, the church set up a Catholic Women's Center for workers. The Center provided women workers with a space for educational and recreational activities. It offered night classes to workers who needed to complete their elementary education and also provided some recreational classes (covering such topics as mask-dance, calligraphy and guitar). In 1987, the classes for "bridal preparation" were very popular among workers, although people outside the church whispered that these classes included Communist political indoctrination in addition to the more standard instruction in etiquette, cooking and family life.

The Masan chapter of JOC was also founded in 1971. It was very active in providing political education to workers in the Zone. The Masan chapter had a small building as its headquarters and was divided into five sections, each of which was stationed at a different neighborhood church. Each section oversaw several teams consisting of three to ten members who got together every week or so to discuss labor issues. These team members did not have to be Catholics, but many eventually converted. At the beginning of 1987, there were about 100 JOC members in the Masan area.

JOC helped coordinate union activity in Masan during the 1987 labor uprising. Its one full-time staff member, Yi Sun-hui, an extremely energetic young woman, was the most important organizer in the Zone (see the Preface). Many of the new union leaders were members of JOC before the uprising began, and Sun-hui sought out and recruited most of those who were not. JOC meetings introduced many women to the concepts of workers' rights and trade unions. And it was at JOC that young workers learned how to unite to fight for their

143

rights. JOC led the struggle in the Zone in the years following the uprising, but it declined rapidly in importance after Sun-hui returned to Seoul in 1990.

In 1986, the Labor Counseling Center (*Nodongmunje Sangdamso*) was opened at the Catholic Women's Center. It was run by three staff members including one woman, Yi Kyong-suk, whose job was to provide help specifically for women workers.[10] This organization sought to help workers organize and teach them how to conduct negotiations. The Labor Counseling Center offered classes to educate production workers about their rights under existing law. Many of these classes were taught by *hak-ch'ul* from the Kyŏngnam Council of Workers. Course titles included "Labor Standard Law" and "Get to Know Our Rights," and classes were packed with ordinary workers (see Chapter 4).

The Kyŏngnam Council of Workers (*Kyŏngnam Nodongja Hyŏbuihoe*) was the first labor group in the Masan area to be organized outside the framework of the Catholic Church. It was started in Ch'angwŏn in 1986 by Mun Sŏng-hyŏn and his wife, Yi Hye-ja. Mun and his wife were dedicated Seoul intellectuals who came to Ch'angwŏn for the purpose of organizing workers. Mun's patience and dedication can be seen in the way he worked in his factory for seven years before revealing his purpose and starting to organize workers. *Hak-ch'ul* provided the Kyŏngnam Council of Workers with important communication and organizational skills, and it rapidly expanded its influence in Masan during the labor uprising.

An important labor body organized following the uprising was the Masan–Ch'angwŏn Coalition of Labor Unions (*Masan–Ch'angwŏn Nodongjohap Ch'ongyŏnhap*). The Alliance was a loose organization of democratic labor unions started during the uprising in response to the need for an umbrella group to oversee the relationship among different enterprise unions. The nineteen democratic unions of the area (with a combined membership of 16,000) came together in the Alliance, and Yi Hŭng-sŏk was elected president in December 1987. The Masan–Ch'angwŏn Coalition of Labor Unions was the first of the eight regional alliances established throughout the country following the uprising. It grew rapidly, and by 1988 included thirty-two unions and 30,000 workers. It was one of the top two regional alliances, equal in standing to the Seoul Alliance of Trade Unions.

---

10 Yi Kyŏng-suk is a woman who has dedicated her life to the struggle for workers' rights. She has a university degree and comes from a conservative, landed rural family. She became involved in labor issues through her work with the Catholic Church. She was in her late forties and single in 1994, and observed that her life of dedication to workers would not have been possible if she were married and had children.

From 1988 to 1990, as the government renewed its suppression of union activity, the Coalition worked closely with the Kyŏngnam Council of Workers, and many activists participated in both organizations. Both organizations also were subject to political pressure from radical students who came to the area in increasing numbers during this period as repression intensified in the Seoul and Inchŏn area. Many students initially became members of the Kyŏngnam Council of Workers. The students helped recruit additional workers, but they also introduced political factionalism into the organization. After a short period many left, claiming that the organization was too backward and ideologically cautious, and they took most of those whom they had recruited into the various splinter groups that they founded.

In 1991, a staff member at the Labor Counseling Center discussed the problems at the Kyŏngnam Council of Workers:

> Mun Sŏng-hyŏn and Yi Hye-ja have been going through rough times since they founded the Kyŏngnam Council of Workers. They embraced all the students fleeing from the Seoul and Inchŏn area, hoping that the Council would benefit from their experience, but they were betrayed by these students. The students just used the Council to recruit workers for their own political agendas. They organized workers into small discussion groups (*haksŭpban*) to study social theory, and once they had organized their own small group they withdrew from the Council. The Council lost large numbers of members three times as students took their followers out.

The Masan–Ch'angwŏn Women Workers' Association (*Masan–Ch'angwŏn Yŏsŏng Nodongjahoe*) was established in 1992 by women who believed that women workers had specific needs that were not adequately addressed by the existing organizations. Its three key organizers were Kang In-sun, a professor of sociology at Kyŏngnam University;[11] Yi Kyŏng-suk, a staff member at the Labor Counseling Center;[12] and Yi Hye-ja, the general secretary of the Kyŏngnam Council of Workers.[13]

---

11 Professor Kang In-sun was active in the Democratic Professors' Association of Kyŏngnam University during the late 1980s.

12 Yi Kyŏng-suk believed that she experienced gender discrimination at the Labor Counseling Center, where she worked for almost five years. There, although she had more experience than other staff members, her salary was the lowest.

13 All three organizers of the Masan–Ch'angwŏn Women Workers' Association were university-educated women with middle-class backgrounds.

Yi Kyŏng-suk became the Association's first president. She had come to Masan in 1981 to work as a coordinator for the Catholic Women's Center. She began working for the Labor Counseling Office when it was opened in 1986. Her conviction that women workers had special needs that had to be addressed separately from those of men workers led her to leave the Labor Counseling Center in order to begin the Women Workers' Association.

Currently, the Association has two officers (both former production workers from the Zone)[14] in addition to the president, and its most important function is running a day-care facility for the children of low-income families. As of January 1994, this facility had three paid teachers and accommodated twenty-five children. It was the only day-care facility in Masan that met the needs of women who worked long hours and could not afford to pay much. In addition to running this facility, the Association provided classes similar to those offered at the Catholic Women's Center.[15]

In 1994, the established workers' political organizations appear to be in decline. JOC had become smaller and increasingly focused on religious issues. The Labor Counseling Center continued to receive financial support from the Catholic Church and Catholic-related international organizations, so it was relatively well funded, but few ordinary workers came to seek counseling. The number of classes offered to union officers had also decreased tremendously. The Kyongnam Council of Workers had been weakened by loss of supporters (especially *hak-ch'ul*). The more radical *hak-ch'ul* split off to found organizations that were more ideological, but that also attracted fewer workers and fragmented the labor movement. More moderate *hak-ch'ul* leftthe labor movement altogether. Factionalism also divided and weakened the Masan–Ch'angwŏn Alliance of Trade Unions. In 1994, fewer than ten unions belonged to the Alliance, and its influence on workers had decreased.

14 One of the officers was Chu Yŏn-ok, who had been a union officer at K.T.E., and the other was a veteran of the struggle at T. C. Electronics Company. Yi Kyŏng-suk, the president, was planning to step down and have Yŏn-ok replace her.
15 The classes on labor issues were having difficulty attracting women workers from the Zone and sometimes had to be canceled because of the lack of interest. The only classes that were doing well were "How to Use Cosmetics Properly," "Sex Education" and "How to Be a Good Wife and Mother."

THE STRUGGLE'S IMPACT ON WORKERS' LIVES

Leaders of the Struggle

This section presents the biographies of three women who were involved in the labor movement and became leaders of their unions during the 1987 labor uprising. One was already a member of JOC, and the other two joined the organization during the uprising. All three showed extraordinary leadership in organizing workers and participated in many different phases of the struggle. Each experienced a prolonged period of imprisonment as a result of her union activities. The common theme that runs throughout their stories is their dedication to improving workers' lives.

All were single when they began their involvement in union activities, and all have now married and started families, but their personal lives have been shaped by their political activism. Each is married to a labor leader whom she met through labor organizations. And each combines loyalty to her husband and children with commitment to the workers' cause.

Family responsibilities prevent all of these women from participating actively in labor politics at present, pointing to a dilemma that confronts South Korean women who bear primary or sole responsibility for child care and other family-related work. Nevertheless, each continues to be involved in the movement through her husband, and each expects to return to more active personal involvement in labor politics when her children are older.

Chŏng-im: From a Worker to a Labor Hero

Chŏng-im transformed herself from a weak, frightened woman to a strong-willed union leader as she organized and led the union at the T. C. Electronics factory (see Chapter 4). She was a twenty-three-year-old assembly line worker in 1987 when the labor uprising erupted in the Zone. She believed that the workers at her factory should join the strike and became the union leader because no one else wanted the position. She knew little about labor organizing, but when she formed the union, members of the JOC contacted her and taught her how to organize it.

She led the fight to keep the factory open when Tandy announced its decision to close. During her struggle with Tandy, she became famous and was frequently interviewed by national and international news organizations.[16] Her struggle lasted for 450 days, and her arrest in December 1989 was reported in all the national newspapers.[17] She spent a year and a half in prison and was released in July 1991 when she was twenty-seven years old. When I met with her a month later, she talked about the day she was released:

> I felt like a hero on the day I was released from Wŏnju prison in Kangwŏn Province. About fifty workers had come from Masan to wait for me to come out, and they brought my mother with them. Normally, prisoners are released at around four or five o'clock in the morning; however, the singing and chanting from outside persuaded the authorities to let me leave earlier. I remember my mother crying and telling me that I must have done something right for this many people to come and greet me. I was warmly welcomed at my village too. Even village people who would normally consider imprisonment to be a disgrace told me that what I had done was courageous and they were proud of me. Everyone regarded me as some kind of hero, and that made me feel a heavy responsibility. I felt that I should continue to participate in the labor movement and lead other workers because that was what was expected of me.

She seemed confused by the changes that had taken place while she was in prison. She believed that students had gained too much influence over workers' organizations. There were many different organizations, unlike the situation in 1987, when there had been only one (JOC). Some even spoke favorably about Kim Il Sung's *Chuch'e Sasang* (Ideology of Sovereignty). She felt ignorant because she could not discuss the theories that had become important to both students and workers and were discussed in every meeting. She was not sure whether workers needed these elaborate theories, but it seemed that almost everyone was committed to them. She wanted to become reinvolved in workers' organizations, but she felt out of place in the new political climate.

She also needed to earn money to support herself and did not know how she would do this. Tandy's factory was closed, so she had no chance of returning to

---

16 I really got to know Chŏng-im after my first fieldwork was over, when she contacted me in New York in an effort to get publicity for her cause. I tried to get several U.S.-based labor organizations interested in the Tandy case but was always told that Tandy's offenses against its workers were relatively minor.

17 Chŏng-im was charged with organizing illegal demonstrations and obstructing the company's lawful activities.

her old job. The union was gone, and although the former members made small contributions of books and pocket money, they were in no position to support her or get her a new job. She was also blacklisted because of her role in the T. C. union. (By contrast, imprisoned male labor activists in heavy industry were frequently able to draw on the support of unions that were still powerful. They usually demanded, and sometimes got, reinstatement after their release.) Chŏng-im returned to her parents' house in the countryside. A few weeks later, her mother was hit by a motorcycle while walking, and Chŏng-im had to stay home to care for her while she recovered.

When her mother recovered, Chŏng-im returned to Masan, where she became involved in setting up the Masan–Ch'angwŏn Women Workers' Association. She also became engaged to and later married a worker at a small company in Ch'angwŏn.

> I was released from prison in July 1991. My husband and I started to live together in November that same year. A friend of mine introduced him to me while I was in prison. He came to visit me twice and sent me letters, so I felt that I knew him well when I got out. My parents had been worried that I might not be able to get married since I was labeled a Communist and spent eighteen months in prison. His parents wanted to have a third daughter-in-law. Our family backgrounds are similar. Both are families of farmers, and neither has money. Although he has been to college, he is the only *hak-ch'ul* in the Ma-Ch'ang area who is still a factory worker. All the others have left the factories. Some do unpaid work for political organizations. Some have gone back to school. But my husband is still at the factory. He can't do unpaid work for political organizations. He has a family to support. If he did not work, I would not be able to earn enough to support our family.

She worked for the Masan–Ch'angwŏn Women Workers' Association from its founding in February until June 1992, when she left to give birth to a daughter. She defended her right to have a family, pointing out that she was twenty-eight years old before she had her first child:

> I know that many people expected a lot from me when I was released. They were disappointed, especially the president of the Association, when I quit after only five months. But I was eight months pregnant. Some thought that I was irresponsible to get pregnant that fast, that I

149

should work for the organization longer. I thought about going back to the Association as a volunteer, but my daughter was too little for me to help at their day-care center. And then when she was just getting old enough, I got pregnant again. Now I really have to stay home because of my daughters. It will be at least two to three years before I can think of any outside work. I will continue to go to the meetings with T. C. friends, though. Frankly, I am not sure that I want to go back to work. (January 1994)

Chŏng-im had just given birth to her second daughter when I visited her in January 1994. She lived with her husband and two daughters (eighteen months old and newborn) in one room in a poor neighborhood in Masan. Her husband was an officer of the union at the small company in Ch'angwŏn where he worked. Her baby was only one week old.[18] The room was extremely small, but they were planning to live there as a family of four for another year. She was playing a recording of workers' songs to her baby when I arrived.[19] Even though she was temporarily cut off from labor activities, the culture of the movement still permeated her life.

Although she was not currently active in the labor movement, many radical workers still considered her a hero (*t'usa*). She was defensive about her temporary absence from the movement. She believed that the public expectations about her life were becoming too much to handle. She was also very much disillusioned about the labor movement and its organizers and condemned the people running it:

I am disappointed at a lot of people, so-called leaders of laborers. Look at the election at Chŏnnohyŏp. People are gossiping about each other who were once their comrades. I am not favoring one party over the other, but the president of Ma-Ch'ang Noryŏn [Yi Hŭng-sŏk (see below)] should be given credit for what he has contributed to workers in the Masan and Ch'angwŏn area. People say bad things about him and don't give him credit for what he has done. There are too many

18 She told other people to wait at least twenty-one days before visiting, but she let me visit her then because I had to return to America.
19 Workers' songs (*Nodongja ui norae*) are sung by workers and students during strikes and demonstrations. They often depict the suffering of factory workers and urge workers to unite to fight against dictatorship in order to achieve democracy in South Korea. Both worker-poets and students write these songs.

groups with too many different ideologies. I was shocked when I first got out of prison, and I still feel disgusted.

She was still proud of her role in the T. C. strike, and felt bad about the comparison people made between the T. C. workers' failure and the Sumida workers' success.

I feel very bad when people mention Sumida's successful case. We fought really hard and long, but people think that Sumida's union suc- ceeded because they got compensation money. We did not get any compensation; we refused to accept whatever they offered us. I won- der why people judge the success or failure of labor unions on the basis of whether compensation money is paid or not. I saw the presi- dent of the Sumida union on TV giving interviews discussing their success. It really hurt me to watch that and hear people talking about our failure at T. C. But I think we are closer and stronger. We still meet and make plans together. Sumida workers were paid over 10 million won ($12,000) a person, but they stopped doing any kind of public work after their success. (January 1994)

Chŏng-im still feels a commitment to improving workers' lives, although, now that she is married and has children, her family has become her chief concern. She still hopes to return to the labor movement, but she recognizes the difficulty involved in balancing obligations to family and the movement. She told me:

For women, marriage and children are the greatest barriers to their in- volvement in the movement. Marriage is a barrier, but a woman can still work after getting married. After having children, however, it be- comes almost impossible.

Chong-yŏp

At the end of 1987, one of the most well-organized unions in the Zone was at Chungch'ŏn, an electronics factory owned by a Japanese firm. The union president was Chong-yŏp, a twenty-six-year-old woman who had already worked in the Zone for nine years, five of them at Chungch'ŏn. Her long experience in the factory was an important reason why workers trusted her and followed her direction. She explained how she came to work in the Zone:

151

I started at a shoe factory. I chose to work for that company because they promised to send me to night school, but after eleven months they told me that they would not send anyone that year. So I moved to Sinhŭng, another shoe factory. Since I had only a middle school education, I could not even apply for a job at an electronics factory. Even at Sinhŭng, they wouldn't pay for me to go to the industrial night school, so finally I had to pay my own tuition. I worked for two and a half years at Sinhŭng and then moved to Chungch'ŏn electronics about five years ago. My plan was to learn as much as possible. I thought that education would solve my problems. I went to private institutes to learn this and that (including English conversation, flower design and telex operating) in the early morning before I went to work, and I went to high school at night. I went around and around like this, as if learning would solve all my problems. I tried four times to start a college correspondence course, but now I have given up since I realize that a college diploma does not mean much. A lot of union officers also took correspondence courses, but they all decided not to continue.

She was angry about how workers were treated, especially at Sinhŭng, and she resolved to do something to improve the situation. She recalled how she had to argue with the line leader every day just to attend her classes.

At Sinhŭng, about a third of the workers were students. The work at a shoe factory is hard, so the management lured young women with promises of education. But whenever they needed overtime work, they would not let students go to school. Workers had to cry, fight and run away to go to school. Seeing what was happening, I got angrier and angrier. These experiences taught me that we needed to organize to protect our rights.

Chong-yŏp was a model worker at Chungch'ŏn. She had an excellent attendance record and consistently topped the list of the most productive workers. She was among the few workers who were sent to Japan for special training, a privilege that was used as a reward for the best workers. Like many of the women who led the unions that sprang up during the labor uprising, she was the workers' representative at the joint labor–management council before becoming the union president. But she felt that management did not treat her with respect because she was a woman. She said:

152

I wished that I could have a sex change operation so that I could become a man. Managers only respect men. Their attitude toward me was "What does a woman know about anything?" They didn't treat me as a serious representative of the workers, but just as an irrational woman. I wonder if this attitude of looking down on women will ever change.

Following the July–August labor uprising, the union that Chong-yŏp led achieved a wage increase of over 20%, the greatest increase attained by any union in Masan. The union was well run and effective. Chong-yŏp was willing to accept advice from close friends at JOC, but she maintained that workers' problems should be solved by workers themselves rather than by student activists from outside.

If we continue to depend on outside people, we cannot achieve anything for ourselves. Even though we may make mistakes, because we do not know exactly what to do, we will learn eventually. When we are trying to solve our problems by ourselves, intellectuals should step aside.

In 1988 the union at Chungch'ŏn had 460 of the company's 670 workers as members. The union vigorously investigated the activities of the company and discovered that although workers were told that factory orders were declining, they were actually being transferred to subcontracting firms outside the Zone. Because the union assembled accurate information about the company's activities, it was able to present a strong and united front in its negotiations with management.

Chong-yŏp's participation in the labor movement went beyond organizing the union in her factory. In 1989 she also became the vice-president of the Alliance of Masan–Ch'angwŏn Workers' Unions (*Ma–Ch'ang Noryŏn*). She took over running the alliance when its president, Yi Hŭng-sŏk (whom she eventually married), was imprisoned. She led the Masan–Ch'angwŏn solidarity strike (*yŏndae p'aŏp*), was arrested for her role in it and was sent to prison in December 1989. Her arrest also marked the end of the union at Chungch'ŏn. The union's vice-president and co-organizer had already left the factory to become a Catholic nun, and with the two top officials gone, the company was able to undermine the union and get rid of it. Most of the core members were fired, and a few were arrested for union-related activities.

Chong-yŏp was in jail for two years. She wrote frequently to Yi Hŭng-sŏk during her imprisonment, and they decided to get married after her release. They were married in March 1992. He continued as president of the *Ma–Ch'ang Noryŏn* (and as a production worker at Takoma in Masan) while she began planning their future, especially their economic future. In late 1993, they and a friend (also a fired worker) opened a small home appliance shop in Ch'angwŏn. When I visited a few months later, the shop was not doing well. No customers entered it during the three hours I spent with her. It was open from 10:00 A.M. to 10:00 P.M. and had only two uncomfortable seats. Chongyŏp said that at first, sitting there alone for twelve hours a day with no one to talk to felt like being back in prison. She was pregnant at the time and said that sometimes her legs got so swollen that she could hardly walk. She told me:

> People would think this is an easy job, but it is really a hard one, especially for me. I would rather go around working for a labor organization than sit here. But one of us has to earn money if we would like to continue the kind of work we believe in.

Many of her friends and comrades in the labor movement reproached her for starting a business, but she defended her actions:

> My husband and I talked things over and decided that I should earn money while he works for the organization full time. We may be able to survive for a short while if both of us are in movement organizations without a steady income, but we cannot do it indefinitely. Who is going to support us both? Eventually, we would both be tired and defeated and would have to leave the movement. We decided against that. People who aren't willing to help us financially are very demanding. They want both of us to be involved, but who is going to buy us rice? When we opened this shop there was all kinds of talk around Masan. People said that since we were involved in a money-making business, we were not concerned about the movement. We did discuss opening this shop with Mr. Mun and Ms. Yi, but now they are accusing us of being selfish. They complained that we should have opened a cooperative with a workers' organization, and contributed half of the profits to the organization and movement people. We have our own plans too, you know. We thought that if our business does well, we could contribute a lot more to the organization. But people did not even give us the chance to show what we can do before they condemned us.

She was especially bitter about the recent election of the National Alliance of Trade Unions (*Chŏnnohyŏp*). Just two days before I talked to her, her husband had been defeated in a close vote for the presidency of the organization. He lost by just 25 votes (148 vs. 177). His supporters were an alliance of workers from various regions who objected to the hegemony of the Seoul organizers. They thought Yi Hŭng-sŏk could best represent the interests of workers throughout the country. The close election reflected wide support, considering the intense opposition he received from Seoul. Ironically, the winning candidate had also been backed by Mun Sŏng-hyŏn, a leading figure in the labor movement in Masan–Ch'angwŏn, whom they had regarded as a friend and political ally. Chong-yŏp was very disillusioned by labor politics and blamed Mun Sŏng-hyŏn and his wife, Yi Hye-ja, for engineering her husband's defeat:

> When I was released from the prison in 1991, I was very sick. At that time, Yi Hye-ja helped me a lot by bringing me to doctors and buying expensive medicine for me. I do appreciate her help. But during this election, I was really disappointed at her and her husband. I acknowledge their contribution to the labor movement in the Masan–Ch'angwŏn area, but they really behaved badly during this election. I understand that they did not want my husband to run for president because they had already decided to back another candidate. However, once my husband started to campaign, they spread all kinds of rumors about him, mostly lies. They even condemned us for having this shop, saying that we are just too selfish to represent workers. I am so disgusted with everything about this election. I have no illusions about those who call themselves movement people, both intellectuals and workers. I stayed out of the campaign because of the business, and so as not to give the impression that my husband was having his wife run his campaign. At first, I was even against his decision to run. But when he made up his mind, I said, "Why not?" I know that my husband is not the greatest orator or organizer, but he has potential.

I upset Chong-yŏp by joking about what people were saying: that she should be the one working for the movement and her husband should work to earn money for their livelihood. Many people told me that she was much more capable, bright, and well organized, as well as being a better orator than her husband. She responded:

155

People think that I am better than my husband, but that is not true. I may be a better speaker and more organized than he is, but he is much more capable than me of thinking broadly and deeply about our region's labor problems. People [in Seoul] just do not know him well enough. As you can see, I am pregnant now. After a baby is born, someone has to take care of the baby while we earn money. We don't have anyone in my family or his family who can take care of the baby for us. It seems best that I take care of the baby while I mind the shop.

All our plans to do things seem useless now because I am so disillusioned about the movement and the people who run it. I believe that *Ma–Ch'ang Noryŏn* will have to go through a difficult period to decide what to do. Even though my husband is still the president, the other staff members of the organization are all *Kyŏngnohyŏp* people [supporters of Mun Sŏng-hyŏn], and they were against him in the election. Now they have to face each other and decide what to do. They either have to kick my husband out or he has to replace the entire staff. I don't know what will happen, but it does not look good at this point.

Their shop also seemed to be failing. They were already planning to sell it and open a dry cleaning shop nearby. They just wanted to stay open until the New Year holiday, which they anticipated would be a peak season for selling appliances. She was worried about the debt that they had acquired when they opened the shop; they were having trouble paying the interest, let alone the principal. She explained the shop's problems to me:

> I think it is wise to cut one's losses early if the business does not look good. This kind of business very much depends on people having extra money because what we sell are not necessities, but luxuries women want only if they have extra money to spend.

I asked Chong-yŏp why she did not get involved in the Masan–Ch'angwŏn Women Workers' Association when Yi Kyong-suk had hoped to train her to take over the running of the organization. She said:

> I know Ms. Yi wanted me to get involved in *Yŏsŏng Nodongjahoe*. I do believe that *Yŏsŏng Nodongjahoe* is important in Masan area because of women workers. But I just was not ready when I was first released, and then my husband and I decided that I would run the shop.

156

What could I do? I could not just push away all the things and become involved in *Yŏnohoe* just because they wanted me to. Again, who is going to support me and my husband? If I became the president of the Association, I would not have any income. Also, I feel more attached to *Ma–Ch'ang Noryŏn* because that was my organization before I went to prison.

A few months later, I heard that Yi Hŭng-sŏk had been ousted from the presidency of the *Ma–Ch'ang Noryŏn*. He and Chong-yŏp had sold their appliance shop and bought a dry cleaning shop. With a child to take care of and a shop to run, it seems unlikely that Chong-yŏp will be able to get back to labor organizing soon.

Ŭn-sun

When I first met Ŭn-sun at a small group discussion at the Catholic Women's Center in June 1987, she was twenty-one years old. She was a fighter; her expression was intense, and she was ready to argue at any time. People joked that she was a gangster (*kkangpae*). She was a garment worker at Soyo Enterprise, and her militant personality made her the logical choice for union president when the first union was organized later that year. It was only after I had gotten to know her fairly well that she was willing to sit down with me and tell me her life story. As was often the case with workers in garment factories, she had experienced considerable hardship and poverty growing up:

After I graduated from middle school I went to Pusan, where I lived with my aunt for two years. While I was there, I took courses from a correspondence high school, and I also learned how to operate a sewing machine. [Ŭn-sun's aunt did subcontracting for a small garment factory.] I worked for my aunt, who did not pay me anything [beyond room and board], although it was understood that she would take care of my wedding expenses in the future. After two years, I moved to Taegu in order to earn wages because my aunt's business was not doing well. I only completed half of my high school course. The place where I worked in Taegu was a small factory in an apartment. There were about 100 workers, ranging in age from twelve-year-old girls to sixty-year-old grandmothers. They did not care whom they hired. Every day I had to work until ten o'clock at night. If we worked the overnight shift on Saturday, then we got Sunday off; if not, we had to work on Sunday too. There was not even one regular day off. We did not receive any overtime wage or any other kinds of allowances at all. On our monthly pay check, there was only one amount (about 100,000 won). I was too ignorant to know anything at that time. Furthermore, we were assigned quotas, and if we did not complete them we had to stay to finish it without getting paid. I worked there for eight months until I could not stand it anymore and ran away. While I was working there, I always sent half of my 100,000-won wage to my parents.

Ŭn-sun rejoined her parents when they moved to Masan in January 1984 and went to work at Soyo Enterprise. She passed a sewing machine test and was given credit for two years' experience. Her daily wage was set at 2,800 won. In 1987 she earned 4,900 won a day, making 160,000 won per month. Out of this, she contributed 100,000 won to her mother to help her family. Her bitterness about her family's poverty led her to get involved in the labor movement. She explained:

I am the oldest of four children (one boy and three girls). My parents worked as tenant farmers, and they were so poor that they decided to move to Masan, where they thought they would be able to get jobs. Now my father works as a day laborer, and my mother works as a cleaning woman at a hospital. Even though four members of my family (father, mother, myself and my younger sister) work hard, we are still poor. Not being able to get out of poverty made me think that something was wrong. With four of us working, we should not be so poor, but still we are. I did not know about how to fight for our rights until I started to go to JOC meetings. I learned that workers have the right to receive enough wages to support themselves, and that we should be united to organize a union to fight against the management. This is how I started to get involved in fighting against the management of the company where I am working.

At Soyo she met Chŏng-ja, who was then president of JOC. Ŭn-sun looked like someone who could fight for the cause, so Chŏng-ja recruited her. Joining JOC transformed her from an angry but ignorant worker to a well-informed leader who was knowledgeable about labor law and other areas.

Her factory was notorious for its difficult work. She complained about how managers forced higher levels of production out of workers.

They put an extra worker at the start of the twenty-worker line. The number of parts increases, and the rest of us have to finish whatever comes down to us. If we do not keep up with that, the manager yells at us. This way, the normal production quota of 200 pairs of pants per person goes up to 240, 280 and they even push us to produce up to 350 a day.

Ŭn-sun frequently argued with her manager, who abused workers verbally and sometimes even physically (he threw scissors at workers on several occasions). Because she was the only one who spoke up, she was chosen as the representative of workers on the joint labor–management council. The council, which consisted of two managers and one worker representative, was supposed to meet once a month, but she had to ask several times to hold the meeting. She tried to bring up issues at the meetings, but the council was not like a union because management controlled it. She felt a strong need for a union in order to achieve better wages and working conditions.

Soyo was one of the rare places where there was no overtime work. According to Ŭn-sun, the reason they did not have overtime work was that the quota system set up by management was so hard to meet that no one could survive additional work. About half of the workers were married women who did not want to do overtime and worked extraordinarily hard to finish the quota. Managers were pleased to be able to achieve high production levels without having to pay overtime. She felt sorry for the married women who worked at Soyo, but she also found them difficult to reach:

> More than half of the sewing machine operators in our factory are married women, and that is why it is so hard to organize. These older women are afraid of losing their jobs because their families cannot survive without their wages. Most of them live in housing units for which they have to pay either a monthly rent or a long-term deposit rent; hardly any own the place where they live. Many women tell me that they never expected to work in a factory again after they were married. However, even though they are married, they clearly need money, and since they know how to operate sewing machines, they come back to work.

Ŭn-sun became president of the union at Soyo in 1987 (see Chapter 4) and proved to be an effective leader. The labor uprising coincided with a particularly difficult time in her life when her mother was hospitalized with a terminal illness. Ŭn-sun would often visit the hospital after work, sometimes bringing her coworkers and me with her. When her mother died that September, Ŭn-sun took the body back to Ch'ungch'ŏng Province for burial.

After her mother's death, her father expected her to take over running the household. He objected to her staying out late after work and was very much against her involvement in labor activities. He demanded that she quit her position at the union so that she could take care of her younger siblings. He sometimes hit her during their heated arguments, but he was unable to persuade her to abandon the union. Even though she felt guilty that she could not do more for her sisters and her brother, she believed her work for the union was too important to give up.

Ŭn-sun continued to lead the union until the end of 1989, when she was arrested during a strike and imprisoned. The union was broken up, and she spent a year in prison. Before her arrest, she had become engaged to a labor activist who worked in Ch'angwŏn. Her fiancé was a disguised worker who had graduated from college (*hak-ch'ul*). Because Ŭn-sun had only completed middle school, the difference in their backgrounds was the subject of considerable comment, and people said he had become involved with her out of pity. He was also arrested and spent more than a year in jail. She was released while her fiancé was still in jail and took up his responsibilities at the Masan–Ch'angwŏn Coalition of Labor Unions (*Ma–Ch'ang Noryŏn*), where he had been in charge of organizing workers. Most people considered her effective, although some believed she was too dictatorial and too rough. Many believed that the job required roughness.

She married her fiancé after his release and continued to work full time at the Masan–Ch'angwŏn Coalition of Labor Unions until their daughter was born in 1991. While she was pregnant with her first child, she told me, "If I see my husband twice a week, I am lucky. He is always going around the area trying to organize and help people. How can I complain about that? I am glad that I am married to him and can continue to work in the organization."

She left her work at the coalition after her daughter was born and found that she needed to devote her time to family responsibilities. She gave birth to a second daughter in 1993 and remained at home to care for her children. Her husband completed his term as general secretary (*ch'ongmu*) of his union in Ch'angwŏn and became a manager for his company. Although labor activists with college degrees were not uncommon, it was highly unusual for a former union officer to join management; I do not know of any other cases. One labor activist who knew the couple commented cynically that he was able to become a manager because he was very careful not to get involved in the union movement too deeply.

I visited Ŭn-sun in January 1994 at the small apartment where she lived with her husband and two daughters (three years old and six months old). The apartment was small (two bedrooms) and not very expensive (about $40,000), but they owned it, although they had had to borrow about half the money needed for its purchase. Ŭn-sun was as energetic as in the past, but in spite of being more financially secure than ever before, she still worried about her large debt. She said, "That is one reason why I cannot be involved in any kind of organization. I cannot afford to pay to leave my daughters at day care to do volunteer work." She also believed that being a mother took precedence over the role of labor organizer:

> I was an organizer even after I got married (I don't think the marriage per se is the problem), but being a mother was completely different. My husband can take care of himself when I am not around, but my daughters need me to feed them and play with them. Although I am not active in any organization, I still see my friends from Soyo. Our monthly meetings are mostly social occasions, though. We talk about our children and husbands, not labor issues. I will come back to work for workers when my children are a little older. People criticize me for not getting involved in the Women Workers' Association, but I cannot do it now when my daughters are so young.

I doubt that Ŭn-sun's involvement in labor activism has ended, but her current situation makes her earlier comments on marriage seem ironic. In 1988 she told me:

> Too many women workers get married for economic reasons (to be supported by their husbands). I wish they could change their way of thinking and become independent human beings. It seems to me that we learn from our family and our patriarchal social structure that we should be subordinate to men. If women get united, we can destroy that kind of ideology, but women give up and subordinate themselves to men. For women workers, marriage seems an easy way out from our low-class, miserable life, but when we see so many married women come back to work, we should realize that marriage is not the answer either. That is why we should unite to fight for better working conditions and better wages and to protect our rights as workers.

161

Class Struggle or Family Struggle?

Ordinary Workers in the Struggle

Chŏng-hui, I-suk and Yŏng-hui were ordinary workers who never became activists. Although each took part in union-related activity during the 1987 labor uprising, politics did not have much appeal for them.[20] In 1987 they joined the unions along with everyone else, but they left when things got difficult. Like most workers, they were happy to go home early during strikes and glad to receive a wage increase, but planning their own lives took precedence over labor politics.

Like most of the young women in MAFEZ, these three women wanted to spend their free time while they were single meeting men, going on dates and planning for their marriages. Rather than having the ambitious social agenda of the activists, their goals were personal and relatively modest, and each has succeeded in those terms. Since 1988, each of them has married a production worker, settled down and started a family. None of them has returned to factory work after marriage, nor are they likely to in the foreseeable future.

My recent meetings with two of them contrasted strongly with my meetings with their activist contemporaries. They spoke of unions and strikes as things from the distant past, events that they had witnessed without altering the course of their lives. For the present, they focused entirely on their families and, in spite of continuing friendships with activists, had no expectations of ever becoming involved in labor politics again.

Chŏng-hui

Chŏng-hui was one of my roommates in 1987. She was from South Chŏlla Province and had a strong regional accent. She was tall and big and had long, straight hair. She was always smiling and had a warm personality. She was the second daughter among four children. Her mother ran a small candy store in Sunchŏn, and her father worked as a day laborer. Her older sister was a good student and was sent to high school, but Chŏng-hui did not do well in school, so her parents did not think it worthwhile to send her to high school. She came to

20 Although Chŏng-hui and I-suk were not especially interested in political causes, they became friends with Sun-hui, the JOC activist. Because of this friendship, both of them were somewhat more involved in union activity than they would have otherwise been. Neither woman, however, became an activist herself, and although both were JOC members, they seemed in all other ways to be typical workers. Our shared friendship with Sun-hui has made it easier for me to stay in touch with them than with other workers whom I knew in 1987–1988.

Masan expecting to be able to continue her education while earning a living. Her junior high school was linked to several factories in Masan and Pusan, and taught students who did not plan to go on to high school sewing in their last year. Through these connections, she came to work at a shoe factory in the Zone.

Her job enabled her to be independent of her family, and she even sent money home when she received a bonus, although she said that the amount she sent (8,000–16,000 won a month) did not make much difference to them. She and her parents agreed that it was now her responsibility to take care of herself and save for her dowry. She said she did not mind the hard work at the shoe factory:

> Even though the work was hard, I did not have anywhere else to compare it with. Since they sent us to high school, we felt that we should obey the managers if we wanted to finish school. Sometimes we even went back to work after school finished at 10:30 P.M. and worked all night. Of course, I did not know anything about the workers' rights then.

After a year and a half, Chŏng-hui's sister asked her to come to live with her in Seoul. She quit her job in Masan and moved to Seoul, but she hated it there and came back after a week. When she returned she was allowed to continue with school, even though she was not given back her job. Usually, a woman who quit her job was automatically dismissed from school because the factory was sponsoring her. The year 1985 was very slow and she could not get another job in the Zone, so she had to go to work at a subcontracting electronics company at lower wages than the factories in the Zone were paying.

When she learned that a new shoe factory had opened in the Zone, she immediately applied and got a job there. She did not tell them that she was a student because it was summer vacation. When school started again, her manager told her that she had to choose either school or work. She chose to go to school and was willing to quit, but another manager intervened and allowed her to keep her job, saying that students work harder than other workers.

During her last year in high school, she changed jobs again. This time she went to an electronics factory. The electronics factory observed more holidays, and the managers treated workers better there. Students even received dinner at the factory before they went to school. Nevertheless, Chŏng-hui did not like the conveyor line work.

At the shoe factory, we could go to the bathroom whenever we wanted to and nobody said anything to us. In the electronics factory, I could not even go to the bathroom and could not move around at all. Furthermore, I could not get along with my coworkers, which made things a lot harder. I could not stand working at the electronics factory. Even if the work was hard at the shoe factory, I liked it there better.

She quit her job at the electronics factory and returned to the shoe factory, where she stayed until it went out of business in May 1987. Sun-hui, a *hak-ch'ul*, was working in her line and sparked her interest in workers' rights. Through Sun-hui she became involved with JOC. She was very impressed by Sun-hui's dedication and knowledge. She told me how she got to know her:

At the shoe factory I met Sun-hui, who later became my roommate. When I first met her, she was trying to organize our line and telling everyone not to sign an agreement to return to work right after the *Ch'usŏk* holiday. Workers often do not come back right after the holiday, so management was worried. Sun-hui told us that they did not have any right to force us to sign anything. I was amazed at how she could persuade the other workers. She was so small and so fragile, but she had lots and lots of energy. Later, when we were roommates, she taught me about labor unions and workers' rights. Sometimes it was boring, but going to JOC and meeting other workers was fun. I want to be like Sun-hui someday, and I have to study hard in order to become like her.

When her shoe factory went bankrupt, Chŏng-hui found a job at Soyo. She became an officer of Soyo's union in 1988 and was fired for her union activities at the end of 1989. For a while after she was dismissed, she went to her factory every day to demand reinstatement, but she did not return to factory work after that.

In 1990 she married a man who worked at Samsong Heavy Industry at Ch'angwŏn and was also a JOC member. After her marriage, she worked as an aide at a day-care center and then as a sales clerk at a department store (see Chapter 3). She experienced more personal tragedy when her first child was born severely deformed and then died in infancy.[21] In 1993 she gave birth to a

---

21 I wondered whether the deformity of Chŏng-hui's baby was related to exposure to chemicals at the factories where she worked, but she never mentioned any such suspicions to me.

healthy son, and things seemed to be going well for her. Her husband was a union member, but not an activist, and his job gave the family financial security. They expected to move into a comfortable apartment in a few months, and Chŏng-hui planned to be a full-time wife and mother.

I-suk

I-suk, another of my roommates in 1987, was eighteen years old and worked at a garment factory. She was a short, stocky young woman who wore glasses. She had been working since she was only eight years old. When she was very young, her family lived comfortably in a rural area. Then her father brought another woman to her house. Her mother left home, abandoning her three children, and her father married the other woman. The three children were mistreated by their stepmother, and the family disintegrated. Her older sister ran away, and I-suk was sent to Pusan to work as a maid for a distant relative. I-suk worked as a maid for various relatives in Pusan and Seoul until she was fifteen years old. Her wages were sent to her stepmother, who told her that she was saving it for her dowry. The only education she received was two years of primary school in Pusan, and she was barely able to add or subtract.

When I-suk was fifteen years old, she wrote to her older sister, who was living in Masan. Her sister invited her to come to live with her. She moved to Masan and found a job at a subcontracting firm outside the Zone that produced gloves. She could not get a job in the Zone because of her lack of education and her age.

She did well at the factory and quickly learned how to use the sewing machine, but she found out that she was being cheated out of her pay because her bosses learned that she was unable to calculate the amount owed to her. She left her first job and went to several other subcontracting factories outside the Zone. Eventually she got a job at the shoe factory where Chŏng-hui was working. She ended up sharing a room with Chŏng-hui and Sun-hui (and eventually me), and when the factory closed, she went with Chŏng-hui to Soyo.

Her friends at the factory persuaded her to attend meetings at JOC and to enroll in night classes to complete her primary education. She earned her primary school diploma and even took some middle school night classes, but eventually she gave up. She justified her decision as follows:

> I don't do well in classes. Maybe it's because I am too old for this. I
> don't want to study anymore. I would like to go out at night some-
> times, but I cannot do that if I go to night classes. I know I'm dumb.

165

> Even if I study I don't do well, so I don't want to go to school. I
> would like to date at night, but my roommates are very strict about
> me going to school. They get mad if I don't go to school. I don't
> know much about labor, unions or demonstrations, and I don't want to
> be involved in that either. But the only people I know are JOC mem-
> bers. I enjoy going to the JOC center and talking to male friends.
> They like me to cook and clean for them, but I get bored whenever
> they start to discuss demonstrations. Of course, I do participate in
> demonstrations and I like shouting, and singing . . . but I really don't
> understand why we have to do this. I would rather go to a movie with
> someone I like or go to a cafe and have a nice dinner.

I-suk spent a lot of the money she earned on clothing and dating expenses. She
also bought furniture and appliances. I felt that she spent her money com-
pulsively after payday, but she argued that the things she bought would be part
of her dowry and thought of them as a kind of savings.

Although she was close to Chŏng-hui, I-suk resented Sun-hui's supervision
and constantly complained about her intervention in her life. She wanted to
move out and eventually did in 1989. I-suk's involvement in JOC was limited
to using their building as a meeting place for her and her male friends. She
joined the organization and the union at her factory but had little interest in the
labor cause.

She quit her job at Soyo in 1989 to become an apprentice hairdresser. Her
goal was to train as a beautician and eventually to have her own beauty shop.
When I saw her in 1991, she was dramatically transformed. She had had plastic
surgery to make her eyes round and larger. She had also lost a lot of weight and
looked very fashionable. But I also heard rumors that she had begun to smoke
and drink heavily. For a time, she had been living with a boyfriend, but their
relationship had recently ended. She told me that she had just taken the written
test for a beautician's license for the third time and finally passed, but this was
untrue. I felt very worried about her future.

She had turned her life around before I saw her again three years later. She
had married a worker at Daewoo Car Company in 1992. In 1994 she was living
in an apartment in Ch'angwŏn with her husband and their infant son. She had
given up trying to become a beautician after failing the written test six times.
She confessed:

> I must be very dumb to fail the written test six times. Everyone else
> passes the written test easily and fails on the practical component, but

166

not me. I pass that part easily, but I cannot pass the written part. I have to give up my plan to become a beautician.

She seemed settled, happy and financially secure. Her husband earned enough money so that she did not have to work, and she no longer worried about opening a beauty shop. She was proud of her accomplishments and was fully occupied as a housewife.

Yŏng-hui

In 1987, Yŏng-hui was a twenty-two-year-old worker at T. C. Electronics. She was also a member of JOC, and through her contact with the organization, she was exposed to ideas about labor organizing and began to be concerned about the exploitation of workers by multinational corporations in MAFEZ. She began working for T. C. in 1986 and became a member when Chŏng-im first organized the union in August 1987. Although she was not a leader, the participation of women like her was essential for organizing the union. But like many workers, her commitment to the union was not strong enough to withstand the pressure placed on her. When management demanded that she withdraw from the union, she meekly obeyed. She explained to me in November 1987 how the managers intimidated her into withdrawing from the union:

My line supervisor called me into his office and told me to sign a withdrawal form. He knew about my JOC membership and in a loud voice asked me why I wanted to become a Communist. He also told me that our wages would be raised and overtime work reduced. And finally, he threatened that I would be fired if I did not withdraw from the union. I did not want to get fired, so I signed the form.

In May 1988, when the T. C. union was organized again, Yŏng-hui again became a founding member. She learned a lot about working conditions in other factories and her own by participating in small group meetings at JOC and talking to other workers. She thought that she was ready to fight against the company. She remained a union member throughout their struggle against the plant closing, but she was not one of the core members who went up to Seoul to occupy the T. C. research institute. After the union disbanded, she moved back to her native city, Taejŏn, and got married.

167

Working-Class Motherhood

With the experience of marriage and motherhood, the lives of activists and ordinary workers have begun to converge. As single women, the activists' personal lives had been overwhelmed by political events. The importance of the labor struggle and their commitment to it emerge dramatically in their accounts of strikes, confrontations and imprisonment. But despite these traumatic experiences, they emerged from their twenties with much in common with their less politically committed counterparts. Their marriages had been delayed a year or two by imprisonment and politics had shaped their choice of husbands, but nevertheless, they had gotten married and started families, the alternative being almost unthinkable.

For all of these women, motherhood represented a personal achievement and a source of fulfillment. It was what their upbringing led them to expect of a proper adult woman, and it was a role that contained enough status and responsibility to be personally satisfying. Motherhood is culturally expected and internalized as a core value by most South Korean women, regardless of social class. For women like Chŏng-hui, I-suk and Yŏng-hui, leaving factory work to marry a successful blue-collar worker represented the successful completion of a strategy for personal development, and they seemed satisfied with exchanging their domestic work for financial security within a patriarchal family structure. They had not eliminated struggle from their lives, because managing a family on a single working-class wage was no easy task, but for the time being they were content with their lot.

The former activists were no less committed to motherhood, but they were also acutely aware of what the role forced them to give up. Motherhood required them to narrow their focus to their own small family and, at least temporarily, to devote themselves to working for the interests of their children instead of those of the working class. This drastic reduction in the scale of their lives was accompanied by a sense of guilt at having abandoned the cause for which they had already given so much.

Despite the way gender inequality permeated the exploitation of MAFEZ factory workers, gender equality was not a central issue in the labor struggle of the 1980s. The labor activists were not especially attuned to gender issues, and within their new families they fit themselves into conventional roles. Motherhood required total devotion to their children's welfare, and in embracing the values of motherhood, they no longer had time to organize workers. Although they felt some guilt at their retreat from activism, Chŏng-im, Chong-yŏp and

Ŭn-sun did not believe that they had made the wrong decision. They believed that they had a right to their families and to lead a full life. This attitude came through clearly when they compared themselves to Yi Kyŏng-suk, who had foregone marriage and family to be a lifelong activist. They admired her commitment, but they also pitied her lack of a family.

Although there was a place in the labor movement for a few lifelong female activists like Ms. Yi, it was as outside organizers fulfilling a charitable role. Chŏng-im, Chong-yŏp and Ŭn-sun had been ordinary workers who organized women of about the same age and whose background they shared. Not only were they now older than most MAFEZ workers, they were no longer workers. Their role as insiders organizing their coworkers was no longer open to them. Chŏng-im, Chong-yŏp and Ŭn-sun still tried to be part of the movement for workers' rights, but they could do so only indirectly as the wives of activists. They were hindered from direct participation not only by their involvement in their families, but also by the gendered structure of the labor market in South Korea.

6

Conclusion

THE period covered by my study of workers in Masan (1987 to 1994) was
one of enormous importance to South Korea. Rapid economic growth was
sustained, but the military dictatorship, with its antilabor policies, came to an
end. The dominance of heavy and advanced-technology industries increased,
while those light industries that employed women as production workers continued their relative decline. For women workers these changes have had
complex and sometimes contradictory effects. The urban working class has
continued to increase in number and has been able to engage in more open
political activity. The end of military rule, however, fragmented opposition
political forces and took away the sense of urgency that had driven middle-
class college students into such activities as labor organizing. Furthermore,
women workers have experienced a diminishing role within the working class
as their jobs as production workers have decreased in number and become less
important to the national economy. The female workforce in Masan is now
only half of its size in 1987, although it is significantly better paid.

Nevertheless, much of what I found in Masan in 1987 remains unchanged.
Factories are still the main employers, and young women still line up every
morning outside the gates of the Zone. Women's jobs are still relatively low
paid, with few prospects for advancement, and their work careers are still
expected to be short, although more women are staying at work after marriage.
Inflation has absorbed much of the wage increase and intensified saving for
dowries has absorbed much of the rest, so factory workers still live poorly.

The decreasing number of factory jobs has limited employment prospects
for the young women of the region, but it is difficult to tell how much hardship
this has caused. Certainly, some women lost jobs that they had expected to
keep for several years more, and others even lost back pay when companies
suddenly closed their doors and pulled out of South Korea. On the other hand,
much of the decrease in the number of jobs occurred gradually through attrition
because women generally planned to leave factory jobs after a few years. Most

170

of the women currently working in Masan factories were school girls in 1986, and most of those working in 1986 are no longer part of the factory labor force. Thus, the women most affected are those who might have become factory workers but have not.

In this study, I have tried not only to show how women factory workers' lives are constrained by age, gender and class, but also to present their energetic and creative responses to an inherently exploitive situation. I found that although women experienced factory work as a hardship, their responses included a mix of resistance aimed at achieving concrete improvements in their lives and accommodation aimed at using the harsh experience of factory work as a foundation for a better future. In this Conclusion, I examine the three themes that emerged as important throughout my study of women factory workers in South Korea: first, how considerations of age and gender dominated all aspects of the lives of factory workers in MAFEZ; second, how these women engaged in various forms of resistance to the powerful social forces that shaped their lives; and third, how women factory workers fit into the class dynamics of the evolving political climate of South Korea in the 1990s.

AGE, GENDER AND FACTORY WORK

Nearly all production workers in MAFEZ were young single women, and this status dominated their lives and their ideas about themselves. Young women and other members of society hold strong cultural expectations about what behavior and attitudes are appropriate to their age and gender status.

South Korea's rapid industrial transformation created new public roles for women and directly involved them in national political struggles. In its initial phase, the cheap productive labor of women factory workers underwrote much of South Korea's export-led development program. In labeling women factory workers "industrial soldiers" (*sanŏp chŏnsa*), the government supplanted the traditional image of young women as vulnerable, fragile and feminine with a very nontraditional association of women with combat, military discipline and casualties. Importantly, this new image did not overturn women's subordinate place in the social hierarchy; rather, it implied that other members of society must be willing to sacrifice because even its least important members were doing so much. Although the government was perhaps engaged in the most cynical and conscious manipulation of gender images, other social forces have also found symbolic significance in young women factory workers. Labor activists drew attention to the plight of these workers by representing them as fragile and vulnerable. And women workers also made use of culturally salient images of feminine vulnerability even as they pursued militant demands in their collective actions.

When young women took factory jobs, they acquired an unprecedented public role outside the household, but the low status and meager wages attached to these jobs were wholly in accordance with the low status with which young women were conventionally regarded. Within traditional Korean society, family was the focus of women's lives, and nearly all women's work was performed within its confines. Family continues to be central to the lives of even those women who do work in factories, many of whom regard themselves as temporary workers and expect to leave the paid labor force in order to become full-time housewives. Women and their employers accorded little importance to women's factory careers, and tended to regard factory work as a transitional phase before a woman took up her primary adult role as a wife and mother.

Nevertheless, the creation of thousands of new factory jobs for women altered the meaning and experience of femininity for South Korean women. Although factories that employed women made use of some aspects of traditional femininity, they undercut others. Factory work itself was very different from the traditional activities of young women, as is clear from the "industrial soldiers" label applied to them. Even work done exclusively by women was physically demanding and unfeminine. Among the roughest and thus least feminine jobs, ironically, were those in the textile and apparel industries, which have the greatest continuity with women's traditional roles in craft production. Not only did workers perform hard physical labor, but they were physically removed from the domestic settings that defined their traditional roles. The long hours of work also precluded much involvement in domestic activities. The main feature connecting the lives of factory workers with traditional expectations for young women was social and economic marginalization. The ranks of the "industrial soldiers" were not meant to include generals.

Workers often found this adjustment to factory work difficult. In a "worker's autobiography," Chang Nam-su comments:

> People say that women's voices should not go over the wall; women
> should be modest, talk in a cultured manner, and behave gently. . . .
> Then what are we? If we measure ourselves in those terms, we are
> nothing. We have to be loud in order to communicate on the shop
> floor; we have to wear uniforms and rush between the machines; natu-
> rally our movements are coarse. If the only price we get paid for our

endless working for our country's industrial development and economic growth is the contemptuous name of *"kongsuni,"* and the deprivation of our "femininity," then, what are we? For whom are we working, and for what are we living? (1984:42–43)

Although women workers perceived that their work in the factories took away their femininity, their experience in the workplace was nevertheless comprehensively genderized. Work discipline was enforced through conventional expectations about gender, which left managerial and supervisory positions reserved for men. Because this subordination of women within the workplace derived from the traditional hierarchical relationship between the genders that permeated society outside the workplace, it seemed natural or common sense (cf. Ong 1987) and was difficult for workers to challenge.

Young single women workers' lives outside the workplace were also dominated by considerations of their age and gender status, and much of their scarce free time and energy was absorbed in preparation for marriage. During the period spent working at factories, young women met and chose potential husbands, arranged weddings, and planned careers as housewives and mothers. They also deferred consumption of their already low wages by saving for dowry and wedding expenses, underwriting their future marriages and relationships with in-laws. Decisions about marriage were fraught with consequences for the future because marriage was the most important event in determining a woman's lifetime status. A woman's best chance for economic security was to marry a man with a well-paid job, so the attention devoted to making the right marriage was warranted on economic grounds alone. Furthermore, because divorce and remarriage were strongly stigmatized, there were few second chances.

If single women were made complacent by their expectation of leaving factory work, those married women who remained in the factory workforce bore a heavy burden of shame for their failure to meet that expectation. Nearly everyone agreed that wives and mothers should not work in factories, and those women who did generally had some specific individual need that made it necessary. The desperation of married women factory workers enabled factories to pay them extra-low wages, for which they were both pitied and despised by other workers. Married women workers were those whose expectations had failed them, and the demands of their families and workplace allowed them very little room to maneuver.[1]

---

1 A recent opinion survey about women's participation in the labor force suggests that attitudes are changing about whether married women should be able to hold jobs (Choe, Kong and Mason

Expectations based on age and gender also shaped the behavior of the women who became labor leaders in MAFEZ. Assertiveness was considered masculine, and so, like other young women, they were expected to adopt a modest, nonconfrontational demeanor in dealing with social superiors. Nevertheless, as we have seen, many young women managed to be assertive and confrontational in the pursuit of the workers' cause. Both Ŭn-sun and Chong-yŏp were examples of women who were said to be, and who said of themselves, that they were like men. Ŭn-sun was frequently described as being rough and gangsterlike, and Chong-yŏp even said she wanted to have a sex change in order to be taken seriously. In spite of their unfeminine aura, however, outside of politics, these women's lives followed conventional scripts, as they both married men they met as workers and started families. Thus, these iconoclastic young women became wives and mothers, burdened with conventional problems of family responsibilities. A few years after leading their unions in confrontational struggles, both women were feeling tension between their new obligations to their families and their continuing dedication to the workers' cause.

The total commitment required of a labor activist was impossible to combine with family life, and there were notable examples of women activists who had forgone the roles of wife and mother because of their dedication to the workers' cause. The Reverend Cho Wha Soon describes how her work occupied her so fully that she was not able to consider marriage (1988:130ff.). Among the leaders I knew in Masan, Yi Kyŏng-suk had a similar total commitment to organizing workers that precluded having a family of her own.[2]

FORMS OF RESISTANCE

Although low pay and unpleasant or even dangerous working conditions ensured a certain level of discontent in the factories of MAFEZ, it was difficult for women workers to organize effective resistance. Most women workers were young and inexperienced, and all had been brought up to accept low status as appropriate to their age and gender. Because most women left their

---

1994). The authors, however, note a discrepancy between their survey, which suggests that most married women (57%) approve of participation in the labor force by married women, and "the actual pattern of female labor force participation, which depends on marital status and the presence of children" (292). I suggest that this discrepancy may exist because women hold themselves to higher standards than they permit in others.

2 The inability of female labor activists to have their own families is without parallel among male activists, even the most self-sacrificing of whom generally manage to marry and have families.

Conclusion

factory jobs when they married, there was little continuity in the workforce at individual factories, and the small to medium-sized firms where they worked were isolated from one another.

In the first fifteen years that MAFEZ was in operation, workers showed their unhappiness largely through unorganized actions such as work slowdowns, small-scale sabotage and the occasional wildcat strike. These actions were responses to specific irritations or complaints and had no lasting impact. No unions or other workers' organizations were formed. Furthermore, regimented factories overseen by sophisticated surveillance techniques made "everyday resistance" (James Scott 1985) difficult, and the authoritarian government aided companies in their efforts to remove troublemakers and keep workers quiescent. Resistance was thus dangerous and uncertain for workers, and a wide array of pressures were used to encourage accommodation.

Overt Resistance

The 1987 labor uprising presented a dramatic opening in this coercive political structure. Suddenly, the women workers of Masan found new allies as part of the national movement for democracy and workers' rights. The result was a burst of political participation.[3] Grievances that had been left unexpressed were given new legitimacy as part of a mass movement. In spite of all the factors discouraging women factory workers from adopting radical positions, many did. The low pay and poor working conditions of factories in MAFEZ aroused a widespread sense of injustice, and a radical leadership developed within the ranks of factory workers.

Although street demonstrations in August and September attracted nearly universal support, the workers of Masan did not sustain this high level of activism. Several factors contributed to the decline of the newly formed unions. Factory owners remained unrelentingly opposed to unions and pressured workers to withdraw their support. For many workers it still seemed inevitable that young women would remain in low-paid, low-status jobs, sub-

---

3 The rebellion of young women, exploited and isolated on the global assembly line, has resulted in similar organized protests in free export zones around the world. These include demonstrations by Jamaican garment and textile workers' (Bolles 1983); demonstrations against the Marcos regime by Philippina textile workers (Enloe 1983); strikes by workers in Barbados and Trinidad (Caribbean Association for Feminist Research and Action *Newsletter* 1988); and strikes in the Mexican *maquiladoras* (Gray 1987). Other, more ambiguous, forms of resistance have also occurred, notably large-scale spirit possession in Malaysian electronics assembly plants (Ong 1987).

ordinate to men. The relatively high prestige of some of the factory jobs in MAFEZ compared to other possibilities also strengthened conservative tendencies among workers (cf. Kim Chang-ki 1991). Electronics workers in the Zone were indoctrinated to see themselves as part of the corporate family, and because this position enhanced their status, many accepted this ascription. Companies defused some of workers' anger by more than doubling wages between 1987 and 1991. Although much of this gain was erased by inflation, real wages for women workers increased by 52% during this period (Korean Women's Development Institute 1994:234).

Actual or threatened factory closings also frightened workers away from union activism. Between 1987 and 1991, the number of factory jobs in MAFEZ declined by almost 50%. Although workers in Masan achieved higher wages and better working conditions, they were unable to stop multinational corporations from leaving South Korea to attain cheaper, unorganized labor. The departure of companies like Tandy and Sumida points to structural problems inherent in export processing zones that unions have been unable to address.

Up to the end of Roh Tae Woo's presidency, political repression continued against workers' organizations in MAFEZ. Union leaders were systematically fired, arrested and imprisoned. The government's removal of union leaders increased the importance of outside organizers and radical ideologies. As the dominant ideology of the organizers in Masan shifted from that of the Catholic JOC to the beliefs of more radical groups run by students from Seoul, workers' organizations became more radical. As workers' groups broke up into rival factions, however, they became less successful in recruiting workers. Many workers were disturbed by the factional conflict and extreme positions of some student groups, and this also contributed to the decrease in labor activity.

Political actions taken by women workers were regarded differently from those taken by men. On the one hand, both the government and opposition groups tended not to take women very seriously. For example, when an American sociologist sought permission to study workers in heavy industry, he was steered toward industries with women workers (Spencer 1988:7–8). On the other hand, because of culturally defined attitudes toward gender, in which the suffering of young women is seen as particularly poignant, the exploitation of women workers has been a rallying point for political opposition. Furthermore, the disregard of women workers by the government allowed sporadic episodes of labor activity to take place among these workers during periods when it was completely repressed among men. Women's actions were thus important both in giving the labor movement a sense of continuity through periods of repression and in providing a symbolic focus for the movement.

Ideas about the historical suffering of the Korean people at the hands of various foreign oppressors, and a sense that righteousness grows out of resistance to this oppression, have been central to the unifying *minjung* ideology (Abelmann 1990). *Minjung* ideology focused on the oppression experienced by the Korean people throughout history, and as the Reverend Cho Wha Soon observed, "Women workers are probably the class that has borne the greatest burden of historical oppression created by human society up to now" (1988:136). Women's suffering can be seen as standing for national suffering, and there is therefore a moral imperative to take political action on behalf of women workers.

The Christian religious organizations engaged in the struggle for workers' rights, UIM and JOC, compared the suffering and martyrdom of women workers to that of Christ. Activists sought to experience that suffering by reading autobiographies of workers and biographies of those who died for the workers' cause. At workers' meetings this suffering was made tangible through close study, and, as Kim Seong Nae states, "reading the biographies of the dead and the reaction of grief to their tragic deaths was like the mourning ritual itself" (1989:10).

In the struggle for workers' rights, women converted their traditionally submissive role into a political weapon. When striking workers were beaten up by hired thugs, an additional level of outrage was reached when the workers were young women. Ideas about female vulnerability thus helped to draw a moral contrast between the workers and those who abused them.

Company executives were surprised by the vehemence of young women during the labor uprising, but they should not have been. Young women working for the few years between the end of their education and the beginning of their marriage were an easily exploitable labor force, but they were also a volatile one because they did not share any long-term interests with their employers. The high turnover rate canceled out companies' efforts to indoctrinate new workers. There were no older workers to illustrate the benefits of selfless service to the company, and the propaganda about loyalty to the corporate family sounded hollow to women who did not expect to remain on the job for even ten years. Women's youth and inexperience made them a cheap and submissive labor force, but it also made them unpredictable.

The institutionalized passivity of women workers concealed an inner indignation and anger, much like that of the colonized people discussed by Frantz Fanon or Emile Zola's archetypal peasant, Jacques Bonhomme (1980; cited in James Scott 1990:214). Women factory workers repressed their anger at their mistreatment, and when it emerged, it resulted in intense and spontaneous action.[4] The rigidly controlled working environment in MAFEZ factories nearly eliminated opportunities for workers to express their anger individually without risking reprisals. Only in the context of the labor uprising did it become practical for workers to speak out on their own behalf.

Everyday Resistance

Returning to Ruth Milkman's observation that recent studies of women and work have created a new myth of "a virtually limitless potential for women's activism" (1985:xii) where previously none had been noticed, I would like to address the more general efflorescence of literature on the behavior of subordinated groups that is now labeled "resistance." Although these studies have helped correct some of the omissions of the past, where women were invisible within workers' struggles or where subalterns were seen principally as a vehicle for false consciousness, this new literature brings its own problems. Seeing resistance everywhere where previously none had been noticed risks presenting a mirror image that is as false a picture as the one it replaces, and one that romanticizes those who experience oppression. Much of this literature on resistance deploys a limited notion of agency, and provides no way of coping with the variability and complexities – ambiguities, nuances and contradictions – of the behavior of real people in real situations.

At times, I myself have found it difficult to maintain a balance between my understanding of the complexities of women workers' lives and my appreciation of the importance of their resistance to self-evidently oppressive forces in their lives. As I have discussed in the Preface, I brought certain attitudes and values to my fieldwork that gave me an affinity to certain people and certain activities. In my writing, I have felt a need to restrain my enthusiasm for "resistance" activities in order to present a balanced account of the workers of MAFEZ.

---

4 Fanon argues that external passivity is produced through enormous efforts of self-repression, and when colonized peoples finally take action against their oppressors, their actions are intense and spontaneous. "Action, not negotiation, is the characteristic response" (Fanon 1969:48, cited in Elson and Pearson 1984:26–27).

Still, resistance needs to be appreciated when it occurs. The major study in English on South Korean women factory workers says nothing about resistance and little about anything that could be taken as resistance (Spencer 1988); indeed, women are more or less overlooked in recent discussions of workers' activism (e.g., Choi Jang Jip 1993; Koo 1993). On the other hand, extravagant claims have been made, especially in Korean language literature, for the political accomplishments of South Korean women workers as activists, particularly during the 1970s (e.g., Choi Jang Jip 1983; Enloe 1983; Jeoung 1993; Karl and Choi 1983; Lee Hyo-chae 1989; Ogle 1990; Sin 1985; Yi Tae-ho 1985). The women factory workers of this period have been at the core of *minjung* rhetoric. It has been important to demonstrate the continuity of Korean resistance in the face of the oppressive events of this century – Japanese colonial rule, the Korean War, and, finally, authoritarian rule and a divided Korea – and the transcendent purpose of representing the continuity of the oppressed soul of the Korean nation has been ascribed to protesting women workers.

A leading figure in the literature on everyday resistance is James Scott, who argues persuasively for a broad notion of resistance not limited to formalized or organized acts. For Scott,

> class resistance includes *any* act(s) by member(s) of a subordinate
> class that is or are *intended* either to mitigate or deny claims . . .
> made on that class by superordinate classes . . . or to advance its own
> claims . . . vis-à-vis those superordinate classes. (1985:290)

In his study of a Malaysian peasant village, Scott usefully details the numerous incidents through which the poor assert their interests, and he argues that the poor have a social consciousness that enables them to understand and act to assert those interests.

In discussing Scott's work, Dorinne Kondo praises his attention to culture and his inclusive notion of resistance but worries about "certain problematic notions of categorization and human agency" (1990:219). One problem involves the assumptions Scott makes about how social classes operate in the Malaysian village, which he divides into "two dichotomous groups, the rich and the poor" (ibid.).[5] Kondo suspects this "simple binary" of concealing complications, contradictions and ironies, but the whole notion of resistance

---

5 Although James Scott's description of village life convincingly describes a dichotomy between the village's rich and poor members, one wonders how distinct these village "classes" look from a regional or national perspective and how they articulate with other national groups.

seems to depend on having such a distinction between a subordinate group and a superordinate group. Binary social distinctions are even more central in Scott's more recent work, which discusses the social consciousness of subordinated groups (1990). Many of his examples of "hidden transcripts" are drawn from slavery in the American South. It seems scarcely surprising that a situation of sharply demarcated groups, enormous inequalities and intense conflict would have elaborate hidden transcripts, and relatively little of the overlapping and compromised interests that Kondo sees as fundamental to social life.

Scott's actors seem inevitably to resist, and any apparent conformity to the desires of superordinate groups is dismissed as merely "a protective disguise" (1985:284). Yet, as Kondo argues:

> That people inevitably participate in their own oppressions, buying into hegemonic ideologies even as they struggle against those oppressions and those ideologies – a familiar fact of life to women, people of color, colonized and formerly colonized people – is a poignant and paradoxical facet of human life given short shrift in Scott's schema. (1990:221)

Based on her research in a small, family-owned factory in Japan,[6] Kondo questions the monolithic notion of power implied in Scott's discussion of resistance. She argues for a "complex view of power and human agency" and sees the need for a theoretical move that would "require seeing people as decentered, multiple selves, whose lives are shot through with contradictions and creative tensions" (ibid.:224) in order to make sense of everyday life. For Kondo,

> A term like resistance, when considered in all its living complexity, seems inadequate at best, for apparent resistance is riven with ironies and contradictions, just as coping and consent may have unexpectedly subversive effects. . . .

She proposes that

---

6 Kondo's study brings up some interesting contrasts with my work in a Korean Free Export Zone. First, in Kondo's small family-owned factory, the social distance between workers and owners is much less, allowing for greater manipulation of social interactions by workers; second, Kondo's women factory workers seem far more accepting of their place than the workers I knew in Masan. Unlike women workers in MAFEZ, Kondo's part-timers did not try to follow the middle-class model of the education mother, or expect their children to do well in school (1990:280–285).

a more complicated view of the agency and selfhood of those who resist would see people caught in contradictions, constructing new arrangements of meaning and power as they craft their lives, but never
"authentically resisting" power to attain some emancipatory utopia (cf.
Foucault 1979, 1980, Butler 1987, Haraway 1989). Such an approach
would not jettison the category of resistance nor would it prevent us
from distinguishing relative vectors of power. (Ibid.:225)

Kondo's critique of Scott can also be applied to the notions of power and
class held by many of the labor activists in Masan. Activists (whose own class
location is often problematic) bring an abstract understanding of social problems to workers' issues and have the sharpest perception of class conflict.
Ordinary workers have greater need to make compromises and accommodations with those who are relatively powerful in their own lives. Their daily
experience of society occurs not so much as capital versus labor but through
more proximate types of unequal relations (line leader–worker, under-
manager–line leader, older sister–younger sister, landlord–tenant, etc.). Ironically, the fact that activists are in the working class voluntarily enables them to
maintain such strongly essentialized notions of class.

Kondo's emphasis on subtlety, irony and contradiction is well suited to her
study of a small, family-owned cake factory in Japan (and perhaps also for
Scott's Malaysian village). In MAFEZ, however, the sides are more clearly
drawn; foreign capital has concentrated power and young South Korean
women workers are relatively weak, and furthermore, they are engaged in
overt resistance. Nevertheless, even here a certain ambiguity begins to creep in
when one recognizes that all managers are Korean and that day-to-day interac-
tion is not between foreign stockholders and Korean production workers, but
among people of more nearly equal status. In MAFEZ, gender divides management from labor, but it also facilitates both love affairs and marriages, which
can occur across this divide. Furthermore, class mobility is perceived as possible by many workers, and claims to be middle class demonstrate an equivocal
commitment to working-class identities.

THE WORKERS' MOVEMENT IN THE 1990s

The end of South Korea's military dictatorship came not with a revolution that
ushered in a just society and a united Korea, but with a partial and forced retreat
by those who had ruled. The leaders of the present democratically elected
South Korean government took control gradually through a series of com-

promises made with the military leaders. Although they have instituted major reforms and popular anticorruption measures, the new regime has substantial institutional continuity with the military dictatorship and, of course, has pursued similar economic policies. The new president, Kim Young Sam, had been imprisoned for his political views under the generals, but he was no radical.[7] The change in regime was, however, far-reaching enough to undermine the sense of common purpose among antigovernment forces. During the military dictatorship, there had been a widespread sense that antigovernment activists associated with the *minjung* movement (students, workers and farmers) were the vanguard of a national crusade and that their militancy was admirable. But after President Kim came to power, militant and extreme antigovernment activity lost its appeal, and many in the political opposition began to question the goals and tactics of the past. Abelmann discusses the fragmentation of the elements comprising the *minjung* movement as political expression became less confrontational in the 1990s (1996:226ff.).

It is not that the opposition was ever united; on the contrary, it was always riven by factionalism, but the dictatorship had provided a common enemy. After the establishment of a civilian government, the *minjung* movement fragmented and lost its central position in the discourse of social activism. Not only did its confrontational tactics seem unnecessary, but its coalition of students, workers and farmers was no longer moved by the same issues.

Some of the support for workers had begun to dissipate in the earliest stages of the transition to democracy. Both the middle class and the workers had participated in the massive street demonstrations that forced direct presidential elections in 1987, but whereas the middle class was placated by the concessions granted by Roh Tae Woo's June 29 declaration (Choi Jang Jip 1993:38), for workers it merely set the stage for the nationwide labor uprising. Roger Janelli, conducting research at a *chaebol* in 1987, found that middle managers

---

7 One interesting aspect of Kim Young Sam's anticorruption campaign was that many of the officials who were accused of wrongdoing blamed their wives. "My wife is the one who takes care of my household finances, so I don't know anything about how much property we own or how much money we have" was a typical answer given by politicians who were accused of abusing their positions to accumulate wealth. The second highest official of Kim Young Sam's Democratic Liberal Party was accused of having a son accepted into college illegally. He admitted his mistake and resigned from his position, but at the same time he blamed his wife, saying that his children's education was his wife's responsibility. "So I did not know anything about what was going on." Many wives came out publicly, accepting blame and claiming that their husbands did not know anything about family finances. The significance of these episodes is that they show both the availability of women as scapegoats and their real role as manager of family finances.

had a great deal of sympathy for the plight of blue-collar workers, but following the June 29 declaration he "saw no further expressions of sympathy for the proletariat" (1993:201). He attributes this change of attitude to the effect that strikes had on managers' lives:

> As a result of these labor disputes, production was disrupted, shipments delayed, plans reformulated, and agreements with customers renegotiated. Lowered estimates of exports for 1987 were widely announced in the press, and many of the white-collar workers' summer vacations were cancelled for the duration of the strikes. (Ibid.)

The loss of ordinary middle-class support for working-class causes began to marginalize labor politics, and "the new middle class became increasingly conservative and somewhat hostile to the aggressive labor movement in the 1990s" (Koo 1993:159).

Among intellectuals, the discourse of social activism has also shifted from the confrontational rhetoric of the 1980s, with its talk of *minjung,* to a more fragmented discourse characterized as *simin* (civil). These *simin* movements advocate social activism but shun the confrontational tactics of the 1980s and, importantly, speak of the "ordinary citizen" rather than "the community of the oppressed." Although *simin* movements do not exclude workers, they are not at the center, as they were with the *minjung* movement. Students are thus no longer drawn to sacrifice for the workers' struggles, but instead pursue middle-class interests at a more moderate pace, and workers are left to press their interests on their own.[8]

Skepticism was expressed about *simin* organizations by most of the labor activists in the Masan area. They believed that these organizations were not interested in representing workers' rights but, instead, were middle-class efforts to coopt workers.

Although the labor movement achieved a dramatic following in the years of transition from dictatorship to civilian government, it has not forged firm links to political institutions. There is as yet no Labor Party or Social Democratic Party on the national scene. Attempts to organize a party to field worker candidates for the 1992 national congressional election failed miserably because of lack of financial resources and divisions among activists.

Women's factory jobs have declined in importance within the national economy, even though manufacturing has continued to grow in importance overall.

---

8 Abelmann (1996) discusses how farmers have reacted to the similar loss of support from students at a time when economic pressures on them have been intensifying.

The present cohort of workers in MAFEZ is much smaller than the one in 1987. It is also slightly older and better paid. Fewer workers are attracted to 1980s-style radical politics.[9] Despite the fact that workers are now allowed to organize freely, they are no longer interested in confrontational tactics. Many of the companies in MAFEZ now have unions, although in 1994 only two were "democratic" unions (i.e., retaining the radical orientation of the 1980s), and workers in some companies seem satisfied with labor–management councils instead of unions. Labor disputes have declined to near nonexistence. I know of no strikes taking place since the 1992 election of Kim Young Sam.

The nationwide labor uprising in 1987 was a turning point in South Korean labor history. Workers and students were instrumental in forcing the end of the authoritarian regime, and the working class gained a sense of its own importance to the country. The new working class has, however, not followed the course that was charted for it, but has stepped back from the confrontational tactics and utopian goals that were so important to the dedicated activists who brought workers' organizations into existence. Continued economic development and rising standards of living have made a deep impression on workers. Ordinary women whom I knew as workers in 1987 believed that their work was paying off when they were able to get modest apartments for their families in the 1990s. At the same time, real needs still exist among workers. Poverty and exploitation have not been eliminated, and the veterans of the struggles of the past decade still see a role for themselves. Wisdom, short-sightedness, self-interest, selflessness, altruism and greed are all part of the behavior of the women factory workers of MAFEZ, and as Kondo suggests, we need to understand them "as decentered, multiple selves, whose lives are shot through with contradictions and creative tensions" (1990:224) in order to make sense of their lives.

9 Whereas in 1987 labor activists offered classes in "bridal preparation" as fronts for political education, when those classes were offered in 1994 they had to teach makeup, flower arranging and sex education in order to draw any workers.

References

Abelmann, Nancy. 1990. The Practice and Politics of History: A South Korean Tenant Farmers Movement. Ph.D. dissertation, University of California at Berkeley.

——— 1996. *Echoes of the Past, Epics of Dissent: A South Korean Social Movement.* Berkeley: University of California Press.

Abu-Lughod, Lila. 1986. *Veiled Sentiments: Honor and Poetry in a Bedouin Society.* New York: Oxford University Press.

——— 1991. Writing against Culture. In *Recapturing Anthropology: Working in the Present.* Richard Fox (ed.). Santa Fe, NM: School of American Research Press.

Acker, Joan, Kate Barry and Johanna Esseveld. 1991. Objectivity and Truth: Problems in Doing Feminist Research. In *Beyond Methodology.* Mary Fonow and Judith Cook (eds.). Bloomington: Indiana University Press.

AMPO. 1977. Special issue on free trade zones in Asia.

——— 1990. Unions' Struggle Across the Border: Mass Dismissals at Korea Sumida. Vol. 21, No. 4.

Amsden, Alice H. 1989. *Asia's Next Giant: South Korea and Late Industrialization.* New York: Oxford University Press.

The Asia Watch. 1990. *Retreat from Reform: Labor Rights and Freedom of Expression in South Korea.* New York: The Asia Watch.

Behar, Ruth. 1993. *Translated Woman: Crossing the Border with Esperanza's Story.* Boston: Beacon Press.

Beneria, Lourdes, and Martha Roldan. 1987. *The Crossroads of Class and Gender: Industrial Homework, Subcontracting, and Household Dynamics in Mexico City.* Chicago: University of Chicago Press.

Bolles, Lynn. 1983. Kitchens Hit by Priorities: Employed Working-Class Jamaican Women Confront the IMF. In *Women, Men and the International Division of Labor.* J. Nash and M. P. Fernandez-Kelly (eds.). Albany: SUNY Press.

——— 1996a. *Sister Jamaica: A Study of Women, Work and Household in Kingston.* Lanham, MD: University Press of America.

——— 1996b. *We Paid Our Dues.* Washington, DC: Howard University Press.

Bookman, Ann. 1988. Unionization in an Electronics Factory: The Interplay of Gender, Ethnicity, and Class. In *Women and the Politics of Empowerment.* A. Bookman and S. Morgen (eds.). Philadelphia: Temple University Press.

Bourdieu, Pierre. 1977. *Outline of a Theory of Practice.* Richard Nice, trans. Cambridge: Cambridge University Press.

185

References

1984. *Distinction: A Social Critique of the Judgement of Taste.* Richard Nice, trans. Cambridge, MA: Harvard University Press.

Braverman, Harry. 1974. *Labor and Monopoly Capital.* New York: Monthly Review Press.

Burmeister, Larry. 1988. *Research, Realpolitik, and Development in Korea: The State and the Green Revolution.* Boulder, CO: Westview Press.

Butler, Judith. 1987. Variations on Sex and Gender: Beauvoir, Wittig and Foucault. In *Feminism as Critique.* Seyla Benhabib and Drucilla Cornell (eds.). Minneapolis: University of Minnesota Press.

Caribbean Association for Feminist Research and Action. 1988. Free Trade Zone Workers Fired. *Newsletter* Vol. 2, No. 2.

Chang Chi-yŏn. 1990. Han'guk Sahoe Chikŏp ui Sŏngbyŏl Punjŏlhwa wa Kyŏngjejŏk Pulp'yŏngdŭng (Gender Segmentation of the Labor Market and Economic Inequality in Korean Society). In *Han'guk Sahoe ui Yŏsŏng kwa Kajok (Women and Family in Korean Society).* Korean Research Center for Social History (ed.). Seoul: Munhak kwa Chisŏngsa.

Chang Nam-su. 1984. *Ppaeatkkin ilt'ŏ (The Lost Workplace).* Seoul: Changjak kwa Pip'yŏng.

Chapkis, W., and C. Enloe (eds.). 1982. *Of Common Cloth: Women in the Global Textile Industry.* Washington, DC: Transnational Institute.

Cho Hye-joang. 1986. Kabujangje ui Pyŏnhyŏng kwa Kŭgbok. (The Transformation of the Korean Patriarchal Family). *Han'guk Yŏsŏnghak (Journal of Korean Women's Studies)* Vol. 2.

1988. *Han'guk ui Yŏsŏng kwa Namsŏng (Korean Women and Men).* Seoul: Munhak kwa Chisŏngsa.

Cho Oakla. 1987. Women in Transition: The Low Income Family. In *Korean Women in Transition: At Home and Abroad.* E. Y. Yu and E. H. Phillips (eds.). Los Angeles: Center for Korean-American and Korean Studies, California State University.

Cho Soon. 1994. *The Dynamics of Korean Economic Development.* Washington, DC: Institute for International Economics.

Cho Soon-Kyoung. 1987. How Cheap Is "Cheap Labor"?: The Dilemmas of Export-Led Industrialization. Ph.D. dissertation, University of California, Berkeley.

Cho Sŭng-hyŏk. 1981. *Tosi Sanŏp Sŏn'gyo ui Insik (Understanding of Urban Industrial Mission).* Seoul: Minjungsa.

1984. *Han'guk Kongŏbhwa wa Nodong Undong (Korean Industrialization and Labor Movement).* Seoul: P'ulbbit.

Cho Wha Soon. 1988. *Let the Weak Be Strong.* Bloomington, IN: Meyer, Stone, and Company, Inc.

Choe Minja K., Kong Sae-Kwŏn, and Karen O. Mason. 1994. *Korean Women's Labor Force Participation, Attitude, and Behavior.* Honolulu, HI: East-West Center, Population Series No. 302.

Choi Jang Jip. 1983. Interest Conflict and Political Control of South Korea: A Study of the Labor Unions in Manufacturing Industries, 1961–1980. Ph.D. dissertation, University of Chicago.

References

1993. Political Cleavages in South Korea. In *State and Society in Contemporary Korea*. Hagen Koo (ed.). Ithaca, NY: Cornell University Press.

Chŏn T'ae-il. 1988. *Nae Chukŭmŭl Hŏttoei Malla (Don't Waste My Life: A Collection of Chun's Writings)*. Seoul: Tolbegae.

Chŏng Hyŏn-baek. 1991. *Nodong Undong kwa Nodongja Munhwa (Labor Movement and Workers' Culture)*. Seoul: Hangilsa.

Christian Institute for the Study of Justice and Development. 1987. *Han'guk Sahoe ui Nodong T'ongje. (Labor Regulations in Korean Society)*. Seoul: Minjungsa.

1987b. *7–8wŏl Nodongja Taet'ujaeng (July-August Laborers' Mass Struggle)*. Seoul: Minjungsa.

Clark, Donald (ed.). 1988. *The Kwangju Uprising: Shadows Over the Regime in South Korea*. Boulder, CO: Westview Press.

Clifford, James. 1988. *The Predicament of Culture: Twentieth-Century Ethnography, Literature, and Art*. Cambridge, MA: Harvard University Press.

Cole, David C., and Park Yung Chul. 1983. *Financial Development in Korea, 1945–1978: Studies in the Modernization of the Republic of Korea, 1945–1975*. Cambridge, MA: Council on East Asian Studies, Harvard University.

Committee for Justice and Peace of South Korea. 1976. A Fact-Finding Survey on the Masan Export Processing Zone. *AMPO* 8(1):58–64 and 8(2):58–69.

Cook, Alice, Val Lorwin, and Arlene Daniels. 1992. *The Most Difficult Revolution: Women and Trade Unions*. Ithaca, NY: Cornell University Press.

Costello, Cynthia. 1988. Women Workers and Collective Action: A Case Study from the Insurance Industry. In *Women and the Politics of Empowerment*. A. Bookman and S. Morgen (eds.). Philadelphia: Temple University Press.

Crapanzano, Vincent. 1980. *Tuhami: Portrait of a Moroccan*. Chicago: University of Chicago Press.

Cumings, Bruce. 1984. *The Origins of the Korean War*. Princeton, NJ: Princeton University Press.

1987. The Origins and Development of the Northeast Asian Political Economy: Industrial Sectors, Product Cycles, and Political Consequences. In *The Political Economy of the New Asian Industrialism*. F. Deyo (ed.). Ithaca, NY: Cornell University Press.

De Bary, William T., and Jahyon K. Haboush (eds.). 1985. *The Rise of Neo-Confucianism in Korea*. New York: Columbia University Press.

Deuchler, Martina. 1977. The Tradition: Women During the Yi Dynasty. In *Virtues in Conflict*. Sandra Mattielli (ed.). Korea: Royal Asiatic Society.

1992. *The Confucian Transformation of Korea: A Study of Society and Ideology*. Cambridge, MA: Harvard University Press.

Deyo, Frederic C. 1987. State and Labor: Modes of Political Exclusion in East Asian Development. In *The Political Economy of the New Asian Industrialism*. F. Deyo (ed.). Ithaca, NY: Cornell University Press.

1989. *Beneath the Miracle: Labor Subordination in the New Asian Industrialism*. Berkeley: University of California Press.

Dong, Won-mo. 1987. University Students in South Korean Politics: Patterns of Radi-

187

References

calization in the 1980s. *Journal of International Affairs* 40(2):233–255.

1988. Student Activism and the Presidential Politics of 1987 in South Korea. In *Political Change in South Korea.* Ilpyong Kim (ed.). New York: Paragon House Press.

Dublin, Thomas. 1981. *Women at Work: The Transformation of Work and Community in Lowell, Massachusetts, 1826–1860.* New York: Columbia University Press.

Eckert, Carter. 1991. *Offspring of Empire: The Kŏch'ang Kims and the Colonial Origins of Korean Capitalism, 1876–1945.* Seattle: University of Washington Press.

Eckert, Carter, et al. 1990. *Korea Old and New: A History.* Cambridge, MA: Korea Institute, Harvard University.

The Economist. 1990. The Drenching of Roh Tae Woo. 315(7654): 12–18.

Ehrenreich, Barbara. 1982. The Nouveau Poor. *Ms.* 10(1):215–224.

Elson, Diane, and Ruth Pearson. 1981. Nimble Fingers Make Cheap Workers: An Analysis of Women's Employment in Third World Export Manufacturing. *Feminist Review* Spring:87–107.

1984. The Subordination of Women and the Internationalisation of Factory Production. In *Of Marriage and the Market.* K. Young, C. Wolkowitz and R. McCullagh (eds.). London: Routledge & Kegan Paul.

Enloe, Cynthia H. 1983. Women Textile Workers in the Militarization of Southeast Asia. In *Women, Men, and the International Division of Labor.* J. Nash and M. P. Fernandez-Kelly (eds.). Albany: SUNY Press.

Fanon, Frantz. 1969. *The Wretched of the Earth.* New York: Penguin Books.

Fernandez-Kelly, Maria Patricia. 1983. *For We Are Sold, I and My People: Women and Industry in Mexico's Frontier.* Albany: SUNY Press.

Ferree, Myra Marx. 1985. Between Two Worlds: German Feminist Approaches to Working-Class Women and Work. *Signs* 10(35):517–536.

Former Y. H. Labor Union. 1984. *YH Nodongjohapsa (The History of YH Labor Union).* Seoul: Hyŏngsŏngsa.

Foucault, Michel. 1978. *Discipline and Punish: The Birth of the Prison.* Alan Sheridan, trans. New York: Vintage Books.

1980. *Power/Knowledge.* Colin Gordon (ed.). New York: Pantheon.

Frobel, F., J. Heinrichs, and O. Kreye. 1980. *The New International Division of Labor: Structural Unemployment in Industrialised Countries and Industrialisation in Developing Countries.* Cambridge: Cambridge University Press.

Fuentes, Annette, and Barbara Ehrenreich. 1983. *Women in the Global Factory.* INC Pamphlet No. 2. New York: South End Press.

Gluck, Sherna B., and Daphne Patai. 1991. *Women's Words: The Feminist Practice of Oral History.* New York: Routledge.

Gray, Linda. 1987. *Global Assembly Line.* Video film.

Grossman, Rachel. 1979. Women's Place in the Integrated Circuit. *Southeast Asia Chronicle.* No. 66:2–17.

Grunwald, Joseph, and Kenneth Flamm. 1985. *The Global Factory: Foreign Assembly in International Trade.* Washington, DC: The Brookings Institution.

References

Gutman, Herbert. 1973. *Work, Culture and Society in Industrializing America: Essays in American Working Class and Social History.* New York: Knopf.

Han'guk Katorik Nodong Ch'ŏngnyŏnhoe (Korean Young Catholic Workers' Organization). 1980. *Masan Such'ul Chayujiyŏk (MAFEZ) Hyup'yeŏp Siltae Pogo (Report on the Reality of the MAFEZ Factory Closings).* Seoul: Han'guk Katorik Nodong Ch'ŏngnyŏnhoe (Korean Young Catholic Workers' Organization).

Han'guk Katorik Nodong Ch'ŏngnyŏnhoe (Korean Young Catholic Workers' Organization). 1986. *Han'guk Katorik Nodong Ch'ŏngnyŏnhoe: 25nyŏnsa (Twenty-Five-Year History of Korean Young Catholic Workers' Organization).* Seoul: Pundo Ch'ulpansa.

Han'guk Kidokkyo Kyohoe Hyŏbuihoe (The National Council of Churches in Korea [KNCC]). 1984a. *Nodongja ui Sallim Sari (Workers' Household).* Seoul: P'ulbbit.

1984b. *Nodong Hyŏnjang kwa Chŭngŏn (The Scene of Labor and Testimony).* Seoul: P'ulbbit.

Han'guk Kidokkyo Sahoe Munje Yŏn'guwŏn (Korean Church Institute for Research on Social Problems). 1987. *7–8wŏl Nodongja Taejung T'ujaeng (July–August Workers' Struggle).* Seoul: Han'guk Kidokkyo Sahoe Munje Yŏn'guwŏn.

Han'guk Minjungsa Yŏn'guhoe (A Society for the Study of the Korean History of the Masses). 1986. *Han'guk Minjungsa I and II (Korean History of the Masses).* Seoul: P'ulbbit.

Han'guk Nodongjohap Ch'ongyŏnmaeng (Federation of Korean Trade Unions). 1979. *Han'guk Nodongjohap Undongsa (History of Korean Labor Union Movement).* Seoul: Koryŏ Sŏjŏk.

Han'guk Yŏsŏng Nodongjahoe (Korean Women Workers' Association). 1987. *Han'guk Yŏsŏng Nodong ui Hyŏnjang (The Scene of Korean Women Workers).* Seoul: Paeksan Sŏdang.

Haraway, Donna. 1989. *Primate Visions: Gender, Race and Nature in the World of Modern Science.* New York: Routledge.

Hareven, Tamara K. 1982. *Family Time and Industrial Time: The Relationship between the Family and Work in a New England Industrial Community.* Cambridge: Cambridge University Press.

Hareven, Tamara K., and Randolph Langenbach. 1978. *Amoskeag: Life and Work in an American Industrial City.* New York: Pantheon.

Harvey, Youngsook Kim. 1979. *Six Korean Women: The Socialization of Shamans.* St. Paul, MN: West.

Hershatter, Gail. 1986. *The Workers of Tianjin: 1900–1949.* Stanford, CA: Stanford University Press.

Hong Young-ju. 1985. Tagukjŏk Kiŏp kwa Yŏsŏng Nodongja (Multinational Corporations and Women Workers). M.A. thesis. Seoul: Ehwa Women's University.

Honig, Emily. 1986. *Sisters and Strangers: Women in the Shanghai Cotton Mills, 1919–1949.* Stanford, CA: Stanford University Press.

Hwang Sŏk-yŏng. 1985. *Chugŭmŭl Nŏmŏ Sidae ui ŏdumŭl Nŏmŏ (Overcoming Death, Overcoming the Dark Period).* Seoul: P'ulbbit.

References

Ilsongjŏng Publishers. 1988. *Haksaeng Undong Nonjaengsa (A History of the Controversial Student Movement)*. Seoul: Ilsongjŏng.

Im Yŏng-il. 1984. Iri Chibang Kongŏp Tanji ui Hyŏnhwang (Fact-finding Survey of the Iri Industrial Estate). *Hyŏnjang* 1:275–336.

Janelli, Roger L., and Dawnhee Yim Janelli. 1982. *Ancestor Worship and Korean Society*. Stanford, CA: Stanford University Press.

Janelli, Roger L., with Dawnhee Yim. 1993. *Making Capitalism: The Social and Cultural Construction of a South Korean Conglomerate*. Stanford, CA: Stanford University Press.

Jayawardena, Kumari. 1986. *Feminism and Nationalism in the Third World*. London: Zed Books.

Jeoung Mi Sook. 1993. A Study on the Women's Labor Movement in the 1970's: The Case of the Textile Industry. M.A. thesis. Seoul: Ehwa Women's University.

Jones, Delmos. 1970. Toward a Native Anthropology. *Human Organization* 29:251–259.

Jones, Leroy P., and Sakong Il. 1980. *Government, Business, and Entrepreneurship in Economic Development: The Korean Case*. Cambridge, MA: Harvard University Press.

Kang In-sun. 1990. Masan, Ch'angwŏn ui Nodongja Kyegŭp ui Kajoksaenghwal (The Family Life of Production Workers in Masan and Ch'angwŏn). In *Han'guk Kajokron (Essays on Korean Family)*. Korean Social Research Center for Women (ed.). Seoul: Kkachi Sa.

——— 1991. 80nyŏndae Masan Chiyŏk Yŏsŏng Nodongja Undong (The Women Workers' Movement in Masan During the 1980s). *Kyŏngnam Taehakkyo Nonmunjip (Kyŏngnam University Collected Papers)*. No. 18.

Karl, Marilee, and Choi Wan Cheung. 1983. Resistance, Strikes and Strategies. In *Of Common Cloth: Women in the Global Textile Industry*. W. Chapkis and C. Enloe (eds.). Washington, DC: Transnational Institute.

Kendall, Laurel. 1985. Ritual Silks and Kowtow Money: The Bride as Daughter-in-Law in Korean Wedding Rituals. *Ethnology* 24(4):253–268.

——— 1988. *The Life and Hard Times of a Korean Shaman: Of Tales and the Telling of Tales*. Honolulu: University of Hawaii Press.

——— 1996. *Getting Married in Korea: Of Gender, Morality, and Modernity*. Berkeley: University of California Press.

Kessler-Harris, Alice. 1981. *Women Have Always Worked*. Old Westbury, NY: Feminist Press.

——— 1982. *Out to Work: A History of Wage Earning Women in the United States*. New York: Oxford University Press.

Kihl, Young Whan. 1994. The Legacy of Confucian Culture and South Korean Politics and Economics: An Interpretation. *Korea Journal* 34:37–53.

Kim Chang-ki. 1991. Largest Labor Union Collapses at Pohang Steel. *Chugan Chosŏn* August 24, 1991:34–37.

Kim, Choong Soon. 1990. The Role of the Non-Western Anthropologist Reconsidered. *Current Anthropology* 31(2):196–201.

References

1992. *The Culture of Korean Industry: An Ethnography of Poongsan Corporation.* Tucson: University of Arizona Press.

Kim, Eun Mee. 1987. From Dominance to Symbiosis: State and Chaebol in the Korean Economy, 1960–1985. Ph.D. dissertation, Brown University.

Kim Eun-Shil. 1993. The Making of the Modern Female Gender: The Politics of Gender in Reproductive Practices in Korea. Ph.D. dissertation, University of California, San Francisco.

Kim Hui-jŏng. 1990. Sanŏpche Tŭkbyŏlhakkŭp Chwihak Nodongja e kwanhan Yŏn'gu (A Study of Special Classes for Adolescent Industrial Workers). M.A. thesis. Seoul: Ehwa Women's University.

Kim Kŭm-su. 1986. *Han'guk Nodong Munje ui Sanghwang kwa Insik (The Circumstances and Interpretation of the Korean Labor Problem).* Seoul: P'ulbbit.

Kim, Myung-hye. 1992. Late Industrialization and Women's Work in Urban South Korea: An Ethnographic Study of Upper-middle-class Families. *City and Society* 6(2):156–173.

Kim Nak-jung. 1982. *Han'guk Nodong Undongsa II (Korean Labor History II).* Seoul: Ch'ŏngsa.

Kim S. H., J. W. Kim, and Herbert Vicks. 1983. *1960nyondae (The 1960s).* Seoul: Kŏrŭm.

Kim Seong Nae. 1989. Gender and the Discourse of Resistance: Reading the Autobiographical Narratives of Militant Factory Women in Korea. University of Michigan CSST Working Paper No. 26.

Kim, Seung-kyung. 1990. Capitalism, Patriarchy, and Autonomy: Women Factory Workers in the Korean Economic Miracle. Ph.D. dissertation, City University of New York.

1992. Export Processing Zones and Worker Resistance in South Korea. In *Anthropology and the Global Factory: Studies of the New Industrialization in the Late 20th Century.* Frances Rothstein and Michael Blim (eds.). New York: Bergin and Garvey.

1995. Field, Subject, Author: Fieldwork With a 'Disguised' Worker in a South Korean Export Processing Zone. *Anthropology Today* 11(3):6–9.

1996. "Big Companies Don't Hire Us, Married Women": Exploitation and Empowerment among Women Workers in Korea. *Feminist Studies* 22(3):555–571.

Kim Yong-ki and Yŏng-il Im. 1991. *A Study of Regional Labor Movements in the 1980s: Focusing on Masan–Ch'angwŏn Area.* Masan, Korea: Labor Welfare Institute, Kyŏngnam University.

Kim Yun-hwan. 1982. *Han'guk Nodong Undongsa I (Korean Labor History I).* Seoul: Ch'ŏngsa.

Kondo, Dorinne. 1990. *Crafting Selves: Power, Gender, and Discourses of Identity in a Japanese Workplace.* Chicago: University of Chicago Press.

Koo, Hagen. 1990. From Farm to Factory: Proletarianization in Korea. *Annual Sociological Review* 55(5):669–681.

1991. Middle Classes, Democratization, and Class Formation. *Theory and Society* 20:485–509.

References

1993. The State, Minjung, and the Working Class in South Korea. In *State and Society in Contemporary Korea*. Hagen Koo (ed.). Ithaca, NY: Cornell University Press.

Korean Women's Development Institute. 1994. *Social Statistics and Indicators on Women*. Seoul: Korean Women's Development Institute.

Korean Young Catholic Workers' Organization (JOC). 1980. *Masan Such'ul Chayujiyŏk hyup'yeŏp e kwanhan Yŏn'gu* (*Masan Export Processing Zone Report on Company Suspension and Closure*). Masan: JOC.

Kung, Lydia. 1976. Factory Work and Women in Taiwan: Changes in Self-Image and Status. *Signs* 2(1):35–58.

1983. *Factory Women in Taiwan*. Ann Arbor, MI: UMI Research Press.

Kuznets, Paul W. 1977. *Economic Growth and Structure in the Republic of Korea*. New Haven, CT: Yale University Press.

1985. Government and Economic Strategy in Contemporary South Korea. *Pacific Affairs* 58:44–67.

Kwangju Taegyogu Ch'ŏngui P'yŏnghwa Wiwŏnhoe (Kwangju Priests for Justice and Peace). 1987. *Owŏl, Kŭnari Tasiomyŏn* (*May, When That Day Comes Again*). Kwangju: Kwangju Taegyogu Chŏngui P'yŏnghwa Wiwŏnhoe.

Kwŏn In-suk. 1989. *Hana ui Pyokŭl Nŏmŏsŏ* (*Overcoming One Barrier*). Seoul: Kŏrŭm.

Kwŏn Sun-taek. 1986. Women College Students' "Factory Lives" and Labor Movement. *Sindonga* September:398–409.

Kyŏngnam Sahoe Yŏn'guso (Kyŏngnam Institute for Social Research). 1993. *Yŏsŏng Nodongja ui Koyong Munje wa Nodongjohap* (*Women Workers' Employment Problem and Labor Union*). Masan: Kyŏngnam Sahoe Yŏn'guso.

Lamphere, Louise. 1987. *From Working Daughters to Working Mothers*. Ithaca, NY: Cornell University Press.

Lamphere, Louise, and Guillermo Grenier. 1988. Women, Unions, and "Participative Management": Organizing in the Sunbelt. In *Women and the Politics of Empowerment*. A. Bookman and S. Morgen (eds.). Philadelphia: Temple University Press.

Lee Ae-suk. 1989. Chŏng Chong-myŏng ui Sam kwa T'ujaeng (Life and Struggle of Chŏng Chong-myŏng). *Yŏsŏng* (*Women*) 3: 255–280.

Lee Hyo-chae. 1983. Iljeha ui Yŏsŏng Nodongmunje (The Female Labor Question Under Japanese Occupation). In *Han'guk Nodong Munje ui Kujo* (*The Structure of the Korean Labor Problem*). Seoul: Kwangminsa.

1986. The Changing Industrial Structure and Its Impact on Women Workers in South Korea. Manuscript.

1989. *Han'guk Yŏsŏng Undongsa* (*A History of the Women's Movement in Korea*). Seoul: Ch'ŏngusa.

Lee Hyo-chae and Cho Hyoung. 1976. Fertility and Women's Labor Force Participation in Korea. In *Recent Empirical Findings on Fertility: Korea, Nigeria, Tunisia, Venezuela, Philippines*. Occasional Monograph Series No.7. Washington, DC: Smithsonian Institution Interdisciplinary Communication Program.

Lee K. S., M. I. Hwang, and H. E. Lee. 1987. *Social and Economic Impacts of Free*

References

Export Zones on Regional Communities in the Republic of Korea. Toronto: International Development Research Center.

Lee, Namhee. 1991. The South Korean Student Movement, 1980–1987. In *Chicago Occasional Papers on Korea.* Bruce Cumings (ed.). Chicago: University of Chicago Press.

Lew Seok-Choon. 1993. Student Movement in Korea: Structure and Functions. *Korea Journal* 33:27–33.

Lewis, Linda. 1988. The "Kwangju Incident" Observed: An Anthropological Perspective on Civil Uprisings. In *The Kwangju Uprising: Shadows Over the Regime in South Korea.* Donald N. Clark (ed.). Boulder, CO: Westview Press.

Lim Hyun-Chin. 1982. Dependent Development in the World-System: The Case of South Korea, 1963–1979. Ph.D. dissertation, Harvard University.

Lim, Linda. 1978. *Women Workers in Multinational Corporations: The Case of the Electronics Industry in Malaysia and Singapore.* Ann Arbor, MI: Michigan Occasional Papers in Women's Studies.

1983a. Capitalism, Imperialism, and Patriarchy: The Dilemma of Third World Women Workers in Multinational Factories. In *Women, Men, and the International Division of Labor.* J. Nash and M. P. Fernandez-Kelly (eds.). Albany: SUNY Press.

1983b. Are Multinationals the Problem? *Multinational Monitor* 4(8):14.

Lown, Judy. 1990. *Women and Industrialization: Gender at Work in Nineteenth-century England.* Minneapolis: University of Minnesota Press.

Luedde-Neurath, Richard. 1980. Export Orientation in South Korea: How Helpful Is Dependency Thinking to Its analysis? *Bulletin* (Institute of Development Studies) 12(1):48–53.

Lutz, Nancy Melissa. 1988. Images of Docility: Asian Women and the World Economy. In *Racism, Sexism, and the World-System.* J. Smith et al. (eds.). New York: Greenwood Press.

MAFEZ Administration Office. Monthly statistics. Masan.

1987. *MAFEZ 15 year History.* Masan: MAFEZ Administrative Office.

McGinn, H. F., et al. 1980. *Education and Development in Korea.* Cambridge, MA: Harvard University Press.

Mies, Maria. 1983. Towards a Methodology for Feminist Research. In *Theories of Women's Studies.* Gloria Bowles and Renate Klein (eds.). London: Routledge and Kegan Paul.

Milkman, Ruth (ed.). 1985. *Women, Work, and Protest: A Century of Women's Labor History.* Boston: Routledge and Kegan Paul.

1987. Women Workers and the Labor Movement in Hard Times: Comparing the 1930s with the 1980s. In *Women, Households, and the Economy.* L. Beneria and C. Stimpson (eds.). New Brunswick, NJ: Rutgers University Press.

Moon, Seungsook. 1994. Economic Development and Gender Politics in South Korea, 1963–1992. Ph.D. dissertation, Brandeis University.

Morawetz, David. 1981. *Why the Emperor's New Clothes Are Not Made in Colombia.* New York: Oxford University Press.

Nakane, Chie. 1970. *Japanese Society.* Berkeley: University of California Press.

References

Narayan, Kirin. 1993. How Native Is a "Native Anthropologist"? *American Anthropologist* 95:671–686.

Nash, June, and Maria P. Fernandez-Kelly (eds.). 1983. *Women, Men and the International Division of Labor.* Albany: SUNY Press.

New York Times. 1988. Some Tandy Work Will Leave Korea. August 26.

Norwood, Stephen H. 1990. *Labor's Flaming Youth: Telephone Operators and Worker Militancy.* Urbana: University of Illinois Press.

Ogle, George E. 1990. *South Korea: Dissent Within the Economic Miracle.* London: Zed Books.

Ohnuki-Tierney, Emiko. 1984. "Native" Anthropologists. *American Ethnologist* 11:584–586.

Ong, Aihwa. 1983. Global Industries and Malay Peasants in Peninsular Malaysia. In *Women, Men and the International Division of Labor.* J. Nash and M. P. Fernandez-Kelly (eds.). Albany: SUNY Press.

—— 1987. *Spirits of Resistance and Capitalist Discipline: Factory Women in Malaysia.* Albany: SUNY Press.

—— 1988. The Production of Possession: Spirits and the Multinational Corporation in Malaysia. *American Ethnologist* 15(1):28–42.

—— 1991. The Gender and Labor Politics of Postmodernity. *Annual Review of Anthropology* 20:279–309.

Pak Young-mi. 1983. The Role of Labor Unions in the Female Labor Movement in South Korea. *Korea Scope* 3(3):3–12.

Pak Yŏng-kŭn. 1984. *Kongjang Oksang e Olla (Going Up to the Roof of a Factory).* Seoul: P'ulbbit.

Park Chung Hee. 1970. *Our Nation's Path.* Seoul: Hollym.

Personal Narratives Group. 1989. *Interpreting Women's Lives: Feminist Theory and Personal Narratives.* Bloomington: Indiana University Press.

Robinson, Michael. 1991. Perceptions of Confucianism in Twentieth-Century Korea. In *The East Asian Region: Confucian Heritage and Its Modern Adaptation.* Gilbert Rozman (ed.). Princeton, NJ: Princeton University Press.

Robotham, Sheila. 1973. *Women's Consciousness, Man's World.* London: Penguin Books.

Rosaldo, Renato. 1989. *Culture and Truth: The Remaking of Social Analysis.* Boston: Beacon Press.

Rosen, Ellen Israel. 1987. *Bitter Choices: Blue-Collar Women In and Out of Work.* Chicago: University of Chicago Press.

Sacks, Karen, and Dorothy Remy (eds.). 1984. *My Troubles Are Going to Have Trouble with Me.* New Brunswick, NJ: Rutgers University Press.

Safa, Helen I. 1981. Runaway Shops and Female Employment: The Search for Cheap Labor. *Signs* 7(2):418–433.

Sanjek, Roger. 1993. Anthropology's Hidden Colonialism: Assistants and Their Ethnographers. *Anthropology Today* 9(2):13–18.

Sanŏp kwa Nodong (The Industry and Labor). 1971. 5(1):4.

Scott, James. 1985. *Weapons of the Weak.* New Haven, CT: Yale University Press.

References

1990. *Domination and the Arts of Resistance: Hidden Transcripts.* New Haven, CT: Yale University Press.

Scott, Joan. 1988. *Gender and the Politics of History.* New York: Columbia University Press.

Sin In-ryong. 1985. *Yŏsŏng, Nodong, Pŏp (Women, Labor, and Law).* Seoul: P'ulbbit.

Society for the Study of Korean Women et al. 1991. *Yŏsŏng Nodongja wa Imgŭm (Women Workers and Wages),* Seoul: Tongnyŏksa.

Sŏk Chŏng-nam. 1984. *Kongjang ui Pulbit (The Light of the Factory).* Seoul: Ilwŏl Sŏgak.

Song Byung-Nak. 1990. *The Rise of the Korean Economy.* Oxford: Oxford University Press.

Song Hyo-sun. 1982. *Seoul ro Kanŭn Kil (A Road to Seoul).* Seoul: Hyŏngsŏngsa.

Sorenson, Clark. 1988. *Over the Mountains Are Mountains.* Seattle: University of Washington Press.

Spencer, Robert F. 1988. *Yŏgong: Factory Girl.* Seoul: Royal Asiatic Society.

Stacey, Judith. 1991. Can There Be a Feminist Ethnography? In *Women's Words: The Feminist Practice of Oral History.* Sherna B. Gluck and Daphne Patai (eds.). New York: Routledge.

Steinberg, David I. 1989. *South Korea: Economic Transformation and Social Change.* Boulder, CO: Westview Press.

Suh Hyong-sil. 1990. A Study of the Women's Movement During the Colonial Period. M.A. thesis. Seoul: Ehwa Women's University.

Sun Chŏm-sun. 1984. *8 Sigan Nodong ŭl Wihayŏ (For Eight-hour Labor).* Seoul: P'ulbbit.

Susser, Ida. 1988. Working Class Women, Social Protest, and Changing Ideologies. In *Women and the Politics of Empowerment.* A. Bookman and S. Morgen (eds.). Philadelphia: Temple University Press.

T. C. Former Labor Union Members. 1991. *T. C. Chŏnja Nodongjohap Undongsa (The History of the T. C. Labor Union).* Seoul: Nŭlbŏt.

Thompson, E. P. 1966. *The Making of the English Working Class.* New York: Vintage Books.

Tilly, Louise A., and Joan W. Scott. 1987. *Women, Work and Family.* New York: Routledge.

Tongil Pangjik Pokjik T'ujaeng Wiwŏnhoe (Tongil Textile Workers' Strike Commitee for Reinstatement). 1985. *Tongil Pangjik Nodongjohap Undongsa (History of Tongil Textile Labor Union).* Seoul: Tolbegae.

Tsurumi, E. Patricia. 1990. *Factory Girls: Women in the Thread Mills of Meiji Japan.* Princeton, NJ: Princeton University Press.

Tu, Wei-Ming. 1984. *Confucian Ethics Today – The Singapore Challenge.* Singapore: Federal Publications.

Turbin, Carole. 1992. *Working Women of Collar City: Gender, Class, and Community in Troy, New York, 1864–86.* Urbana: University of Illinois Press.

U.S. Department of Labor. 1990. *Worker Rights in Export Processing Zones: Korea.* Washington, DC: Bureau of International Labor Affairs.

References

Wall Street Journal. 1973. September 20.

Willis, Paul. 1977. *Learning to Labor: How Working-Class Kids Get Working-Class Jobs.* Westmead: Saxonhouse.

Wolf, Diane. 1992. *Factory Daughters: Gender, Household Dynamics, and Rural Industrialization in Java.* Berkeley: University of California Press.

——— 1996. *Feminist Dilemmas in Fieldwork* (ed.). Boulder, CO: Westview Press.

Wolf, Margery. 1992. *A Thrice Told Tale: Feminism, Postmodernism and Ethnographic Responsibility.* Stanford, CA: Stanford University Press.

Won Yong-suk. 1975. *I Am a Textile Worker.* Nodong: Office of Labor Affairs.

Woo, Jung-en. 1991. *Race to the Swift: State and Finance in Korean Industrialization.* New York: Columbia University Press.

Yi Eunhee Kim. 1993. From Gentry to the Middle Class. Ph.D. dissertation, University of Chicago.

Yi Tae-ho. 1985. *Pulkkotiyŏ I Ŏdumŭl Palkyŏra: 70nyŏndae Yŏsŏng Nodongja ui T'ujaeng (Flames, Brighten This Darkness: The Struggle of Women Workers in the 70s).* Seoul: Tolbegae.

——— 1986. *Choegŭn Nodong Undong Kirok (Records of the Recent Labor Movement).* Seoul: Ch'ŏngsa.

Yu, Eui-young. 1990. Regionalism in the South Korean Job Market: An Analysis of Regional-Origin Inequality among Migrants in Seoul. *Pacific Affairs* 63:24–39.

Zaretsky, Eli. 1976. *Capitalism, the Family, and Personal Life.* New York: Harper & Row.

Index

197

Index

hak-ch'ul, 144, 146, 149
half-arranged/half-love marriages, 67
Hamsŏng (A Great Outcry), 119
Han'guk Katorik Nodong Ch'ŏngnyŏnhoe, 20
Han'guk Kidokkyo Kyohoe Hyŏbuihoe, xiii, 101n8
Han'guk Kidokkyo Sahoe Munje Yŏn'guwŏn, 113
Han'guk Minjungsa Yŏn'guhoe, 97, 98, 99, 99n4
Han'guk Nodong Ch'ŏngnyŏnhoe, 101n8
Han'guk Nodongjohap Ch'ongyŏnmaeng, 98n3
Han'guk Tongkyŏng Chŏnja (Korea Tongkyŏng Electronics; KTE); see KTE
Han'guk Yŏsŏng Nodongjahoe, 46, 47
Haraway, Donna, 181
Hareven, Tamara K., 11
Harvey, Youngsook Kim, 8n8
health and safety issues, 40, 43–4, 45
heavy industry, 12, 13, 101, 109, 170
Heinrichs, J., 10n14
Hershatter, Gail, 11
hierarchical relationships, 5–6, 7, 50–2, 94, 173; see also gender hierarchy
hiring policies, 16; age in, 28–30
"home work," 85
Hong Young-ju, 3
Honig, Emily, 11
housemaids, 57, 58
housewife, becoming, 66–75; see also wife/mother role
husbands; character and economic security of, 67; meeting potential, 64, 67, 69–70; and returning to work, 89–90, 95–6; wages, 87, 94, 95
Hwang, M. I., 23
Hwang Sŏk-yŏng, 35n9, 132n5
Hye-in, 84–5
Hye-jong, 87–9
Hye-sun, 58–9
Hyundai Group Labor Unions Alliance, 112

Ilsongjŏng Publishers, 132n4, 133
Im Yŏng-il, 16, 55, 56n23, 115
imprisonment, 18, 134n6, 137, 147, 148, 153–4, 160, 168; of men leaders, 149; of students, 134, 135
Inchŏn, 138, 145
income: and age, 87f; single women's use of, 65–6, 65t
independence, 37, 38, 97
individualism, 37–8, 62–3, 64–5
industrial soldiers, 2–9, 57, 171, 172

industrialization, 2–3, 16–17, 97–8, 100, 129; low-wage, 9–14; rapid, 140, 171; see also export-led industrialization
industries, movement between, 38, 38t, 39
informal labor movement, 104–5
In-ja, 89
in-laws, 77, 79
In-suk, 64–5, 69–70
intellectuals, 17–18, 183; and labor movement, 108, 113; role of, xvii, xviii; and workers, 100, 129; and working-class consciousness, 130, 132
international business community, 125
international division of labor, 9–10, 13, 16
I-suk, 162, 165–7, 168

Janelli, Dawnhee Yim, 7n6
Janelli, Roger L., 2, 7n6, 12n16, 46, 48nn13–14, 51n19, 52, 52n20, 67n5, 182–3
Japan, 121, 152; foreign investment, 10n13; modernization, 3
Japanese colonial rule, 97–8, 104, 179
Japanese companies in South Korea, 13, 20, 49, 53
Jayawardena, Kumari, 104
Jeoung Mi Sook, 5, 32, 52, 179
jobs: source of, 39–40, 39t; status differences, 58–62; see also factory jobs
JOC; see Young Catholic Workers' Organization (JOC)
joint labor-management councils (nosa hyŏbuihoe), 23, 56, 102–3, 152, 159, 184
joint venture companies, 20
Jones, Delmos, ix
Jones, Leroy P., 2
"June 29 Declaration," 111–12, 113, 182, 183
just society, 18, 97, 132, 133, 141; as goal, 142

Kang Chu-ryŏng, 104n14
Kang In-sun, 23, 145
Karl, Marilee, 2, 179
Kendall, Laurel, xiin5, 8n8, 76, 77
Kessler-Harris, Alice, 11
Kihl, Young Whan, 7
Kim Chang-ki, 142n9, 176
Kim Chŏng-im, 122, 125–6
Kim Chŏng-ja, 118n28
Kim, Choong Soon, ix, 2, 39n10, 40n11, 48n14, 49, 49n15
Kim Dae Jung, 112n26
Kim, Eun Mee, 2
Kim Eun-Shil, 3, 5n5, 32, 67n5
Kim Hui-jŏng, 31

205

Printed in the United States
154472LV00006B/33/P